GLOBE FEARON'S

World Literature

Globe Fearon Educational Publisher
A Division of Simon & Schuster
Upper Saddle River, New Jersey

We are grateful to the following educators. They served as reviewers during the various stages of product development. Their valuable comments and suggestions served to enhance the quality of this book.

Renée Floyd, Special Education Teacher, English
G.F. Brewer High School
Fort Worth, TX 76108

Carolyn Lambert, Special Education Teacher
Lower Pioneer Valley Educational Collaborative
Wibraham, MA 01095

Henry M. Marcet, Special Education Teacher
East Bay High School
Tampa, FL 33534

Special thanks to Isabel Geneste at Caldwell College for providing phonetic translations of character names in "A Piece of String."

Project Editor: Renée E. Beach
Senior Editor: Nance Davidson
Editorial Assistant: Marilyn A. Bashoff
Production Editor: Rosann Bar
Electronic Page Production: Margarita Giammanco, José López, Mimi Raihl,
              Heather Roake
Cover Photo: John Paul Endress
Photo Research: Jenifer Hixson

ISBN 0-835-93458-6

Printed in the United States of America
3 4 5 6 7 8 9 10 02 01 00 99

GLOBE FEARON EDUCATIONAL PUBLISHER
A Division of Simon & Schuster
Upper Saddle River, New Jersey

Contents

A Note to the Student

The world is a big place with many possibilities. One way to explore some of these possibilities is through literature.

In *Globe Fearon's World Literature,* you will find stories, myths, poems, and biographies by well-known authors from all over the world. Some of the selections are from well-known writers from the past. Other selections are from exciting authors writing today. You will share the experiences and ideas of people from other cultures. This will open new doors for you.

You will find several study aids as you read each chapter of this book. At the beginning of each chapter, you will find **Learning Objectives.** Take a moment to study these goals. They will help you focus on the important points covered in that chapter. You will also find **Words to Know.** This is a look ahead at new vocabulary you may find difficult. The first time you see one of the Words to Know in the chapter, it will appear in dark type. A **Chapter Review** at the end will give you a quick summary of what you have just read. A **Unit Review** also follows each unit.

In addition, special features throughout the book explore topics of interest that are related, in some way, to the selection. Sometimes the connection may be historical. At other times, it may be interesting information that ties in to the selection.

Finally, look for notes printed in color in the margins of the pages. These friendly notes are there to help guide you through the selection. Sometimes they comment on the material you are learning or they ask you questions that make you think about the selection in a new or different way.

We hope you enjoy reading this collection of world literature. Everyone who put this book together worked hard to make it interesting as well as useful. The rest is up to you. We wish you well in your studies.

Unit One

NEW DIRECTIONS

▲ In *Tentation de St. Antoine,* two armies are resolving their conflict in battle. Sometimes resolving a conflict can take our lives in a new direction. The artist of the painting is Jerome Bosch.

Chapter Learning Objectives

- Learn about myths.
- Understand the use of conflict in a story or poem.
- Learn about the narrator of a story.
- Identify the setting of a story.
- Learn about irony of situation.
- Recognize the tone of a poem.
- Understand how imagery is used.

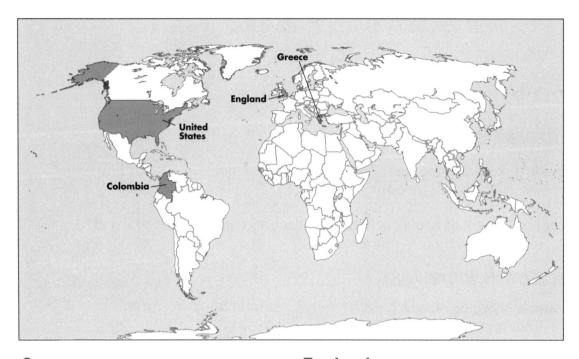

Greece
Arachne
a myth retold by Olivia E. Coolidge

Colombia
Lather and Nothing Else
an adapted story by Hernando Téllez

England
The Interlopers
an adapted story by Saki

United States
Bering Coast
a poem by Fred Bigjim

In our lives we often face conflict. Each conflict is a chance to learn
something new. In this chapter, you will read about people who have
conflicts within themselves and with other people. In the process, they
take their lives in new directions.

Arachne

a myth retold by Olivia E. Coolidge

Words to Know

LITERARY TERMS

myth a story that teaches a lesson about human behavior or tells how something in nature came to exist

conflict a fight or battle between two or more characters; the problem that needs to be solved in a story

SELECTION VOCABULARY

loom a machine on which cloth is woven

embroidery detailed needlework on cloth

shuttle a card or spool that moves thread back and forth to weave cloth

immortal living forever

challenged called to a fight or contest

dazzling bright

insult something said that hurts someone's feelings

Arachne (ah-RAK-nee)

Myths often teach lessons about human faults. In this myth, Arachne learns that a human being can never win in a conflict with a goddess.

⎯⎯ ⦿⦿⦿ ⎯⎯

Arachne was not beautiful or well-born. But she became famous all over Greece.

Arachne lived in a little village with her father, who dyed wool. Her father was very skillful at this. He made many different and wonderful colors. He was famous for the clear, bright red he made.

◀ Looms have been used for many centuries. Here a woman is seated at her loom in this painting by an unknown artist.

This was the most beautiful of all the colors used in ancient Greece.

Arachne was even more skillful than her father. She spun the wool into a fine, soft thread. She wove the thread into cloth on the high **loom** in their cottage.

Arachne was small and pale from all the work she did. Her eyes were light, and her hair was a dusty brown. Yet she was quick and graceful. Her rough fingers moved so fast it was hard to follow them.

Soon Arachne was known all over Greece. No one had ever seen work like hers before. They had never seen thread so soft and even, or cloth so fine. They had never seen **embroidery** so beautiful.

People used to come from far and wide to see Arachne working. Even the nymphs would come from the streams or the forests to peek shyly through the cottage door. They would watch in wonder as Arachne worked. They watched Arachne throw the **shuttle** from hand to hand between the hanging threads.

They would watch her draw out the long threads of
wool as she sat spinning.

People would say to each other, "Surely Athena
herself must have taught her. Who else would know
the secret of such great skill?"

Arachne was used to being wondered at. She was
very proud of her skill. Praise was all she lived for. It
made her angry when people thought Athena had
taught her.

Arachne would turn to the crowd of people and say,
"I have my skill because of hard practice. I work from
early morning until night. As for Athena's skill, how
could it be greater than mine? If she came down to
compete with me, she could do no better than I."

One day when Arachne spoke this way, an old
woman answered her. She was a gray old woman and
very poor. She leaned on a staff, looking at Arachne
through the crowd of people. The old woman said,
"Foolish girl! How dare you say you are equal to the
immortal gods? I am an old woman. I have seen many
things. Take my advice and ask pardon of Athena. Be
happy that your spinning and weaving is the best that
mortals can do."

Arachne said, "Stupid old woman! Who gave you
the right to speak to me this way? It is easy to see you
were never good at anything. That is why you come
here in rags to watch my skill. If Athena dislikes my
words, let her answer me. I have **challenged** her to a
contest. But she, of course, will not come."

At these words, the old woman threw down her
staff. She grew tall and beautiful. She was dressed in
long robes of **dazzling** white. The crowd of people was
terribly afraid. They knew this was Athena herself.

Arachne turned red. She had never really believed
the goddess would hear her. But she would not give in.
She pressed her pale lips together with pride.

Arachne led Athena to one of the great looms.

Athena (ah-THEEN-uh) is
the Greek goddess of
wisdom and the arts.

This is the first hint of a
conflict. As you read, you
will see the conflict
increase between
Arachne and Athena.

Greek gods and
goddesses often punish
humans who anger them.

Greek gods and
goddesses can shape
themselves into other
forms. Here, Athena
tricks Arachne by
appearing as an old
woman.

Arachne stood before the other loom. Without a word, they began to work. They threaded the long wool strands that hung from the rollers. Between these strands, the shuttles move back and forth. Many colors of wool were ready for them to use: white, gold, red and others. The colors Arachne's father made were as wonderful as the cloth she wove.

Soon the room was almost silent. There was the creaking of the looms as the threads were pressed into place. Another sound was the breathing of the crowd of people. They were excited.

The crowd began to see that the skill of Arachne and Athena was almost equal. But the goddess was the quicker of the two.

Arachne also noticed how quickly the goddess was working. She had never matched her skill against anyone like this. She saw the goddess working quickly, calmly, and always a little faster than herself. Instead of

Who do you think will win the contest? Why?

◀ Stone sculpture of the Greek goddess Athena.

What do you think the warning might be?

Poseidon (puh-SEYE-duhn) is the Greek god of water, earthquakes, and horses. Athena won the contest with Poseidon. She claimed Athens as her own special city.

Athena allows Arachne to live. Did you expect this? Why?

being frightened, she became angry. An evil thought came into her head.

Meanwhile, on Athena's loom, a pattern of many pictures was growing. At each side of the cloth were branches of Athene's favorite tree, the olive. In the middle, figures began to appear. The crowd saw that Athena was weaving a warning to Arachne.

In the center was Athena herself. She was competing with Poseidon for the city of Athens. But in the four corners were mortals who had tried to compete with the gods. Terrible things had happened to them.

Athena finished a little before Arachne. She stood back to see what the young woman was doing. On Arachne's loom were scenes showing evil things the gods had done. The pictures showed how gods tricked young women. They showed how gods came to Earth pretending to be poor people.

When Athena saw this **insult**, her gray eyes blazed with anger. She tore the cloth in half. Then she hit Arachne across the face.

Arachne stood there, feeling anger, fear, and pride. She said, "I will not live under this insult."

She grabbed a rope from the wall. She made it into a noose. She would have hanged herself, but Athena stopped her.

The goddess touched the rope and touched Arachne. She said, "Live on, evil girl. Live on and spin. You shall spin and so shall your descendants. You will remind people that it is not wise to compete with Athene."

The body of Arachne shrank up. Her legs grew tiny. She became a little dusty brown spider on a thin thread.

All spiders are descendants of Arachne. As the Greeks watched them spin their fine thread, they remembered that even the most skillful of mortals must not try to be equal with the gods.

Literature Practice

Answer these questions on a separate sheet of paper.

1. What skill is Arachne known for in Greece?
2. What causes Athena to be angry with Arachne?
3. What warning does Athena weave into her cloth?
4. What happens to Arachne?

The World of Spiders

The Greek myth, "Arachne," explains how spiders came to exist. The Greek word *arachne* means "spider." Today, spiders and other eight-legged creatures are called arachnids.

In the Greek myth, "Arachne," Athena turns Arachne into a little dusty brown spider. Spiders come in all sizes and shapes. The smallest spider is four hundredths of an inch long. The biggest spider is almost four inches long. Most spiders have eight eyes and four pairs of legs.

Spiders weave their webs with fine silken threads. They catch their prey, mostly insects, in the sticky webs. Not all spider webs are woven in the same shape. The wolf spider traps its prey in woven tunnels. The comb-footed spider shoots its web strands in many different directions. The sheet-web weaver spins a horizontal web that looks like a bed sheet. The trap-door spider weaves a tunnel with its own trap door. Some spiders even weave their webs in the shape of funnels.

Lather and Nothing Else

an adapted story by Hernando Téllez

Words to Know

LITERARY TERM

narrator the person who tells the story

SELECTION VOCABULARY

wearily in a tired way

mangled cut and bruised

rebel a person who is against the ruling government

dedicated devoted

humbly with meek or modest feeling

cowardly lacking courage

In this story, the narrator is a skilled barber. One day, the feared leader of the army enters his shop. This terrifying meeting forces the barber to face a difficult conflict.

———❈———

The narrator in this story is a barber. The narrator uses *I* to refer to himself.

He came in without a word. I was sharpening my best razor. When I saw who it was, I started to shake. But he did not notice. To cover my fright, I went on sharpening the razor. I tried the edge with the tip of my thumb. Then I took another look at the blade in the light.

Meanwhile, he was taking off his bullet-trimmed belt with a pistol holster hanging from it. He put it on a hook in the closet and hung his cap above it. Then he turned full around toward me. Loosening his tie, he remarked, "It's hot as the devil. I want a shave." With that he took his seat.

I guessed he had a four-days' growth of beard.

They were the four days he had been gone rounding up our men. His face looked burned, tanned by the sun.

I started to work carefully on the shaving soap. I scraped some slices from the cake and dropped them into the mug. Then I added a little warm water and stirred with the brush. The lather soon began to rise.

"The fellows in the troop must have just about as much beard as I," he said. I went on stirring the lather.

He said, "But we did very well, you know. We caught the leaders. Some of them we brought back dead. Others are still alive. But they'll all be dead soon."

"How many did you take?" I asked.

"Fourteen. We had to go pretty far to find them. But now they're paying for it. Not one will escape; not one," he said.

He leaned back in the chair when he saw the brush full of lather. I had not yet put the sheet on him. I was very troubled. Taking the sheet from the drawer, I tied it around his neck.

He went on talking. He seemed to believe that I backed the present government.

"The people must have gotten a scare the other day," he said.

"Yes," I replied. I finished tying the knot behind his neck. His skin smelled of sweat.

"Good show, wasn't it?" he asked.

"Very good," I answered. Now I turned my attention to the brush. The man closed his eyes **wearily**. He waited for the gentle touch of the cool lather.

I had never had him so close before. The day he made us file through the schoolyard, our paths had crossed briefly. We were to look upon the four rebels hanging there. But the sight of those **mangled** bodies kept me from looking at the man in charge of it all. Now I had him in my hands.

Lather is a light foam made with soap and water to be put on the face for shaving. Another meaning for lather is to be excited or nervous. Both meanings are used in the story.

The story takes place in a South American village. For many years, government and rebel forces have battled for control of Colombia.

The barber in this painting by Ilya Bolotowsky called *In the Barber Shop* is probably as proud of his job as the barber in the story. ▶

It was not a bad face certainly. The beard, which aged him a bit, was not ugly. His name was Torres. Captain Torres.

I started to lay on the first coat of lather. He kept his eyes closed.

"I would love to catch a nap," he said. "But there's a lot to be done."

I lifted the brush. Then, trying to sound casual, I asked, "A firing party?"

"Something like that," he replied, "but slower."

"All of them?"

"No, just a few."

I went on lathering his face. My hands began to shake again. The man could not be aware of this. That was lucky for me. But I wished he had not come in. Probably many of our men had seen him enter my shop. With the enemy in my house, I felt a kind of duty.

I would have to shave his beard like any other beard. I would be careful and neat, as though he were a good customer. His skin should not ooze a single

Captain Torres makes the narrator feel nervous. What details in the story tell you this?

drop of blood. I would see to it that the blade did not slip in the small folds of skin. The skin would be left clean and soft. When I passed my hand over it, not a single hair should be felt. Yes. I was secretly a **rebel**. Yet I was also a **dedicated** barber, proud of my work. That four-day beard was a challenge.

The narrator's two roles cause a conflict. Why?

I took up the razor and opened the blade. Then I began working downward in front of one ear. The blade worked perfectly. The hair was tough and hard; not very long, but thick. Little by little the skin showed through. The razor gave out its usual sound as it scraped layers of soap and bits of hair. I paused to wipe it clean. Then I sharpened the blade once more. I am a careful barber.

The man had kept his eyes closed. Now he opened them. He put a hand out from under the sheet. He felt the part of his face that rose from the lather.

"Come at six o'clock this evening to the school," he said.

"Will it be like the other day?" I asked, stiff with horror.

"It may be even better," he replied.

"What are you planning to do?" I asked.

"I'm not sure yet. But we'll have a good time," he replied.

Once more he leaned back and shut his eyes. I came closer, the razor held high.

"Are you going to punish all of them?" I meekly asked.

"Yes, all of them," he said.

The lather was drying on his face. I must hurry. Through the mirror, I took a look at the street. It seemed about as usual. There was the grocery shop with two or three people inside. Then I took a quick look at the clock. Two-thirty.

I kept moving the razor down. He had a blue beard, a thick one. He should let it grow like some

Franciso Goya's painting *The 3rd of May* catches the drama of men facing a firing squad. The rebels in the story faced the firing squads of Captain Torres. ▶

poets or priests. It would suit him well. Many people would not know him. That would be a good thing for him. I thought this as I went gently over his throat. At this point, you really had to handle your blade with skill. That's because the thin hairs often fall into small folds of skin. It was a curly beard. The skin might open a tiny bit and let out a drop of blood. A good barber like myself builds his good name by not letting that happen to his customers.

This was surely a special customer. How many of ours had he sent to their death? How many had he cut to pieces? It was best not to think about it. Torres did not know I was his enemy. Neither he nor the others knew it. It was a secret known to very few. This made it possible for me to tell the rebels about Torres's actions. I could tell them what he planned to do when he went to hunt rebels. So this was going to be very hard to explain. How was it that I had him in my hands and let him go, alive and clean-shaven?

His beard had now almost disappeared. He looked years younger than when he had come in. I suppose that always happens to men in barber shops. Under my razor, Torres was refreshed. Yes, I am a good barber, the best in this town. I say this **humbly**.

A little more lather here under the chin near the large vein. How hot it is! Torres must be sweating just as I am. But he is not afraid. He is a calm man. He is not even thinking of what he will do to his prisoners later. I, on the other hand, clean him with this razor. I am careful not to draw blood. I cannot keep my thoughts in order.

What kind of man is Captain Torres?

Curse the hour he came into my shop! I am a rebel but not a murderer. It would be so easy to kill him. He has it coming, or does he? No! No one deserves what it costs those who become killers. What is to be gained by it? Nothing. Others and still others keep coming. The first kill the second. Then these kill the next. In the end everything becomes a sea of blood. I could cut his throat, so, swish, swish! He would not even have time to moan. His eyes are shut. He would not even see the shine of the razor or the gleam in my eye.

But I'm shaking like a murderer. From his throat a stream of blood would flow on the sheet. It would run over the chair on my hands then onto the floor. I would have to close the door. But the blood would go on flowing. Along the floor, warm, long-lasting, and unstoppable until it reached the street. A small red river.

I'm sure that with a good, deep cut, he would feel no pain. He would not suffer at all. What would I do then with the body? Where would I hide it? I would have to flee, leave all this. I would find a home far away, very far away. But they would follow until they caught up with me. The murderer of Captain Torres. He slit his throat while he was shaving him. What a **cowardly** thing to do.

If you were the narrator, what would you choose to do?

At last, the narrator makes his decision.

Captain Torres surprises the narrator with his final words. What is the surprise?

Others would say, "The hero of our people. A name to remember. He was the town barber. No one knew he fought for our cause."

So, which will it be? Murderer or hero? My fate hangs on the blade of this razor. I can turn my wrist a little and press the blade in. The skin will part like tissue, like rubber. There is nothing softer than a man's skin. The blood is always there, ready to burst out. A razor like this cannot fail. It is the best one I have.

But I don't want to be a murderer. No, sir. You came in to be shaved. I do my work with honor. I don't want to stain my hands with blood. Just with lather and nothing else. You are a killer. I am only a barber. Each one to his job. That's it. Each one to his job.

The chin was now clean and soft. The man got up and looked at himself in the glass. He ran his hand over the skin. He felt its freshness, its newness.

"Thanks," he said. He walked to the closet for his belt, his pistol, and his cap. I must have been very pale. I felt my shirt soaked with sweat. Torres put on his belt, tightened the buckle, and patted his gun. After smoothing his hair out of habit, he put on his cap. From his pants pocket he took some coins to pay for the shave. He started toward the door. At the door he stopped and turned toward me.

"They told me you would kill me. I came to find out if it was true. But it's not easy to kill. I know what I'm talking about."

Literature Practice

Answer these questions on a separate sheet of paper.

1. How does Captain Torres make the narrator feel?

2. What kind of man is Captain Torres?

3. Why does the narrator take pride in his work as a barber?

4. What conflict does the narrator face?

5. Why do you think the narrator makes the decision that he does?

A Barber's Many Jobs

The narrator in "Lather and Nothing Else" is proud of his work as a barber. To him, being a barber is more than just a job. He takes special care to do his work well and to take good care of his customers.

The barber profession is an old one. In the 1300s, you could visit the barber to have your hair cut or to have your teeth pulled. Barbers even performed surgery.

Today barbers still hang red and white striped poles outside their shops. The red and white pole recalls the barber's early job as a surgeon. The red stripes on the pole stand for blood. The white stripes stand for white bandages. Luckily for all of us, barbers today stick to cutting hair and trimming beards.

The Interlopers

an adapted story by Saki

Words to Know

LITERARY TERMS

setting the time and place of the action in a story

irony of situation an event that is not expected

SELECTION VOCABULARY

game wild animals hunted for sport or for food

lawsuit a disagreement brought to court

generations the time between the birth of parents and the birth of their children

feud a long quarrel between families

civilized educated or refined

hesitated stopped for a moment

clumsiness awkwardness

possibility chance

Two neighbors have been in conflict with one another for many years. One winter night the two men come face to face in a dark forest. Unfortunately, they learn about friendship much too late.

———◦◦◦———

The setting of this story is a forest at night. The Carpathian (kahr-PAY-thee-uhn) Mountains are in central Europe.

In a forest somewhere in the eastern Carpathians, a man stood. It was a winter night. He watched and listened like a man who is hunting. But the **game** he looked for was not usually hunted. Ulrich von Gradwitz searched the dark forest for a human enemy.

The forests of von Gradwitz were large and well supplied with game. The small strip of steep woods on its border, however, was not known for good hunting. There was not much game. But it was the most carefully guarded area of von Gradwitz's land.

A famous **lawsuit**, in the days of von Gradwitz's grandfather, took it from a neighbor. The neighbor was a small landowner with no legal right to the land. They lost the case. But they did not agree with the Court's ruling. As a result, there were many fights that followed over hunting rights. It caused a bitter feeling between the families. This feeling lasted for three **generations**.

The **feud** became personal once Ulrich became head of his family. The man he hated most in the world was Georg Znaeym. Znaeym was the head of the neighboring family. The feud might have died down. The families might have reached an agreement. But both men continued to fight each other. As boys, they thirsted for each other's blood. As men, each prayed bad luck might fall on the other.

On this windy winter night, Ulrich called together his men to watch the dark forest. They were to keep a lookout for prowling thieves. The deer usually kept under cover during a storm. Tonight, however, these creatures were uneasy. Instead of sleeping as usual, they were running like driven things. Clearly there was something troubling in the forest. Ulrich could guess from where it came.

He walked away by himself. The men on lookout duty were waiting on the crest of the hill. Ulrich wandered far down the steep slopes into the wild tangle of bushes. He looked through the tree trunks for sight or sound of the thieves. He thought to himself what it might be like if he came across his enemy, Georg Znaeym. To meet him alone, that was his chief thought. As he stepped round the trunk of a huge tree, he came face to face with the man he wanted to see.

Ulrich von Gradwitz [OOL-rihk vawn GRAHD-vihtzh]

The conflict in this story is between two families who disagree about the ownership of a piece of land.

Georg Znaeym [GAY-awg ZAI-ehm]

Artist Roger de la Fresnaye shows the beauty of a small village in his painting *La Cheminée d'usine Paysage de Meulan*. The von Gradwitz and Ulrich families probably lived in a quiet village like this one. ▶

What role does nature play in the conflict between Ulrich and Georg?

The two enemies stood glaring at one another for a long, silent moment. Each held a rifle. Each had hate in his heart and murder on his mind. The chance had come to play out the hatred of a lifetime. But a **civilized** man cannot easily bring himself to shoot down his neighbor. One kills in cold blood and without a word only for a crime against his home and honor.

While the men **hesitated**, there was a splitting crash over their heads. Before they could leap aside, a huge falling tree thundered down on them. Ulrich von Gradwitz found himself stretched on the ground. One arm lay numb beneath him. The other was held in a tangle of branches. Both legs were pinned beneath the fallen mass. His heavy boots had saved his feet from being crushed. His broken bones were not as serious as they might have been. Yet it was clear that he could not move until someone came to free him. The falling twigs had slashed the skin of his face. He winked away some drops of blood from his eyelashes. Only then could he get a view of the disaster.

At his side lay Georg Znaeym. He was so close to Ulrich, the two men could have touched. Georg Znaeym was alive. He was also helplessly trapped. All round the men lay thick piles of splintered branches and broken twigs.

The men were glad to be alive. But they were angry at being trapped. It brought on mixed feelings. Solemn thanks and sharp oaths came to Ulrich's lips. Georg was nearly blinded by blood dripping across his eyes. He stopped struggling for a moment. He listened. Then he gave a short, mad laugh.

"So you're not killed as you ought to be. But you're caught, anyway," Georg cried. "Caught fast. Ha! What a joke. Ulrich von Gradwitz is trapped in his stolen forest. There's justice for you!"

He laughed again.

"I'm caught in my own forest land," returned Ulrich. "When my men come to free us, you will wish you were in some other spot. Caught hunting on a neighbor's land. Shame on you."

Georg was silent for a moment. Then he answered quietly.

"Are you sure your men will find much to free? I have men, too. They were in the forest tonight. They will be here first. They will do the freeing. They will drag me out from under these branches. With a little **clumsiness** on their part, they might roll this huge trunk on you. Your men will find you dead. To make it look good, I will send my regrets to your family."

"Good," snarled Georg, "good. We'll fight this out to the death. You, I, and our men. No outsiders will come between us. Death and hell's fires to you, Ulrich von Gradwitz."

"The same to you, Georg Znaeym," said Ulrich. "Land thief, game grabber."

Both men spoke with the bitter **possibility** of losing. Each knew that it might be a long time before his men found him. It was a plain case of who would come first.

Notice how the two men act as they discover they are both caught under the tree.

Both had given up the useless struggle to get free. The mass of wood held them down. Ulrich tried only to bring one partly free arm to his coat. He hoped to reach his water. Even after he reached it, it was a long time before he got any water down his throat. But what a heaven-sent swallow it was! It was winter, and little snow had fallen as yet. Because of this, the captives suffered less from the cold than might be expected. Even so, the water was refreshing to the injured man. He looked across at his enemy with a small throb of pity. Georg could just barely keep the groans of pain and weariness from his lips.

"Could you reach this water if I threw it over to you?" asked Ulrich suddenly. "One should be as well off as possible."

This winter forest in V. Grubicy's *Poema Pantersta* is like the forest in the eastern Carpathians where von Gradwitz and Znaeym happen to meet. ▼

"No, I can hardly see anything. There is so much blood caked around my eyes," said Georg. "In any case, I don't take water from an enemy."

Ulrich was silent for a few minutes. He lay listening to the low whistle of the wind. An idea was slowly growing in his brain. It became stronger every time he looked across the branches. In the pain Ulrich was feeling, his old hatred seemed to be dying.

"Neighbor," he said at last. "Do as you please if your men come first. It was a fair deal. But as for me, I've changed my mind. If my men come first, you shall be the first to be helped. You will be treated as my guest. We have fought like devils all our lives. Fought over this stupid strip of forest. A place where the trees can't even stand up in the wind. Lying here tonight, thinking, I've learned we've been fools. There are better things in life than winning a quarrel over land. Neighbor, if you will help me to bury the old quarrel, I—I will ask you to be my friend."

Georg Znaeym was silent for a long time. Ulrich thought perhaps he had fainted from his injuries. Then Georg spoke slowly and in jerks.

"How the market square would stare and talk if we rode into the town square together. No one living can remember seeing a Znaeym and a von Gradwitz having a friendly talk. What peace there would be among the forest folk if we were to end our feud. If we were to make peace among our people, no outsider could meddle. You would spend nights under my roof. I would feast with you at your castle. I would never fire a shot on your land except as your guest. You could shoot with me down in the marshes where the wild birds are. In all the countryside, none could stop us if we chose to make peace. I thought I would hate you all my life. Now I think I have changed my mind about things. You offered me water. . . . Ulrich von Gradwitz, I will be your friend."

Ulrich's feelings toward Georg begin to change. Why?

The scene of *Wolves Trailing a Man's Trace* is an illustration by an unknown artist. ▶

For a time both men were silent. They turned over in their minds the great changes of this sudden friendship. In the cold, gloomy forests, the wind tore in gusts at the branches and trees. The two men lay and waited for the help that would bring freedom. Each prayed secretly that his men might be the first to arrive. Then he might be the first to attend to the enemy that was now a friend.

Presently, as the wind dropped for a moment,

Ulrich broke the silence.

"Let's shout for help," he said. "In this lull, our voices might carry."

"They won't carry far though the trees and brush," said Georg. "But we can try. Together, then."

The two raised their voices in a long hunting call.

They listened. There was no answer. "Together again," said Ulrich a few minutes later.

"I heard something that time, I think," said Ulrich.

"I heard nothing but the deadly wind," said Georg.

There was silence again for some minutes. Then Ulrich gave a joyful cry.

"I can see figures coming through the wood. They are following the way I came down the hill."

Both men raised their voices in as loud a shout as they could gather.

"They hear us! They've stopped. Now they see us. They're running down the hill toward us," cried Ulrich.

"How many of them are there?" asked Georg.

"I can't see clearly," said Ulrich. "Nine or ten."

"Then they are yours," said Georg. "I had only seven out with me."

"They are making all the speed they can. Brave lads," said Ulrich gladly.

"Are they your men?" asked Georg. "Are they your men?" he said again eagerly. Ulrich did not answer.

"No," said Ulrich with a laugh. It was the silly laugh of a man who is suddenly very afraid.

"Who are they?" asked Georg quickly. He strained his eyes to see what the other wished he had not seen.

"Wolves."

The ending of the story is an example of irony of situation. What did you expect to happen?

Literature Practice

Answer these questions on a separate sheet of paper.

1. What is the setting of the story?
2. What is Ulrich doing in the forest on a windy winter night?
3. How do Ulrich and Georg feel toward each other when they meet in the forest?
4. How do Ulrich and George become trapped in the forest?
5. What happens when the two men call for help?

Bering Coast

a poem by Fred Bigjim

Words to Know

LITERARY TERMS

tone the feeling a writer has toward the subject of a story or poem

imagery words that help the reader to "see" how something looks, sounds, feels, or tastes

SELECTION VOCABULARY

relics objects that have been left behind, usually by a culture or group of people

Eskimos people native to the Arctic coastal areas of North America

culture the customs and beliefs of a group of people

interwoven woven together

Sometimes people are in conflict with nature. The speaker in this poem learns that his mixed feelings about the Bering Coast are an important part of who he is.

———— ✸✸✸ ————

Your shores hide the Eskimo's past,
Covering it with sands of time.

Every once in a while,
You uncover jewels of **relics**,
As if to remind the world
That once, in times past,
Eskimos shared the shore with you.

The speaker in this poem talks directly to the Bering Coast.

Eskimo hunters used float racks to keep their harpoons, spears, and floats in place. Four small seals decorate one side of the rack. ▶

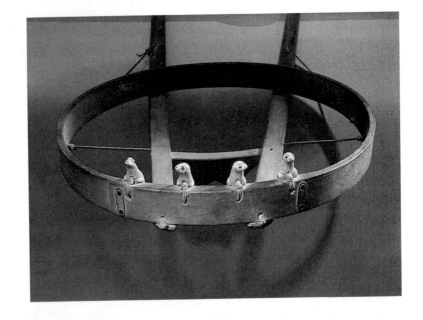

How did the speaker in this poem feel about the Bering Coast when he was nine years old?

When I was nine,
I walked your shores
Nearly every day.
Once, I found a baby seal.
When I approached,
It looked at me
With tears in its eyes.

The Eskimo in me said,
"Take it for its fur and liver."
The child in me said,
"I need to care for it."

Eskimo,
   Seal,
      Together a **culture.**
So **interwoven** like braided hair,
Shedding the same kind of tears.

"Interwoven like braided hair" describes the close connection between Eskimos and seals.

The child in me carried the
seal
And it disappeared off the
Bering Coast.
The Eskimo in me went
with it.

◀ This is a seal-oil lamp
used by Eskimos.

Literature Practice

Answer these questions on a separate sheet of paper.

1. Who is the speaker talking to in the poem?

2. What are the speaker's feelings about the coast?

3. What kind of relationship do the Eskimos have
   with the Bering Coast?

4. What image shows how the baby seal feels?

5. What internal conflict does the speaker struggle
   with?

Chapter Review

Summaries

- **Arachne**—Arachne is a young maiden in Greece. She is known for her beautiful weaving. People come from all over Greece to see her work. Arachne is proud of her skill. She thinks she can weave as well as the goddess Athena. Arachne's pride angers Athena. Arachne challenges Athena to a weaving contest. Athena teaches Arachne a lesson about having too much pride.

- **Lather and Nothing Else**—The narrator is a skilled barber who takes pride in his work. The barber is also a secret rebel. He does not approve of the army leaders who run the government. When the captain of the army visits his shop, the barber struggles with his feelings. He must decide between killing the captain or giving him a good shave.

- **The Interlopers**—For many years the von Gradwitz and Znaeym families have disagreed about who owns a piece of land. Ulrich von Gradwitz and Georg Znaeym are bitter enemies. One night, the two men happen to meet in the forest. They are trapped by a fallen tree. While they are trapped, both men learn that their fight with each other is silly. But they have a new struggle to face.

- **Bering Coast**—The speaker in this poem writes about the Bering Coast. He wants to protect and care for the coast. At the same time, he knows that he must depend on the coast to survive.

Chapter Quiz

Choose the letter of the correct answer. Rewrite the sentences on a separate sheet of paper.

1. Arachne suffers from having too much
   a. talent.
   b. pride.
   c. money.
   d. beauty.

2. The narrator in "Lather and Nothing Else" chooses to do his job as a
   a. rebel.
   b. soldier.
   c. surgeon.
   d. barber.

3. In "The Interlopers," Ulrich and Georg are
   a. best friends.
   b. brothers.
   c. school mates.
   d. enemies.

4. In the forest, Ulrich and Georg are discovered by
   a. Ulrich's men.
   b. Georg's men.
   c. wolves.
   d. a herd of deer.

5. The speaker's feelings in "Bering Coast" are expressed with a tone of
   a. anger.
   b. happiness.
   c. sadness.
   d. worry.

Thinking and Writing

Write answers to the following questions on a separate sheet of paper.

1. Think about the conflict between Arachne and Athena. In what way is Arachne responsible for her punishment from Athena?

2. Why do you think Hernando Téllez gave his story the title "Lather and Nothing Else"?

3. Why do Ulrich's and Georg's feelings toward each other change in "The Interlopers"?

4. How does the speaker in "Bering Coast" solve his conflict?

▲ *Retrato del Turista* by
Maria Izquierdo shows a
man having his portrait
painted. The portrait
shows another view of the
man. In a moment of
truth, we see ourselves
differently.

Chapter Learning Objectives

- Identify the main character in a story.
- Discover the use of description in a story.
- Identify clues about character.
- Recognize alliteration in a poem.

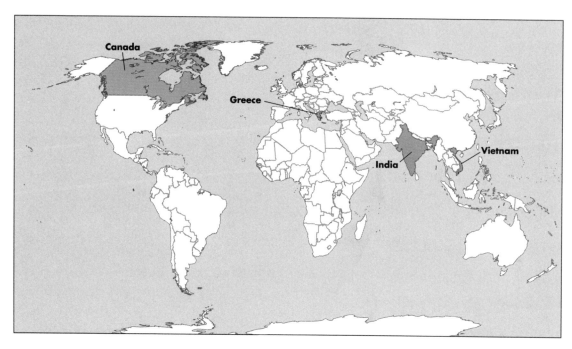

Greece
The Golden Touch
a myth retold by Mary Pope Osborne

Vietnam
The Fly
an adapted story by Mai Vo-Dinh

India
By Any Other Name
an adapted story by Santha Rama Rau

Canada
The Small Cabin
a poem by Margaret Atwood

At some point, there are moments when we must honestly face who we are and who we want to become. These moments force us to be stronger and more confident. In this chapter, you will read about people who use these moments to find new directions for their lives.

The Golden Touch

a myth retold by Mary Pope Osborne

Words to Know

LITERARY TERMS

main character the central figure in a story

climax the most exciting part of a story that comes near the end

SELECTION VOCABULARY

goblet a drinking glass

hospitable friendly and generous

nugget a small lump of gold

pillars tall columns

mansion large house

exhausted very tired

overjoyed very happy and satisfied

King Midas is granted everything he wished for. Then he learns a lesson about the evil of greed.

————— ⊗⊗⊗ —————

The main characters are King Midas and Bacchus, who is a Greek god. In Greek myths, gods and goddesses teach important lessons to people. King Midas will learn a lesson from Bacchus.

Bacchus, the merry god of the vine, raised his **goblet.** "To you, King Midas," he said, "and because you have been so **hospitable** to me—ask for anything you wish, and I will grant it to you."

"What an idea!" said Midas. "Anything I wish?"

"Indeed, anything," said Bacchus.

"Anything?"

"Yes! Yes!"

"Ah, well," said the king, chuckling. "Of course, there's only one thing: I wish that everything I touch

would turn to gold!" Midas looked sideways at Bacchus, for he couldn't believe such a gift could really be his.

"My friend, you already have all the gold you could possibly want," said Bacchus, looking disappointed.

"Oh, no! I don't!" said Midas. "One never has enough gold!"

"Well, if that's what you wish for, I suppose I will have to grant it," said Bacchus.

Bacchus took his leave. As Midas waved good-bye to him, his hand brushed an oak twig hanging from a tree—and the twig turned to gold!

This describes the kind of man King Midas is.

King Midas is surprised and thrilled that Bacchus has granted his wish.

The king screamed with joy, then shouted after Bacchus, "My wish has come true! Thank you! Thank you!"

The god turned and waved, then disappeared down the road.

Midas looked around excitedly. He leaned over and picked a stone up from the ground—and the stone turned into a golden **nugget**! He kicked the sand—and the sand turned to golden grains!

King Midas threw back his head and shouted, "I'm the richest man in the world!" Then he rushed about his grounds, touching everything. Everything, everything turned to gold: ears of corn in his fields! Apples plucked from trees! The **pillars** of his **mansion**!

Everything turns to gold when King Midas touches it. How might this cause trouble?

When the king's servants heard him shouting, they rushed to see what was happening. They found their king dancing wildly on his lawn, turning the grass to glittering blades of gold. Everyone laughed and clapped as Midas washed his hands in his fountain and turned the water to a gleaming spray!

Finally, **exhausted** but **overjoyed**, King Midas called for his dinner. His servants placed a huge banquet meal before him on his lawn. "Oh, I'm so hungry!" he said as he speared a piece of meat and brought it to his mouth.

But suddenly King Midas realized his wish may not have been as wonderful as he thought—for the moment he bit down on the meat, it, too, turned to gold.

Midas laughed uneasily, then reached for a piece of bread. But as soon as his hands touched the bread, it also became a hard, golden nugget! Weak with dread, Midas reached for his goblet of water. But alas! His lips touched only hard, cold metal. The water had also turned to gold.

Covering his head and moaning, King Midas realized his great wish was going to kill him. He would starve to death or die of thirst.

"Bacchus!" he cried, throwing his hands toward heaven. "I've been a greedy fool! Take away your gift!

◀ The artist, James Reynold Draper, calls this painting *Show of Hands*. King Midas could use his hands to turn anything he touched to gold.

Free me from my golden touch! Help me, Bacchus!"

The sobbing king fell off his chair to his knees. He beat his fists against the ground, turning even the little anthills to gold. His servants grieved for him, but none dared go near him, for they feared he might accidentally turn them to gold, too!

As everyone wailed with sorrow, Bacchus suddenly appeared on the palace lawn. The merry god stood before the sobbing king for a moment and said, "Rise, Midas."

This is the climax of the myth. What does King Midas learn about himself?

Stumbling to his feet, King Midas begged Bacchus to forgive him and to take away the curse of the golden touch.

"You were greedy and foolish, my friend," said Bacchus. "But I will forgive you. Now go and wash yourself in the river that runs by Sardis, and you'll be cleansed of this desire to have more gold than anyone else!"

King Midas did as Bacchus said. He washed in the river, leaving behind streams of gold in the river's sands. Then he returned home and happily ate his dinner.

Literature Practice

Answer these questions on a separate sheet of paper.

1. What does King Midas wish for?
2. What does the king's wish reveal about the kind of man he is?
3. What happens when the king touches objects?
4. What is the climax of the myth?
5. What lesson does the myth teach?

The Fly

an adapted story by Mai Vo-Dinh

Words to Know

LITERARY TERM

clues about character thoughts, actions, and words in a story that help the reader find out what the character is like

SELECTION VOCABULARY

marketplace a public square where goods are bought and sold

bamboo a kind of tropical grass that has hollow woody stems

witness a person who sees or hears something

clever smart and quick

firmness solid manner

explanations answers

chuckling quietly laughing

A rich, older man tries to trick a young boy and his family. Instead, the man learns the importance of keeping a promise.

————

Everyone in the village knew the moneylender. He was a rich and smart man. Having made a great fortune over the years, he settled into an easy life in his big house. The house had a huge garden and was guarded by a pack of fierce dogs. But still he was not happy with all he had. He went on making money by lending it to people all over the county. He charged them a very high rate for the loans. The moneylender was the most powerful man in the area, for many were in debt to him.

What do you learn about the moneylender?

One day, the rich man set out for the house of one of his poor farmers. Even though he had been warned many times, the poor farmer could not pay off his debt. Even working himself to a shadow, the poor farmer could barely make ends meet. The moneylender was therefore set on getting his money back. If he could not get his money back, he would take some of the poor farmer's best belongings. But the rich man found

The young boy is the main character in the story.

This portrait of Hidetada is by an unknown artist. ▶

no one at the farmer's house but a small boy of eight or nine. He was playing alone in the dirt yard.

"Child, are your parents home?" the rich man asked.

"No, sir," the boy replied. He went on playing with his sticks and stones. He paid no attention at all to the man.

"Then where are they?" the rich man asked, rather angrily. Still the little boy went on playing and did not answer.

When the rich man repeated his question, the boy looked up and answered slowly. "Well, sir, my father has gone to cut living trees and plant dead ones. My mother is at the **marketplace** selling the wind and buying the moon."

The boy tells riddles instead of telling the man where his parents are.

"What? What in heaven are you talking about?" the rich man commanded. "Quick, tell me where they are, or you will see what this stick can do to you!" The **bamboo** walking stick in the big man's hand surely looked frightening.

Even after he questioned him again and again, the boy gave the same reply. Being very upset, the man told him, "All right, little devil, listen to me! I came here today to take the money your parents owe me. But if you tell me where they really are and what they are doing, I will forget all about the debt. Is that clear to you?"

"Oh, sir, why are you joking with a poor little boy? Do you expect me to believe what you are saying?" For the first time the boy looked interested.

"Well, there is heaven and there is earth to hear my promise," the rich man said. As he spoke, he pointed up to the sky and down to the ground.

But the boy only laughed. "Sir, heaven and earth cannot talk and therefore cannot tell anyone about your promise. I want some living thing to hear your promise."

The rich man caught sight of a fly landing on a bamboo pole nearby. Then laughing inside because he was fooling the boy, the rich man made an offer.

"There is a fly. He can be our **witness**. Now, hurry and tell me what you mean. How can your father be out cutting living trees and planting dead ones? How can your mother be at the market selling the wind and buying the moon?"

Looking at the fly on the pole, the boy began to speak. "A fly is a good enough witness for me. Well, here it is, sir. My father has simply gone to cut down bamboo. He will make a fence with it for a man near the river. And my mother . . . oh, sir, you'll keep your promise, won't you? You will free my parents of all their debts? You really mean it?"

"Yes, yes, I do honestly swear in front of this fly here." The rich man urged the boy to go on.

"Well, my mother has gone to the market to sell fans. She will use the money to buy oil for our lamps. Isn't that what you would call selling the wind to buy the moon?"

The rich man shook his head. He had to admit to himself that the boy was **clever**. However, he thought the little genius still had much to learn. A clever person would never believe that a fly could be a witness to anyone. Saying good-by, the man told the boy he would soon return to keep his promise.

A few days passed. Then the moneylender came back. This time he found the poor farmer and his wife at home, as it was late in the evening. A nasty scene followed. The rich man demanded his money, and the poor farmer said he was sorry and begged for more time. Their fighting woke up the little boy. He ran to his father and told him, "Father, father, you don't have to pay your debt. This gentleman here has made a promise to me. He has promised that he would forget all about the money you owe him."

"Nonsense," the rich man shook his walking stick at both father and son. "Nonsense. Are you going to stand there and listen to a child's stories? I never spoke

The rich man makes a promise in front of the witness he and the boy have chosen. Do you think the rich man intends to keep his promise to the boy?

Why does the rich man think that he will be believed rather than the boy?

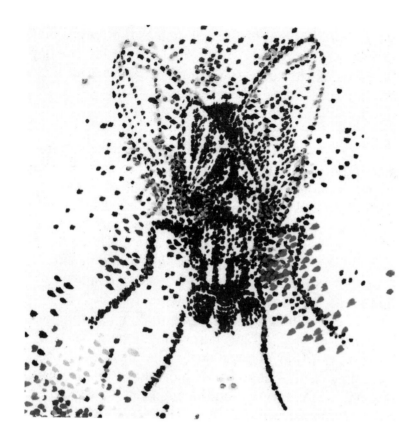

◀ The fly is an important witness in the story. Artist Phong Bin drew this *Study for a Fly.*

a word to this boy. Now, tell me, are you going to pay, or are you not?"

The whole matter ended by being brought to the judge in charge of the county. The poor farmer and his wife did not know what to believe. All they could do was take their son with them to court. The boy's **firmness** about the rich man's promise was their only hope.

The judge began by asking the boy to tell exactly what happened. Happily, the boy quickly told about the **explanations** he gave the rich man in return for forgetting the debt.

"Well," the judge said to the boy," if this man here has made such a promise, we have only your word for it. How do we know that you have not made up the whole story yourself? In a case such as this, you need a witness to prove your story. You have none." The boy stayed calm. He said that, of course, there was a witness to his talk with the rich man.

"Who is that, child?" the judge asked.

"A fly, Your Honor."

"A fly? What do you mean, a fly? Watch out, young man. Daydreams are not allowed in this place!" The judge's kind face suddenly became stern.

"Yes, Your Honor, a fly. A fly which was landing on this gentleman's nose!" The boy jumped from his seat.

"Rude little devil, that's a pack of lies!" The rich man roared in anger. His face was like a ripe tomato. "The fly was not on my nose; he was on the pole. . . . " But he stopped dead. It was, however, too late.

The great judge himself could not help bursting out laughing. Then the crowd burst out laughing. The boy's parents, too, laughed shyly. The boy, and the rich man himself, also laughed. With one hand on his stomach, the judged waved the other hand toward the rich man.

"Now, now, that's all settled. You, dear sir, have indeed made your promises to the child. Pole or no pole, your talk with this boy did happen after all! The court says that you must keep your promise."

Still **chuckling**, he told all to go.

> The color of the man's face is compared to that of a ripe tomato. Why is his face turning red?

> What lesson does the boy teach the moneylender?

Literature Practice

Answer these questions on a separate sheet of paper.

1. Why does the rich man visit the boy?

2. Who is the main character in the story?

3. What promise does the rich man make to the boy?

4. Who witnesses the promise?

5. Why does the rich man think he can trick the boy?

By Any Other Name

an adapted story by Santha Rama Rau

Words to Know

LITERARY TERM

description words that create a clear picture of a person, place, or thing

SELECTION VOCABULARY

Anglo-Indian English and Indian

headmistress school principal

glittered sparkled or shined

stubborn firm

civil service having to do with the part of the government that deals with employment

twilight faint light after sunset

whitewashed painted white

guarded cautious or watchful

Sometimes challenges help us to grow stronger. Two Indian sisters try hard to fit in at a British-run school. The struggle ends when one sister refuses to accept their unfair treatment.

———∞∞∞———

At the **Anglo-Indian** day school in Zorinabad, they changed our names. We were sent to this school when my sister was eight years old. I was five and a half. The first day of school was a hot, windless September morning. Such mornings came often in north India. We stood in the **headmistress's** study. She said, "Now you're the new girls. What are your names?" My sister answered for us. "I am Premila." She turned to me. "This is Santha."

Zorinabad [zoh-REHN-ah-bad]

How does the
headmistress feel about
Indian names?

The headmistress had been in India fifteen years. She still smiled at her helpless lack of skill when saying Indian names. Her rimless, half-glasses **glittered**. The loose bun on her head trembled as she shook her head. "Oh, my dears, those are much too hard for me. Let's give you pretty English names. Wouldn't that be more jolly? Let's see, now Pamela for you, I think." She looked at my sister. "That's as close as I can get. As for you," she said to me, "how about Cynthia? Isn't that nice?"

Premila keeps silent.
Imagine how it would feel
to have someone change
your name.

My sister was always less easily frightened than I was. She kept a **stubborn** silence. I said, "Thank you," in a very tiny voice.

We were sent to that school because my father worked in the area. As an officer of the **civil service**, he had to inspect the villages. His headquarters at the time were in Zorinabad. He made his shorter inspection tours on horseback. A week before the first day of school, we had waved good-by to him. It was a stale, hot day after the rainy season. Such days were normal that time of year. An assistant, a secretary, two bearers, and a man to look after the bedding and luggage were with him. They rode away through our large garden. We turned back into the **twilight** of the house. We could hear the sounds of fans whispering in every room.

The British ruled India for
90 years. The mother's
comment suggests her
belief that people do not
change.

Up to then, my mother had refused to send Premila to the British run school. She used to say, "You can bury a dog's tail for seven years, and it still comes out curly. You can take the British away from home for a lifetime, and they'll still remain narrow-minded." Diplomas from Indian schools were not thought to be any good in those days. In my case the question of school had never come up. It probably never would have if Mother's good health had not broken down. For the first time in my life, she could not go on giving us lessons every morning. So our Hindi books were put away. We were sent to the Anglo-Indian school.

I still remember that first day of school. At that age, if one's name is changed, one becomes almost two people. I remember having a distant interest in the actions of "Cynthia." Yet I certainly did not feel I had to answer for them. So, I followed the thin, stiff back of the headmistress down the porch to my classroom. I felt only a brief interest in what was going to happen to me. This was a strange, new place they called School.

The building was Indian in appearance. It had wide porches opening onto a courtyard. Indian porches are

How does Santha feel about her first day of school?

◀ A 17th century watercolor by artist Murad shows two women seated in the courtyard of a house in India.

usually **whitewashed** and have stone floors. These, in the style of British schools, were painted dark brown. In addition, they had mats on the floors. The mats seemed to add to the heat.

I think there were about a dozen Indian children in the school. It held about forty students in all. Four Indian students were in my class. They were all sitting at the back of the room. I went to join them. I sat next to a small, serious girl who didn't smile at me. She had long, glossy-black braids. She wore a cotton dress, but she still kept her Indian jewelry. She wore a gold chain around her neck, thin gold bracelets, and tiny rubies in her ears. Like most Indian children, she had a rim of black powder around her eyes. The cotton dress should have looked strange. All I could think of was asking my mother if I couldn't wear a dress to school, too. It would replace the Indian clothes I now wore.

I can't remember too much about what went on in class that day. However, I do remember how it began. The teacher pointed to me. She asked me to stand up. Then she said, "Now, dear, tell the class your name."

I said nothing.

"Come along," she said, frowning slightly. "What's your name, dear?"

"I don't know," I said, at last.

There were about eight or ten English children in the front of class. They giggled and twisted around in their chairs to look at me. I sat down quickly and opened my eyes very wide. I hoped in that way to dry them off. The little girl with the braids put out her hand. Very lightly, she touched my arm. She still didn't smile.

Most of that morning I was quite bored. I looked briefly at the children's drawings pinned to the wall. Then I watched a lizard hanging to the ledge of the high, barred window behind the teacher. From time to time it would shoot out its long, yellow tongue for a fly. Then it would rest with its eyes closed and its belly throbbing.

What words describe the small, serious girl?

It seemed as though it were swallowing several times very quickly. The lessons were mostly about reading and writing and simple numbers. These things my mother had already taught me, so I paid little notice. The teacher wrote on the board words like "bat" and "cat." These seemed babyish to me. Only "apple" was new and hard to grasp.

When it was time for lunch, I followed the girl with the braids onto the porch. The children from other classes were also there. I saw Premila. I ran over to her, as she had our lunch boxes. The children were all opening packages and sitting down to eat sandwiches. Premila and I were the only ones who had Indian food. Our lunch boxes held thin wheat chapatties and some vegetable curry. There were also bottles of buttermilk for us to drink. Premila thrust half of the lunch into my hand. Then she whispered fiercely that I should sit with my class. That was what the others seemed to be doing.

The huge black eyes of the little Indian girl looked at my food longingly. I offered her some. But she only shook her head. She plowed through her sandwiches.

I was very sleepy after lunch. At home we always took a nap. This was usually a pleasant time of day. The bedrooms were darkened against the harsh afternoon sun. I would drift off to sleep to the sound of Mother's voice reading a story. Finally, the shrill, fussy voice of the ayah would wake us for tea.

At school, we rested for a short time on low cots on the porch. After that we were expected to play games. During the hot part of the afternoon, we played indoors. After the shadows got longer and an evening breeze came up, we moved outside to the courtyard.

I never really grasped the idea of games that were contests. At home, whenever we played a game like tag, I was always allowed to "win." "Because she is the youngest," Mother used to tell Premila. I had often heard her say it. So I had no idea what "winning" meant.

The word "apple" is hard for Santha to understand because she has never seen an apple. Apple trees do not grow in India.

Chapatties are thin pieces of bread baked in a hot pan. Curry is a combination of strong spices used in a sauce for vegetables, rice, and meat dishes.

An ayah (EYE-yuh) is an Indian nurse or maid.

Santha does not
understand that she
cannot always win a
game. The other children
want her to join in and
play fairly.

When we played twos-and-threes that afternoon, I let
one of the small English boys catch me. This is what I
was trained to do. So I was, of course, puzzled when the
other children did not return the favor. I ran about for
what seemed like hours without catching anyone. I ran
about until it was time for school to close. Much later I
learned my idea was called "not being a good sport." I
therefore stopped letting myself be caught. It was years
later that I really learned the spirit of the thing.

When I saw our car come up to the school gate, I
broke away from my classmates. Rushing toward it, I
yelled, "Ayah! Ayah!" It seemed like forever since I had
seen her that morning. This wise, loving figure in her
white sari had given me so much useless advice. All of
it was on how to be a good girl at school. Premila
followed more calmly. On the way home, she told me
never to do that again in front of the other children.

A sari is a dress worn by
Hindu women in India
and Pakistan. It is made
from many yards of
lightweight cloth. The
cloth is wrapped to form
a skirt and a shoulder
covering.

When we got home, we went straight to Mother's
high, white room. There we had tea with her. I quickly
climbed onto the bed and bounced on the springs.
Mother asked how we had liked our first day in school.
I was pleased to be home. I was pleased to have left
that odd Cynthia behind. So I had nothing whatever to
say about school, except to ask what "apple" meant.
But Premila told Mother about the classes. She added
that in her class they had weekly tests. These were
given to see if they had learned their lessons well.

I asked Premila, "What's a test?"

Premila said, "You're too small to have them. You
won't have them in your class for donkey's years." She
had learned the phrase that day. Now she was using it
for the first time. We all laughed loudly at her wit. She
also took Mother to one side to say we should take
sandwiches for lunch. Not, she said, that she minded.
But they would be simpler for me to handle.

What is the real reason
Premila asks for
sandwiches?

That whole lovely evening I didn't think about
school at all. I dashed barefoot across the lawns with

◄ The seated woman in this 18th century painting is being waited upon. The artist of the work is unknown.

my best friend, the cook's son. Together we ran to the stream at the end of the garden. We quarreled in our usual way. Then we waited for the night to bring out the smell of flowers. I listened closely to his stories of ghosts and demons. By dark I was too scared to cross the garden alone. The ayah found me. She shouted at the cook's son. Then she scolded me. She hurried me in to supper. It was a wonderful evening.

It was a week later that our lives changed suddenly. It was the day of Premila's first test. I was sitting in the back of my class. As usual, I was only half listening to the teacher. I had started a rather **guarded** friendship with the girl with braids. Her name turned out to be Nalini (Nancy, in school). The other three Indian children were already fast friends. Even at that age, one thing was clear to us. Becoming friends with the English children was out of the question. Sometimes during the class, my new friend and I would draw pictures. We would show them to each other secretly.

The door opened sharply, and Premila marched in. At first, the teacher smiled at her kindly. Then she said, "Now, you're little Cynthia's sister?"

Premila didn't even look at her. She stood with her feet planted firmly apart. Her shoulders were stiff as she spoke straight to me. "Get up," she said. "We're going home."

What details help you see how brave and confident Premila is?

I didn't know what had happened. I could tell that it was a turning point of some kind.

"Bring your pencils and your notebook," she said.

I went back for them. Then together we left the room. The teacher started to say something just as Premila closed the door. But we didn't wait to hear what it was.

In total silence we left the school and started to walk home. I asked Premila what the matter was. All she would say was, "We're going home for good." It was a very tiring walk for a child of five and a half. I dragged along behind Premila. My pencils were growing sticky in my hand. I can still remember looking at the dusty hedges and tangles of thorns. They lay in ditches by the side of the road. I also remember smelling the faint perfume of the trees. I wondered if we would ever get home. Now and then a horse-drawn cart passed us. The women in their pink and green silks stared at us as we trudged along the road. A few workers and women with baskets of vegetables on their head smiled at us. But it was nearing the hottest time of the day. Therefore, the road was nearly empty. I walked more and more slowly. I shouted to Premila from time to time. "Wait for me!" I yelled in a voice that became more and more cranky. She spoke to me only once. That was to tell me to carry my notebook on my head. It would shield me from the sun.

When we got home, the ayah was just taking lunch into Mother's room. She immediately started asking us questions. Her questions were all about what we were doing back here at this hour of the day.

Mother looked surprised and very concerned. She asked Premila what had happened.

Premila said, "We had our test today. She made me and the other Indians sit at the back of the room, with a desk between each one."

Mother said, "Why was that, darling?"

"She said it was because Indians cheat," Premila added. "So I don't think we should go back to that school."

Why is Premila upset by the teacher's comment?

Mother seemed far away. She was silent for a long time. At last she said, "Of course not, darling." She sounded displeased.

We all shared the curry she was having for lunch. Afterwards I was sent off to the beautiful bedroom for my nap. I could hear Mother and Premila talking through the open door.

Mother said, "Do you think she understood all that?"
Premila said, "I shouldn't think so. She's a baby."
Mother said, "Well, I hope it won't bother her."

Of course, they were both wrong. I understood it perfectly. I remember it all very clearly. But I put it happily away because it had all happened to a girl called Cynthia. I was never really very interested in her.

What do you learn about Santha at the end of the story?

Literature Practice

Answer these questions on a separate sheet of paper.

1. What happens to Premila and Santha on their first day of school?
2. How does the mother feel about British-run schools?
3. How would you describe Premila?
4. What kind of person is the headmistress?
5. What causes Premila to walk out of school?

What's in a Name?

The headmistress in "By Any Other Name" decides it is easier to give Premila and Santha English names. Premila, whose Indian name probably means "first", is given Pamela, which means "all honey." Santha is renamed Cynthia, a Greek name for "goddess of the moon."

Giving a child a name is an important act. Some parents pass on to their child a name that has been in the family for many years. Others may give a name based on a child's features or qualities. Often a child is named for a saint or other religious person, such as Jerome or Mary. In Native American cultures, a child is given a name that relates to an animal, a dream, or a successful life event.

Whatever the reason for giving a name, each name has its own meaning or history. For example, the name Philip means "lover of horses." The name Theodore comes from the Greek meaning "given by god." In Spanish, the name Rosa means "rose." The Irish name Meghan means "pearl."

The Small Cabin

a poem by Margaret Atwood

Words to Know

LITERARY TERM

alliteration the repeating of consonant sounds that begin words

SELECTION VOCABULARY

gradually slowly

crumple fold or wrinkle

collapsing caving in or falling down

After a fire destroys the family's cabin, the speaker in this poem has difficulty believing the tragedy actually happened.

The house we built **gradually**
from the ground up when we were young
(three rooms, the walls
raw trees) burned down
last year   they said

I didn't see it, and so
the house is still there in me

among branches as always   I stand
inside it looking out
at the rain moving across the lake
but when I go back
to the empty place in the forest

There is a pause in the line. It shows that the speaker of the poem is only repeating what she heard. Perhaps she still cannot believe the news.

The pause lets you feel the speaker move from the thought of the burned cabin to the thought of how lovely the cabin was.

▲ The title of the painting by Jasper Francis Cupsey is *A Cabin in Greenwood Lake.*

The repeated letter sounds in "collapsing like a cardboard carton" sound a little bit like the crackling of a fire.

the house will blaze and
crumple
suddenly in my mind

collapsing like a cardboard
carton
thrown on a bonfire,
summers
crackling, my earlier
selves outlined in flame.
Left in my head will be
the blackened earth: the
truth.

Where did the house go?
Where do the words go
when we have said them?

Literature Practice

Answer these questions on a separate sheet of paper.

1. What happens to the cabin?

2. How does the poet describe the burning house?

3. Who are the "earlier selves outlined in flame"?

4. Why do you think the memory of the small cabin is important to the speaker?

Chapter Review

Summaries

- **The Golden Touch**—King Midas asks the Greek god Bacchus to grant him a wish. Midas wishes that everything he touches would turn to gold. Bacchus grants his wish. King Midas is thrilled. Now he is even richer than he was before. But King Midas soon comes face to face with his own greed.

- **The Fly**—A rich moneylender visits a poor farm family that owes him money. The parents aren't home. Their clever son answers the man's questions with a riddle. The man promises to forget the debt if the boy will explain the riddle and reveal where his parents are. The man thinks he can deceive the boy. Instead, he learns a lesson in keeping promises.

- **By Any Other Name**—Premila and Santha are sisters who live in India. On their first day at the Anglo-Indian school, the headmistress gives them English names to use at school. Most of the students at the school are British. The sisters try to fit in with the other students. Premila, however, refuses to stay in a school where teachers are prejudiced against Indian students.

- **The Small Cabin**—The speaker remembers a small house that her family built when she was young. The house stood in a forest near a lake. Then the small cabin burns down. The speaker finds it difficult to believe the cabin is no longer standing. Finally, the speaker understands that she can always see in her mind the cabin as it once was.

Chapter Quiz

Choose the letter of the correct answer. Rewrite the sentences on a separate sheet of paper.

1. In "The Golden Touch," King Midas thinks that one can never have enough
   a. friends.   c. servants.
   b. gold.   d. food.

2. In "The Fly," the rich moneylender learns the importance of
   a. forgetting a debt.   c. collecting debts.
   b. keeping a promise.   d. a judge's decision.

3. The main character in "The Fly" is the
   a. young boy.   c. moneylender.
   b. judge.   d. boy's father.

4. The teacher in "By Any Other Name" changes the sisters'
   a. room assignments.   c. grade levels.
   b. names.   d. test scores.

5. The house in the poem "The Small Cabin"
   a. is sold.   c. burns down.
   b. collapses.   d. is empty.

Thinking and Writing

Write answers to the following questions on a separate sheet of paper.

1. In "The Golden Touch," why do you think Bacchus is surprised by King Midas' wish?

2. How would you describe Premila and Santha in "By Any Other Name"?

3. Does the speaker in the poem "The Small Cabin" believe the house has burned down? Explain your answer.

Unit One Review

A. The following questions are about some of the selections you read in this unit. Answer each question by writing one or two sentences on a separate sheet of paper.

1. What conflict does the narrator face in "Lather and Nothing Else"?

2. Why is setting important? Consider the setting in "The Interlopers" and in "Bering Coast" in your answer.

3. How would you describe the main character in "The Fly"?

4. Do you think Premila in the story "By Any Other Name" does the right thing by walking out of school? Explain your answer.

5. What does the speaker in the poem "The Small Cabin" learn about herself?

B. Choose two of the essay questions below. Answer them on a separate sheet of paper. Write one or two paragraphs for each one.

1. Each time we understand something new about ourselves, we grow. Such moments of truth can change our lives. Think about the selections you read in this unit. How are people's lives changed by the lessons they learn?

2. Solving a conflict can take people in a new direction. Choose a character from a story or a speaker from a poem. Tell what you believe happens to this person one year after the story or poem ends. Explain the reasons for the new direction.

3. The values and traditions that we get from our ancestors are part of who we are. In "Bering Coast" and "By Any Other Name," the characters and the speaker have a strong connection to their heritage. How does this connection lead each of them in a new direction?

4. In "The Small Cabin," the speaker in the poem faces an important moment. How does the way the poem is written help to support the ideas that are important to the speaker?

Unit Two

DARE TO BELIEVE

▲ The difficulty of meeting a challenge becomes clear in Paul Klee's painting *Drum Organ*. It shows a man lost in a world of cubes. His challenge is to find a way out.

Chapter Learning Objectives

- Learn about a folktale.
- Identify the first-person point of view.
- Learn about the setting of a story.
- Recognize nonfiction.
- Learn about an autobiography.

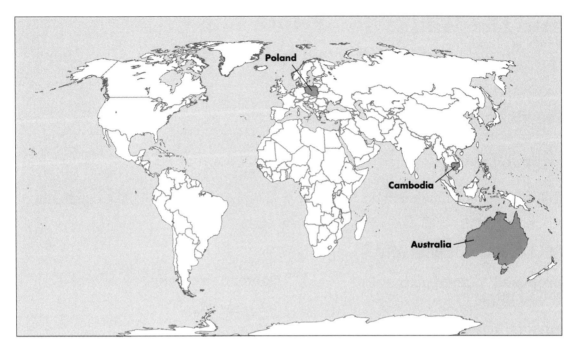

Cambodia

**The Mountain of the Men
and the Mountain of the Women**

*an adapted folktale retold by Touch
Neak and Alice Lucas*

Poland

The Endless Steppe

*adapted from the autobiography of
Esther Hautzig*

Australia

My Brilliant Career

an adapted story by Miles Franklin

Some challenges greet us in our own backyards. Others happen far from home. If we dare to believe in ourselves, we can face any challenge. We can find the courage and determination to meet it. In this chapter, you will read about challenges that range from changing an old custom to lifting cows.

The Mountain of the Men and the Mountain of the Women

an adapted folktale retold by Touch Neak and Alice Lucas

Words to Know

LITERARY TERM

folktale a story handed down for many years among the people of a community or region

SELECTION VOCABULARY

proposed offered marriage to someone

custom a usual way of acting

ministers people who help the king run the country

lantern a covering for a light

slender thin

Even if something has been done the same way for thousands of years, that does not mean it is right. In this story, some women dare to challenge an old custom.

———∞———

Kampong Cham [KAHM-pahng CHAHM]

This folktale takes place a little more than one thousand years ago.

Long ago, in the Kampong Cham province of Cambodia, marriage was very different from how it is today. In those days, girls **proposed** to boys. If the boy said yes, the girl had to pay for the wedding. She also had to buy expensive gifts for the boy.

This **custom** went on for many years. The young women thought it was very unfair. They were not as strong as the young men. It was harder for them to make money.

▲ This is a stone carving on one of the towers of Angkor Wat. The building, which is one of the largest monuments in the world, is a symbol of hope and pride for the people of Cambodia.

Jayavarman [ji-yuh-VAR-muhn]

Cambodian kings ruled from Angkor for more than 500 years.

All over the country, girls talked about this problem. They decided to go to the king. At that time, Jayavarman the First was king of Cambodia. He was the king who had brought together two kingdoms: the kingdom of the north and the kingdom of the south. He made them into the mighty Angkor Empire.

The king had made great cities. His buildings had beautiful stone carvings. He was a very good king. The girls trusted that he would help them. But one girl reminded them that the king himself was a man. Men liked the marriage custom very well.

Another girl said, "We must trick the king. We must think of a way to get him to change the marriage custom!" So the girls made a secret plan. The young women who were the best speakers traveled to the city of Angkor to visit the king.

The young women met with the king Jayavarman. They bowed and said, "Most high Lord, we ask that you listen to our story. We girls are weak compared to the strong men of our country. Yet we are the ones who must propose marriage to a boy. And we must pay for the wedding! We must buy fine gifts for him and his family! It is very hard for us to do these things. Why not have the boys propose marriage to us? It would be easier for them to pay for the wedding and the gifts. Do you not agree?"

What do you think the king will say to the girls?

King Jayavarman was silent for a long time. He looked down at the bowed heads of the girls. At last he said, "Perhaps you are right, beautiful daughters of the Khmer. But what am I to do? This is the custom of our land. How can I change the Khmer way of proposing marriage?"

The Khmer [kuh-MEER] are one of the first groups of people to live in Cambodia.

The boldest girl raised her head and spoke. She pressed her hands together to show respect. She said, "Great leader of the Khmer people, may we tell you of a plan?"

The king nodded.

The girl said, "Call all the young men and women

of our country together. Tell each group they will build a mountain to show respect for you. Give them five days to finish the task. On the morning of the fifth day, the work must stop. Count the days from the time the Morning Star rises in the dark sky. That is the time before the sun shows its face.

"When the Morning Star rises on the first day, the work must begin. When the Morning Star rises for the fifth time, the work must stop."

The king liked the idea of having two mountains built to honor him. There were not many mountains in Kampong Cham province. The king thought he could stand on the top of these mountains and be closer to heaven. He could also watch for enemies from the mountain top. Since he himself was a man, he believed the men would win this contest.

The king agreed to the girls' plan. The next day, his **ministers** called all the young people to the king's palace. As they bowed before him, the king said, "The young women are unhappy with our country's marriage customs. They want the men to propose to them and pay for the wedding!"

The young men laughed at such a foolish idea.

The king shouted, "Silence! To be fair to the girls, I have made a plan. Listen carefully." The king told the young people about the plan to build two mountains. He explained how the days would be counted by the rise of the Morning Star.

Then the king said, "Come with me. I will show you where to build." He walked along the east bank of the Mekong River. He showed them the place where the mountains were to be built.

The king said, "Tomorrow, as the Morning Star rises, I will beat the royal drum. That will be the signal for work to begin. You may work both day and night for five days. But remember: When the Morning Star rises for the fifth time, you must stop work. Do you understand?"

The Morning Star is the planet Venus. It shows just above the horizon before sunrise. Why do you think the people in this story tell time by the sky?

The King says it is his plan. What does that tell you about the king?

The women are planning to trick the men and the king. What do you think they will do?

The young men and women nodded.

The king said, "When the day is light, I will come to see your work. If the men have built a higher mountain, the women must keep the marriage customs we have now. But if the women's mountain is higher, the customs will change. The men will propose to the women and pay for the wedding and the gifts."

When the king had left, the men laughed and joked about the plan. They said, "No woman can do such hard work. We will win easily. Let us go home and rest so we are ready to work tomorrow."

This is a puppet from a Thai Buddhist drama. The three women seem to be working together just as the women do to build their mountain. ▶

That night, while the men were sleeping, the women met. They were afraid they might lose unless they started work right away. Quietly, they walked to the building place by the river. They dug the dirt to make it loose. The next day it would be easy for them to dig up big stones. They would roll the stones together to make the base of their mountain. When the women finished, they hid their work with branches. No one would guess they had already started.

The "trick" begins.

When the Morning Star rose the next day, the king beat the royal drum. The work began. The men worked all day. The women worked all day, too. When evening came, the men rested and drank cool drinks. They were sure they were ahead of the women. But the women kept working all night. They took turns resting for only short periods of time.

The Morning Star rose on the second day.

The women stopped working and had a meeting. The men saw them sitting and talking. They said, "Ha, look at those lazy women. We don't have to work too hard." That night, while the men slept, the women worked.

On the third day, as the Morning Star rose, some of the women went to the market. They bought thin, clear paper, string, and a candle. Some other women went to the forest to cut bamboo.

The women buy materials that they will use in their plan to trick the men and the king.

The men said, "Look, some women are going to the market. Others are going to the woods to get out of the hot sun." The men stopped their work, too. They sat in the cool shade. On the third night, the women worked while the men slept.

On the fourth day, the men saw the women sitting beside their small mountain. The man said, "Look at those foolish women! They must be chewing betel nuts instead of working!" The men worked for a while, then rested under a tree.

The betel nut is a nut that many Asians chew just as many Americans chew gum.

What do you think the women had been doing? They had been making their own Morning Star! They cut the bamboo into thin pieces. They arranged the pieces in the shape of a star. They tied the corners together with strong grass. Then they covered the star with clear paper. Now the star looked like a **lantern.** They tied a long string to their star. Then they hid it in the grass.

That night the women worked again while the men slept. But after only a few hours, they took the star lantern from its hiding place. They put the candle inside. The evening breeze lifted the lantern high in the sky.

The women began to cry. They said, "Oh no, the Morning Star has risen for the fifth time. We must stop building. Oh, we have certainly lost the race."

The men said, "Listen to those crying women. We have certainly won the race. Let us sleep a little longer. We will rest for a big celebration tomorrow."

So the men went back to sleep. The women worked for the rest of the night. When the true Morning Star rose, they stopped.

When the sun came up, the king and his ministers came to look at the mountains. The king saw the women's tall mountain with its **slender** peak.

The king saw the men's mountain. It had a strong, wide base. But it was flat on top. It had no peak at all! It was plain to see the women had won.

The king kept his word. This was his order: "From this day on, it must be the man's responsibility to propose to the woman. He must buy fine gifts for her and her family. And he must also pay for the wedding feast. In this way, the men of the Khmer Kingdom will honor the women."

If you travel up the Mekong River on the way to the Kampong Cham, you will see two mountains. One is the Mountain of the Men. The other is the Mountain of the Women. You will see for yourself which mountain is higher and more beautiful.

The women do many clever things. Do you think they are being fair to the men?

The women's mountain is better than the men's mountain in at least two ways. What are they?

Literature Practice

Answer these questions on a separate sheet of paper.

1. This folktale explains how something changed long ago in Cambodia. What changed?

2. What challenges do the women face?

3. How do the women in this story show that they dare to believe in themselves?

4. The men and the women view the contest in different ways. What are the differences?

5. How would you describe the king?

Cambodian Wisdom

Every culture has proverbs, or short, well-known sayings that contain wise thoughts. Here are some proverbs, along with their meanings, from Cambodia.

- Don't let an angry man wash dishes. (An angry man who washes dishes may break all the dishes.)

- Don't let a hungry man guard rice. (The hungry man will eat the rice while he is guarding it.)

- If a tiger lies down, don't say, "The tiger is showing respect." (Be careful that the tiger is not getting ready to attack.)

- Don't take the straight path or the winding one. Take the path your ancestors have taken. (The path your ancestors have taken is one that has been well used. You can be sure of succeeding if you follow it.)

- No cleverness can ever overturn wise rules set out in distant times. (It does not matter how smart you think you are. You cannot change customs that have been followed for a long time.)

The Endless Steppe

adapted from the autobiography of Esther Hautzig

Words to Know

LITERARY TERMS

nonfiction a story that is about real places, people, and events

autobiography the story of a person's life written by that person

SELECTION VOCABULARY

steppe a large area of dry, flat, grass-covered land

manure animal waste

whitewash a mixture that is used like paint to make something white

cubbyhole a small shelf or cupboard, often used to store things

pumice a type of rock, sometimes used to scrub away dead skin

gauze a thin, see-through cloth used for bandages

outcast a person whom other people do not accept

cast off sent or driven away

When life presents challenges, we can give up, or we can find the strength and beauty inside to keep going. This is a story about dealing with a challenging place and a challenging person.

In 1941, Esther and her family were sent from their home in Poland to Siberia.

Spring came to the **steppe** of Siberia. When I think of spring there, I always think of the thick mud. When the snow melted, the steppe became an ocean of mud. Walking through it was like walking through knee-deep molasses. It took energy to pull a foot up from the bottom of this mud. Often one of my shoes would get

▲ The man walking through the muddy field in *The Tramp* by Jean François Raffaëlli seems lonely and sad. Vanya the bum seems very lonely and sad in the same way.

Svetlana (SVEHT-lah-nah)

The person who tells the story in an autobiography is the author. Autobiographies are one kind of nonfiction.

stuck. I would have to go back and look for it.

Mud or no mud, I was happy in spring. I had a friend to whisper and gossip with—Svetlana. I played tag and hopscotch. Svetlana and I helped each other in school. She helped me with grammar and spelling. I helped her with ideas for writing. Going to school in Siberia was wonderful. Coming back home to the hut was not.

There were ten of us living in the hut—several other people beside our family. When summer came, the heat was terrible. The hut was an awful little oven with the ten of us inside it. Our tempers rose.

Father decided to look for a new place for our family to live.

On the north side of the village, there were some empty huts. They were empty for a reason. They had no heat, no floors, and no glass in the windows. But they were empty. Father asked the village housing chief if we could live in one of the huts.

A miracle happened. We were allowed to move in to one of the empty huts. Our family would be alone at last.

That little hut became my dream house. Every day, after working in the potato patch, I went to the hut and cleaned it. Also, we picked up **manure,** mixed it with clay, and made new bricks. We fixed or replaced the old bricks in the walls. Father got some **whitewash** at his job. We painted the walls with it. Someplace or other, we found glass for the windows.

The family seems to make the best out of what they have. How will the new hut be better than the old one?

Father made an outdoor stove out of bricks for summer cooking. We could cook our own little flour cakes or soup. We wouldn't have to line up with other people to eat.

There was a public bath in the village. To go there was Mother's dearest wish. We would have to save up for such a treat. It would mean eating a little less for a week or two. But wouldn't it be wonderful to feel clean before we moved into our own home?

The bath was a small building with two doors—one for women and one for men. We found that Mother was not the only woman who wanted to be clean. The line was long. The wait would be a couple of hours, at least. We waited.

What problems are involved in getting a bath?

There were two rooms in the bath. One had faucets along the walls. The other was a steam room. In there, you used twigs to rub and clean yourself.

We were sent to the faucet room. We were given a **cubbyhole** for our clothes, a bowl, and **pumice.** We filled our bowls at the faucet, sat down on a stone bench, and scrubbed ourselves. The water was hot. Mother was delighted. Now we were really ready to move.

The simple pleasure of taking a bath is a great event for Esther and her family. This helps to show how challenging their everyday life is.

Outside our hut, there was a small piece of land that no one seemed to be using. We would turn it into a vegetable patch. We had potatoes, tomato plants, and corn seed.

Things were hard to come by in this land. Whenever something came your way, you took it. Svetlana's father had gotten a large amount of **gauze** from a hospital. (I did not know how he had gotten it. I did not want to ask.) Svetlana asked me if I wanted some. I said yes. I would use it for curtains.

Svetlana said, "You're going to use white hospital gauze for curtains, Esther?"

I said, "You will see."

I began to save onion peels. I asked Svetlana to do the same. In school, we had learned that if you boil onion peels in water, you get a yellow dye.

Notice the details about making curtains. These details help readers see that Esther is clever and can figure things out.

When I had a big pile of onion peel, I boiled it in water. The water became a pot of pale yellow dye. I put the gauze in this and let it stay for several hours. It worked! The gauze was now a pretty yellow. I dried it out in the sun and then I made my curtains.

The hut was heaven. We ate when we wanted to. We slept when we wanted to. At night we would sit

Imagine what it would feel like to be told that a stranger was moving in with your family.

Vanya (VAHN-yah)

Esther and her family may have used a stove like this one for cooking. This is *Franklin Stove* by Wanda Hazel Gay. ▼

outside and watch the Siberian sky. There was always something to see. We would sit there quietly, quietly.

It was too good to last.

One day the village housing chief came to our hut when I was alone. He told me that the next day someone would be coming to live with us.

I said, "Who is it going to be?"

The housing chief said, "Vanya the bum."

This was awful.

I had been taught never to call anyone names. But everyone called this man with one leg, "Vanya the bum." He was the village beggar. People said he stole. Now this dirty bum was going to live with us.

When I gave the news to my parents, they couldn't believe it either.

Father said, "Vanya, the bum …?"

Mother coughed. That was a signal to my father. She did not like the way he was speaking. She said Vanya should not be called a bum. In fact, he should not be called Vanya, either. He must have a proper name. When we met him, we should introduce ourselves as usual.

Father agreed. He gave the old speech about not judging people by the way they looked.

I stood on one foot and then the other, listening. To me, Vanya the bum was coming to live with us.

The idea made me scared and sick.

The next evening, Vanya the bum stood at our open door.

He said, "May I come in?"

Mother said, "Of course you may."

Father went toward him. He said, "Good evening."

I felt Mother's eyes on me. I said, "Good evening. My name is Esther Rudomin. What's yours?"

He said, "Vanya."

His eyes went from Father to Mother and back to me.

He added, "My name is Ivan Petrovich, my child." There was a tiny spark in his eyes.

Father said, "Welcome to our house, Ivan Petrovich."

The change from village bum to Ivan Petrovich did not happen overnight. At first he was a shadow from the dark world of the homeless, an **outcast.** He left very early in the morning. When he came home, he went right to his corner of the hut. He talked very little. He would eat bits of food he had picked up, then go to sleep.

After a few weeks, he began to change. He started to eat with us. He would share whatever food he brought.

"Vanya" is a nickname for "Ivan." The narrator's mother feels that a more formal name should be used for the man.

Describe the family's manners. Describe Vanya's manners.

▲ One day Vanya just walked away. No one ever heard from him again. This painting of an *Old Man Walking in a Rye Field* is by Lauritz Andersen Ring.

Then he began to talk. Ivan Petrovich was a shoemaker from the Ukraine. He had read many books. But once he had talked too much or talked too carelessly. Maybe he had been misunderstood. He had been sent to prison in Siberia. He never knew why. When they finally let him out of prison, he had only one leg left. He had gone from village to village, begging.

The Ukraine is a country in Russia.

Soon he began to wash himself. That made us happier than I can tell. He began to comb his beard. He began to walk tall. He became Ivan Petrovich.

As Ivan Petrovich began to look at himself with new eyes, so did the people in the village. They did not think of him as a bum anymore. They thought of him as just another human being **cast off** on the great steppe of Siberia.

How did Ivan Petrovich become Vanya the village bum?

One day he disappeared. He left one morning as always but did not come back that night. That was the last time we saw Ivan Petrovich, who used to be called Vanya the bum.

Literature Practice

Answer these questions on a separate sheet of paper.

1. Why is "The Endless Steppe" nonfiction?
2. How would you describe the family in this story?
3. What challenges does life in Siberia present?
4. What challenges does living with Vanya present?
5. How does Vanya change?

Big, Bad Siberia

When people think of Siberia, two words often come to mind—big and bad. A giant part of Russia, Siberia covers millions of square miles. In much of the region, summers are hot and winters are cold. Imagine living in a place where it is 93 degrees below zero.

Not much food can grow there. Part of the reason is the climate. In addition, the soil is poor. With extra hard work, people do manage to grow crops such as potatoes and wheat. Still, not many people live there. Life is too hard. Animals, on the other hand, manage to do well in Siberia. Foxes, otters, wolves, elk, reindeer, seals, and bears live in Siberia in large numbers.

For hundreds of years, criminals and people who questioned the way the Russian government was run were sent to prison camps in Siberia. This practice was at its worst in the early 1900s. At that time, tens of millions of people were sent to camps in Siberia to do hard labor. Many died there. Some people, like Vanya, never even found out why they were sent there.

My Brilliant Career

an adapted story by Miles Franklin

Words to Know

LITERARY TERMS

first-person point of view the use of the words *I, me,* and *my,* to tell a story

setting the time and place in which a story occurs

SELECTION VOCABULARY

veranda a large, open porch

drought a long period of time without rain

tripod a stand with three legs

lever a rod or bar used to lift things

weariness tiredness

career the work a person chooses to do in life

bulwarks strong supports

The kinds of challenges people face often depend on where and how they live. In this story the narrator faces the challenge of hard work in the hot sun. She also faces the challenge of making a better life for herself.

⸻⸎⸻

Possum Gulley, Australia, 1890

My father called to me, "Sybylla, what are you doing? Where is your mother?"

I said, "I'm ironing. Mother's taking care of some chickens. What do you want?"

It was two o'clock in the afternoon. The thermometer hanging in the shade of the **veranda** said 105 degrees.

The story takes place more than one hundred years ago in Australia.

Sybylla [SIH-bih-lah] the narrator refers to herself as *I*.

Father said, "I see Blackshaw coming across the flat. Call your mother. You bring the leg-ropes. I've got the dog-leg. Come at once. We'll get these cows back on their feet. Poor devils — they're so weak they're falling down. We might as well kill them now. But there might be rain by the next moon. This **drought** can't last forever."

I called my mother, got the leg-ropes, and started off. I pulled my sunbonnet closely over my head. Clouds of dust were blowing from the west. I needed to protect my eyes.

An Early Settler's Homestead, New Zealand by John Weeks looks very much like the home of Sybylla and her family. ▼

The dog-leg that father was talking about was three poles about eight or ten feet long. They were strapped together to make a **tripod.** Father had made the dog-leg to help us lift cows that had fallen down.

We stood the tripod up on the ground. Across the top of the tripod, we placed a longer pole. We used this as a **lever,** putting our weight at one end to lift the cow at the other end. The cow was tied to the lever with leg-ropes. One rope went around the cow near its front legs. The other rope went close to its back legs.

New cows were not used to the dog-leg. We had a hard time with them. But the cows who were used to it would help themselves. Up they would go, nice as a daisy.

The only trick to the dog-leg was to pull the pole back quickly, before the cow could move. Otherwise, the ropes would trip the cow, and it would fall again.

On this afternoon we had six cows to lift. We struggled hard and got five cows back on their feet. Then we walked to where the last cow was lying. It was a stony spot on the side of a hill. There was no shade.

Blackshaw turned her around by her tail. Mother and I fixed the dog-leg and got the ropes ready. We got the cow up, but the poor animal was so weak that she fell down again.

We decided to let her rest a few minutes before trying to lift her once more. There was not a blade of grass to be seen. The ground was too dusty to sit on. We were so hot and tired, we could not say more than one word to each other. We waited in silence in the blazing sun. We closed our eyes to shut out the dust.

Weariness! Weariness!

Weariness was on my mother's delicate face. Weariness was in my father's dusty face. Blackshaw was weary and said so. He wiped the dust from his face. His sweat had turned the dust to mud. The poor cow lying at our feet was weary.

The cows suffer so much in the heat that they fall over and must be lifted. Think of how difficult it is to lift a cow.

Try to see in your mind what is happening here. Describe what you see in your own words.

The details here help you learn more about the setting. What is it like?

The narrator repeats the words *weariness* and *weary* a number of times. Why does she do this?

Does the narrator really mean that her career is brilliant? What does she mean?

The narrator thinks the life of a peasant is not bad, but she knows it is not the life for her.

All of nature was weary. It seemed to sing a sad, tired song with the hot wind. The wind was like the breath of a furnace. It roared among the trees.

Everything was weary, everything but the sun. He felt his power. He was never tired. He would never let up. He swung boldly in the sky, looking down on his helpless victims.

Weariness! Weariness!

This was life—my life! This was my **career,** my brilliant career! I was fifteen—fifteen!

It seemed that in a few short hours I would be as old as the adults who stood around me. I looked at them as they stood there. They were weary. They were on their way down the other side of the hill of life.

When they were young, I'm sure they had dreamed of the better life. Maybe they had even known a better life. But here they were. This had been their life. This was their career. It would probably be mine, too. My life—my career—my brilliant career!

I say nothing against the lower life. Peasants are the **bulwarks** of every nation. For someone who has a peasant's soul, it is a good, honest life. When times are good and the seasons are kind and gentle, a peasant's life is a grand life. But to me the life of a peasant is awful. The people around me work from morning until night. Then they enjoy their hard-earned sleep. They have only two things in their life—work and sleep.

Work and sleep were not enough for me. There was a third part in me which cried out to be fed. I longed for the arts. Music was a great love of mine. I borrowed every book in the neighborhood. I stayed up late to read them when I should have been sleeping. Since I slept less, my work was harder for me than for other children my age.

That third part of me was the strongest part. I live a dream-life with writers, artists, and musicians. Hope whispered sweet, cruel lies to me. It told me that one day my dream-life would be real. That dream-life was like a shining lake I could see in the distance. The lake called to me to come and sail on its silver waters. But I was inexperienced. It was blind, self-centered inexperience that kept me from seeing the pit—the enormous pit between me and that shining lake.

The narrator does not think she can reach her "shining lake." Why not?

Literature Practice

Answer these questions on a separate sheet of paper.

1. What is the challenge the farmers in this story face?

2. How is the narrator like the other characters?

3. How is the narrator different from the other characters?

4. How does the setting influence the life of the narrator?

5. Do you think the narrator might have a "brilliant career" ahead of her? Why or why not?

Chapter Review

Summaries

- **The Mountain of the Men and the Mountain of the Women—**
  The women are unhappy with the custom for proposing marriage.
  The king agrees with their plan for changing the custom. The
  women win in a contest against the men. As a result, the men now
  propose marriage and pay its costs.

- **The Endless Steppe—**The narrator remembers growing up in
  Siberia. She and her family are pleased to be able to move into
  a tiny, one-room hut. One day the family is told that Vanya the bum
  must move in with them. Although they do not like the idea, they are
  polite and respectful. In time, their kindness helps Vanya regain his
  self-respect.

- **My Brilliant Career—**The narrator and her parents lead a hard life
  on their farm. The narrator realizes she needs more in life. Yet there
  is a huge distance between her present life and the life she dreams
  about.

Chapter Quiz

Choose the letter of the correct answer. Rewrite the sentences
on a separate sheet of paper.

1. In "The Mountain of the Men and the Mountain of the Women,"
   mountains are built to decide
   a. who will be king of Cambodia.
   b. whether the marriage
   custom should change.
   c. where to build the
   kingdom.
   d. whether men and women
   are equal.

2. In "The Endless Steppe," a small hut is
   a. a welcome home.
   b. a prison cell.
   c. Vanya's place of birth.
   d. turned into a garden.

3. The narrator's family learns that Vanya the bum
   a. cannot speak.
   b. has suffered in his life.
   c. deserves to be treated badly.
   d. can never change.

4. The problem the narrator and her family face at the beginning of "My Brilliant Career" is
   a. being weak from hunger.
   b. lifting fallen cows.
   c. finding enough food.
   d. finding books to read.

5. In "My Brilliant Career," Sybylla wishes for
   a. a life on the farm.
   b. the end of the hot weather.
   c. more cows.
   d. a different life.

Thinking and Writing

Write answers to the following questions on a separate sheet of paper.

1. The men in "The Mountain of the Men and the Mountain of the Women" believe that women are not able to do any hard work. How does this thinking affect the way the men meet the challenge of building a mountain?

2. At the end of "The Endless Steppe," Vanya disappears. What do you think happens to him?

3. How does the use of first–person point of view in "My Brilliant Career" help you learn about the hopes and dreams of the narrator?

Chapter 4 Heroes

▲ The artist Paolo Uccelo shows Saint George bravely fighting a dragon in *Saint George and the Dragon*. Sometimes people who dare to believe become great heroes.

Chapter Learning Objectives

- Identify clues about character.
- Learn about the resolution of a story's conflict.
- Learn how descriptive details are used.
- Understand personification.

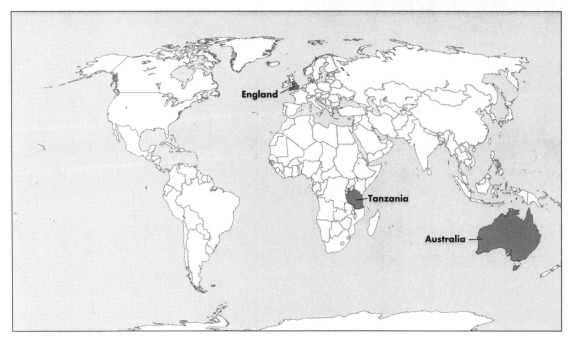

Australia
The Heroic Fisherman
*an adapted myth retold
by Louis A. Allen*

England
Beowulf and the Fire Dragon
*an adapted story retold
by Robin McKinley*

Tanzania
Unanana and the Elephant
*an adapted folktale retold by
Kathleen Arnott*

When people dare to believe, they can sometimes do the impossible. In these stories, you will meet heroes who put their own lives in extreme danger to save the lives of others.

The Heroic Fisherman

an adapted myth retold by Louis A. Allen

Words to Know

LITERARY TERMS

character clues thoughts, actions, and words in a story that help the reader find out what a character is like

hero the main character in a story

SELECTION VOCABULARY

wallaby a small kangaroo

reef a ridge of coral in the sea

whirlpool fast-moving water from the sea that turns in a circle

ancestor a person who lived long ago and is related to someone living many, many years later

grieve to feel or show great sadness

messenger person who carries news or other information

Heroes have a lot of courage. In this story, a great fisherman, Munjurr, knows that his friend is about to drown. Only the very bravest of actions can save his friend.

———∞———

For the native people of Australia, the Dreamtime is when the world began.

Manggalilji (mahn-gah-LIHL-jee)

In the Dreamtime, in the country of the Manggalilji people, there lived a great fisherman called Munjurr. In his canoe made of bark, he went far out to sea. He speared kingfish and dugong for the people of his camp. Munjurr was wise in the ways of wind and tide.

When the waves rolled high, he alone could steer his canoe between them. Sometimes the surf was so rough others were afraid to fish in it. But Munjurr would calmly paddle through the waves to the fishing grounds beyond.

One morning, Munjurr came to the campfire of his friend, Nurru. Nurru was the best drone piper in the camp. Nurru was practicing power notes on his didjeridu. He was getting ready for a ceremony that would be held before the moon died.

Munjurr said, "Come fish with me, Nurru."

Nurru said, "The waves are high today. The canoe will tip over."

Munjurr said, "This is a fine time to catch the big fish. When the surf runs high, they come close to shore."

Munjurr (MUN-jur) is the hero in this myth. Look for clues that describe the qualities that make him great.

A drone is a single sound. Nurru (NYOO-ryoo) plays one very powerful, long note on his drone pipe, or didjeridu (dij-uh-ree-do). His pipe is probably about 5 feet long.

The village of Munjurr and Nurru is near the sea like this Mayan village. This is a mural painting in the temple of Chichen-Itza. ▼

In this dialogue, you learn about Munjurr and Nurru. How are these characters different?

The details here describe Munjurr's great skills.

The man in this painting by Paul Klee battles a huge fish. If he is as skilled a fisherman as Munjurr, he will not be afraid. ▼

Nurru said, "Let us hunt the **wallaby.** Tomorrow, when the wind dies, we can fish."

Munjurr said, "You are known as a brave man, Nurru. You and I will bring back a great catch today. Our friends will be proud that we were the only ones who faced such rough waters. If we run into trouble, you can sound a power song on your didjeridu to help us."

Munjurr had touched Nurru's pride. Nurru followed Munjurr to the beach. They pulled the canoe from the bushes and checked to make sure it was watertight. Then they splashed into the surf and quickly began to paddle.

Almost at once, a great wave caught them. It took all of Munjurr's skill to steer through the waves, which were like mountains. But slowly Munjurr moved away from the dangerous shore and into the calmer waters

that were beyond the **reef.** There the two men turned their attention to fish.

Walu, the Sun Woman, had just started moving across the sky when Nurru suddenly grabbed Munjurr's arm.

Nurru said, "A whale! It comes this way."

Munjurr looked. A large whale was moving toward them. Water ran down its sides as it cut through the sea. The story of deimiri, the whale spirit, was often told around the camp fires. Munjurr remembered hearing of deimiri's three mouths. Two of those mouths were in the whale's tail. He also remembered how the whale tipped over the canoes of fishermen.

Munjurr shouted to Nurru, "Paddle hard!"

The great whale came toward them. It came faster than they could get away. When they could see the whale's eyes, Nurru picked up his drone pipe and blew a power song with all his might. The whale was almost beneath them. Then suddenly it dove down under the water. The water became a spinning **whirlpool.** It sucked the canoe into its center. The canoe tipped over, and the men were thrown into the sea.

Munjurr saw the spears pop up to the surface of the water. He swam toward them. He was quick, but they floated beyond his reach. Nurru tried to grab his drone pipe, but it floated away.

Finally, Munjurr grabbed a paddle. He pointed toward the shore. He shouted to Nurru, "This way." He began to swim. He held onto the paddle so he could rest when he grew tired.

Nurru swam also but more slowly. As the two men came close to shore, the surf grew rough. Even Munjurr had to rest on his paddle. But Nurru could not rest. His arms grew heavy and slow. His feet hardly moved. He began to sink.

Munjurr turned and saw what was happening to his friend. He swam toward Nurru and shoved one end of the paddle at him. Munjurr said, "Take hold of the paddle!"

The people who lived in the Dreamtime called the sun Walu, (WAH-lyoo) the Sun Woman. What time of day do you think it is?

deimiri (dih-MEH-rih)

Nurru grabbed the paddle. But it was too light to hold up both men. Munjurr let go of his end of the paddle. He said, "Hold onto it!" Then he swam away.

The last rays of Walu, the Sun Woman, were sinking when the tide carried Nurru onto the beach. He lay there, hardly breathing. He still held the paddle in his hands.

Munjurr shows that he is a hero. What does he do?

But Munjurr did not return. Not that day, or the next, or even the day after that. His people searched the beaches but did not find him. The waves had taken his body. They carried it far out to sea. His spirit had gone to the Sky World. There, Barama, the powerful creator **ancestor,** waited to greet him.

Barama said to Munjurr, "When you saved Nurru, you lost much. You lost your family, your friends, and the land of your birth. But you will not **grieve** for them. I will make you my **messenger.** You are to carry my words to the people on earth and bring back their messages to me. In this way, you will be happy."

Munjurr made his camp beside the Milky Way, the great river that flows across the Sky World. He made a canoe like the one he had used on earth. He paddled it on the river and fished as happily as before. From time to time, Barama sent Munjurr to earth with messages. When he made these journeys, Munjurr always came back happy.

When he dies, Nurru joins Munjurr.

Below, in the land of the Manggalilji, wet season followed dry. Dry season followed wet, until Nurru's eyes grew dim. His shoulders stooped. His feet no longer went far from the camp fire. One morning, when the surf ran high and the winds blew strong, Nurru's spirit joined the spirit of Munjurr. In that great river the Milky Way, they fish forever. Sometimes they hunt the turtle and water birds that make their homes along its banks.

Literature Practice

Answer these questions on a separate sheet of paper.

1. How does Munjurr encourage Nurru to go fishing?
2. What kind of man is Nurru?
3. What happens to Munjurr at the end of the story?
4. What happens to Nurru at the end of the story?
5. Munjurr is called "the heroic fisherman." Why?

The Munjurr Way

Munjurr is a myth told by the aborigines, the native people of Australia. Here are some words that tell you about the lives of the aborigines.

If you lived with Munjurr and you wanted

- to drink, then you would go to the **billabong,** or water hole.

- to hunt, then you would pick up your **boomerang,** a curved, flat weapon that comes back to you when you throw it.

- to eat, then you might eat a **witchetty grub,** which is a large, early form of a moth.

- to have fun, then you might enjoy the **playabout,** where you would sit around the campfire and pretend to be different animals or act out scenes from your life with singing and dancing.

- to carry something, then you might pack it up in your **dilly bag,** a big bag woven from bark, string, or grass.

Beowulf and the Fire Dragon

an adapted story retold by Robin McKinley

Words to Know

LITERARY TERMS

resolution the point at which the conflict in a story ends

descriptive details details of how something looks, feels, smells, or tastes

SELECTION VOCABULARY

slithering sliding smoothly, like a snake

scaly covered with scales

armor a covering that protects a fighter in a battle

slay to kill

invaders people who take over other people or places

gushed flowed or poured out quickly

shattered broke into many pieces

Heroes often fight difficult battles. In this story, a wise, old king knows he must fight his last battle. But even the thought of death does not stop him.

The Geats (GEETS) were a people who lived in southern Sweden.

Long, long ago in the land of the Geats, a large family of mighty warriors won a war. They hid the treasures from that war in a cave. This cave was under a great hill overlooking the sea. Over time, these families were destroyed in a number of wars, and the hidden treasure was forgotten.

One day a fire dragon was looking for a place to hide among the rocks. As it looked, it found the door to the cave. **Slithering** inside, it saw the gleaming treasures. The dragon fell in love with them. It twisted its large, **scaly** body around the sparkling **armor,** silver coins, and jeweled cups. Then it fell asleep for three hundred years.

After three hundred years, a runaway slave came across the dragon's treasure. The slave feared that his master would catch him and punish him for running away. He hoped to buy his freedom by returning with a beautiful gold cup. As the slave ran off with the cup, the fire dragon awoke.

The creature smelled the man's scent. It knew at once that part of its treasure had been stolen.

Spreading its great scaly wings, the dragon flew off. It wanted to take revenge on all people. It began making nightly raids on anyone who lived nearby. Flames shot from the dragon's terrible nostrils. Each night, people were swallowed up by these flames. Homes and farms became smoking ruins.

During this time, the king of the Geats was the hero named Beowulf. As a young man, he had killed a monster from the swamps known as Grendel. This earned him much fame and glory. He led his people to victory in many battles against their enemies. Then, for fifty years, he ruled in peace.

Now he was an old man. However, he knew that it was his fate to **slay** the dragon. Deep in his heart, he also knew that this battle would be his last.

Still, he did not hesitate. He called the man who made his armor. "The shield I now own is made of wood. It will give me little safety from a fire-breathing dragon," he said. "Make me a new shield of thick iron."

He called twelve of his best warriors together. "We will go and seek the dragon that is destroying our land," he told them.

Eleven of the warriors shook with fear. Still, they did not dare to say no to Beowulf. The twelfth warrior

In this paragraph, you meet the great fire dragon who falls in love with the treasure. As you continue to read, notice how the dragon is described.

This is the beginning of the conflict in the story.

These details give information about Beowulf. What kind of man is he?

was called Wiglaf. He was the grandson of another brave warrior. Many years ago, Wiglaf's grandfather had battled the wicked Grendel with Beowulf. Wiglaf spoke up. "I will go and fight by your side. I will fight to my death if need be!" he promised.

"Go and find the slave who stole the golden cup from the dragon," said Beowulf. "This man can lead us to the dragon's cave."

Jahn Michael Rysbraeck named this sculpture *The Saxon God Thunor Enthroned.* ▶

Beowulf woke early the next morning. He put on his best armor for the last battle of his life. He took his new iron shield and the heavy sword. He had won it for killing Grendel many years ago. Then the king and his men set off. They rode two days to the fire dragon's cave. When they reached the cave, Beowulf allowed the slave to leave. The man ran away as fast as his legs could carry him.

Beowulf sat alone on the stump of a fallen tree. There he began to sing his death song. He sang of his happy boyhood and of his victory over Grendel. He also sang of battles with **invaders** and of his many years ruling the peaceful Geats. The warriors listened. They knew that their king did not expect to survive this battle. When they saw that Beowulf planned to face the dragon alone, they were secretly pleased. Only one of them spoke up.

"Let me come with you," said brave Wiglaf. But Beowulf only smiled and shook his head. Then, lifting his sword and shield, Beowulf went to the dragon's cave alone.

When he reached the mouth of the cave, Beowulf began beating his sword against his shield. This was followed by his war cry. The fire dragon awoke. It heard a man shouting curses and insults. It became very angry. It snorted in fury and shot flames from its mouth. Beowulf held out his iron shield to guard himself from the fierce heat. Even in the valley, the warriors of Geat felt the earth shake as the dragon trudged forward.

The dragon spread its leather-like wings and rushed at the man who had awakened it. Instantly, Beowulf brought his heavy sword down hard on the creature's head. Blood **gushed** forth, but the monster's skull did not break. The dragon's fury only grew. Beowulf's armor glowed bright red as the wounded dragon blasted him again with its fiery breath.

When the warriors of Geat saw the dragon, they

Beowulf shows his greatness by allowing the slave to leave. After all, the slave is in some ways responsible for the terrible problem that Beowulf faces.

Once again, Wiglaf steps forward. What do his actions say about him?

These details describe the dragon. Which words help you to see the dragon?

▲ A man fights a dragon in this scene from the work of the Reverend Father Kircher. The scene is called *Dragon of the Caverns of Mount Pilatus.*

were terrified. All but one, Wiglaf, turned and ran. Wiglaf ran after them. He reminded them of their promise to Beowulf. Soon he saw that his words would not stop the cowards. Wiglaf rushed back to fight at his king's side.

Beowulf welcomed the faithful youth. Together they faced the dragon's fury. A blast of the creature's breath turned Wiglaf's wooden shield to ashes. Beowulf called the brave lad to take shelter behind his iron shield. He swung again at the dragon. This time his mighty sword **shattered** against the dragon's scaly neck.

At the same moment, the beast rushed forward. It blasted Beowulf with its fiery breath. Its razor-sharp teeth sank into Beowulf's throat.

The king's lifeblood gushed from the wound in his throat. The sight filled Wiglaf with rage. He plunged his own sword deep into the dragon's unguarded belly. Even as the dragon's fiery breath burned Beowulf's flesh, Beowulf pulled out his knife. He slashed again and again at the weakened dragon. At last, the creature fell wounded on the ground.

Only then did Beowulf give in to his own terrible pain. Holding his bloody throat, he collapsed near the mouth of the cave. Wiglaf filled his helmet with water from the nearby stream. He used it to wash the king's face and neck. Beowulf's wounds were deep, and they kept bleeding. His body was covered with burns. One arm had been burned all the way to the bone. Wiglaf was also hurt. His hair and eyelashes had been scorched by the monster's fiery breath. Seeing tears in Wiglaf's eyes, the kindly old king tried to comfort the brave youth.

"I have lived long," he said. "I have always tried to do the right thing. If I must die now, I do so with no regrets." He gazed once more upon the slain dragon. The beast's belly still gushed blood. Its tail twitched as it slowly died.

Many strong words help you see and feel the action. What are some of these words?

Beowulf and Wiglaf succeed in killing the dragon. Why is this the resolution of the story?

Beowulf proves he is a hero through his actions. How do his words also show that he is a hero?

Information in a story can help you figure out words you do not know. Because of what has already been told, you can figure out that "noble deeds" means "great actions."

Wiglaf becomes king. Why do you think it is important to Beowulf to name a new king?

Then Beowulf asked Wiglaf to show him some of the treasures hidden in the cave. Wiglaf went inside. He came out with his arms full of gold jewelry and cups sparkling with rare gems. Beowulf was pleased. He knew his people would be well taken care of.

Beowulf then gazed at the hill above the cave. He told Wiglaf that he wanted to be buried on the cliff overlooking the sea. A great monument of stone should be built at his grave.

"When ships pass," he said, "let them see Beowulf's grave. Let our people not forget that their king loved them always."

Wiglaf promised to do as the king commanded. He swore that no one would ever forget the noble deeds of Beowulf.

Then Beowulf removed the blood-soaked golden collar from around his neck.

"You are the last and most worthy of the Geats," he said. Then he handed the collar of kingship to Wiglaf. "Rule wisely as I have always tried to do."

With these words, noble Beowulf closed his eyes for the very last time.

Literature Practice

Answer these questions on a separate sheet of paper.

1. Why does the dragon suddenly cause trouble?

2. Why does Beowulf feel that he must kill the dragon?

3. Why do you think Wiglaf is in this story?

4. What words and phrases are used to give you pictures of what is happening? Think about the dragon and Beowulf's battle.

5. What makes Beowulf a great hero?

Dragons

Dragons are monsters that appear in stories from all around the world. Often, they are pictured as snakes with wings. Like snakes, they have scales covering their bodies. They hide in holes and caves.

Unlike snakes, dragons often have wings. They have huge, sharp claws. Some dragons, like the one in this story, can breathe fire.

Not all dragons are evil, though. The Greeks and Romans believed dragons could protect people. Because of this belief, the Romans put pictures of dragons on their flags. In northern Europe, people carved dragons out of wood and put them on the front of their ships. In China, the dragon is still a sign of good fortune.

In this story, the dragon is such a powerful creature that only a true hero like Beowulf can kill it.

Unanana and the Elephant

an adapted folktale retold by Kathleen Arnott

Words to Know

LITERARY TERM

personification giving human characteristics to nonliving things

SELECTION VOCABULARY

baboon a large monkey

gazelle a small, fast antelope

tusk a long, curving tooth that usually grows in pairs and sticks out of the sides of the mouth of an elephant

gulp a large swallow

flesh the soft parts of an animal's body that are covered with skin

groaned made a deep, sad sound

bleats the cries of a goat, sheep, or calf

Heroes are always brave. Sometimes they are also clever. In this story, a mother proves that she will stop at nothing to save her children. That means she will be both brave and smart.

———— ❧ ————

Unanana (yoo-nah-NAH-nah)

Just before each animal appears, the children hear a little noise. This creates a mood of suspense.

Many, many years ago there was a poor woman called Unanana. She had two beautiful children. People always noticed their smooth skin and bright eyes.

Early one morning, Unanana went into the bush to collect firewood. She left her children playing with a little cousin.

The children were playing when they heard a noise in the grass. It was a curious **baboon.**

The baboon said, "Whose children are those?"
The cousin said, "They belong to Unanana."

The baboon said, "Well, well, well! I have never seen such beautiful children before."

The baboon disappeared, and the children went on playing. Later the children heard a twig crack. They looked up and saw a **gazelle** staring at them.

The gazelle said, "Whose children are those?"

The cousin said, "They belong to Unanana."

The gazelle said in her soft voice, "I have never seen such beautiful children before." Then the gazelle disappeared into the bush.

The children were getting a drink when they heard a noise. It was a leopard.

The leopard said, "Whose children are those?"

The cousin's voice shook with fear. She said, "They belong to Unanana." She backed up slowly toward the door of the hut. She was afraid the leopard might jump at her.

But the leopard was not interested in a meal. He said, "I have never seen such beautiful children before."

The children were afraid of these animals who kept asking questions. They called loudly to Unanana. But she did not come. Instead, a huge elephant with one **tusk** came out of the bush.

The elephant said, "Whose children are those?"

The cousin said, "They . . . they belong to Unanana."

The elephant said, "I have never seen such beautiful children before. I will take them with me." He opened his mouth wide. He swallowed Unanana's two children in one **gulp.**

The little cousin screamed and ran into the hut.

Soon Unanana came home. When she heard what happened, she said, "Did the elephant swallow them whole? Do you think they might be alive in his stomach?"

The cousin cried loudly. She said, "I don't know."

Unanana said, "There's only one thing to do. I must ask the animals if they have seen an elephant with one tusk. But first of all I must get ready."

Talking animals is an example of personification.

Elephants usually have two tusks. This elephant is strange.

The cousin is so scared that she hesitates as she speaks.

Another mother might scream and cry when she heard that her children were eaten by an elephant. What does Unanana do?

Unanana cooks a pot of beans and grabs a knife. What do you think will happen next?

Unanana cooked a big pot of beans. She put the pot on her head and got her large knife. She told the little cousin to look after the hut. Then she went off into the bush to look for the elephant.

Soon Unanana found the elephant's tracks. She followed them a long way, but she could not find the elephant. As she walked through some tall trees, she met the baboon.

Unanana begged, "O baboon, help me! Have you seen an elephant with one tusk? He has eaten both my children. I must find him."

The people in this scene are trapped, just like Unanana's children, inside a large elephant. The artist is unknown. ▼

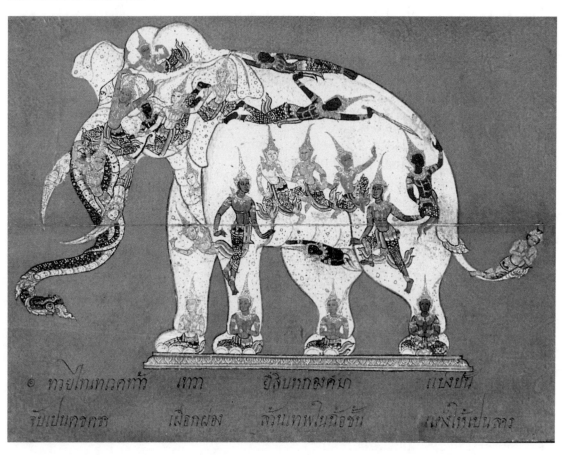

The baboon said, "Keep going along this track. You will come to a place with high trees and white stones. There you will find the elephant."

Unanana went along the track for a very long time. Suddenly, a gazelle leaped across her path.

Unanana said, "O gazelle! Help me! Have you seen an elephant with only one tusk? He has eaten both my children. I must find him."

The gazelle said, "Keep going along this path. You will come to a place with high trees and white stones. There you will find the elephant."

Unanana said, "O dear! It seems such a long way. I am so tired and hungry." But Unanana did not eat the food she carried. That was for her children.

Unanana went on and on. She saw a leopard sitting outside his cave. He was washing himself with his tongue.

Unanana said, "O leopard! Have you seen an elephant with only one tusk? He has eaten my children. I must find him."

The leopard said, "Keep going on this track. You will come to a place where there are high trees and white stones. You will find the elephant there."

Unanana said to herself, "My legs will not carry me much further."

She went on a little more. Suddenly she saw high trees ahead. Below the trees were large white stones spread out on the ground.

Unanana said, "At last!" She hurried forward. A huge elephant lay in the shade of the trees. He had only one tusk.

Unanana came as close to the elephant as she dared. She shouted, "Elephant! Elephant! Are you the one who has eaten my children?"

The elephant said, "O no! Keep going straight on this track…." But he did not finish what he was saying. Unanana ran up to him, waving her knife.

Unanana screamed, "Where are my children?

Unanana meets all the same animals in the same order in which they appeared to her children.

Unanana is very tired, but she does not stop. Another mother might be afraid to meet an elephant that eats children. But Unanana, who is a hero, keeps going.

How can Unanana be sure this is the right elephant?

Where are they?"

The elephant opened his mouth. He did not even bother to stand up. He swallowed Unanana and the pot of beans in one gulp. This was just what Unanana wanted.

Down, down, down Unanana went in the darkness. She reached the elephant's stomach. What a sight she saw there! The walls of the elephant's stomach were like hills. There were small groups of people camped on the hills. There were dogs and goats and cows and her own two children.

The children said, "Mother! Mother! How did you get here? Oh, we are so hungry."

Unanana took the pot off her head. She began to feed her children the beans. All the other people crowded around. They begged for just a little food.

Unanana said to them, "Why not get your own food? It is all around you."

She took her knife and cut large pieces of **flesh** from the elephant. She built a fire in the middle of the elephant's stomach and cooked the meat. Soon everyone was eating elephant meat, even the dogs and goats and cows.

The elephant **groaned** so loudly that he could be heard all over the bush. Animals came to the elephant to find out what was the matter. The elephant told them, "Ever since I swallowed a woman called Unanana, I have felt bad inside. I don't know why."

The pain got worse and worse. Finally, the elephant dropped dead. Then Unanana took her knife and cut a door between the elephant's ribs. The dogs, goats, cows, men, women, and children walked outside. They shouted with joy to be free.

The animals thanked Unanana with moos, barks, and **bleats.** The human beings gave Unanana all kinds of presents. With so many presents, Unanana and her children were not poor any more.

Brave Unanana actually planned on being swallowed by the elephant.

Why does Unanana cut up the elephant?

The animals coming to "find out what was the matter" is another example of personification. The animals are showing a human sense of concern.

Literature Practice

Answer these questions on a separate sheet of paper.

1. What happens to Unanana's children?
2. What makes Unanana a hero?
3. How is Unanana rewarded for what she has done?
4. How does the writer create a mood of suspense in the story?

Chapter Review

Summaries

- **The Heroic Fisherman**—One day the great fisherman Munjurr and his friend Nurru are fishing. A whale makes a whirlpool that tips their canoe into the sea. Munjurr could have saved himself, but instead he gives Nurru the one paddle they have. Nurru makes it to shore alive. Because of this, Munjurr's spirit is rewarded in the Sky World. He becomes the happy messenger of Barama.

- **Beowulf and the Fire Dragon**—A fire dragon sleeps in a cave for three hundred years. When he is suddenly awakened by a thief, he begins killing people. Beowulf, a great king, must kill the dragon to protect his people. He chooses twelve warriors to join him, but only the brave Wiglaf goes to battle with him. They kill the dragon, but Beowulf dies. Before he dies, he makes Wiglaf king to make sure the people will be taken care of.

- **Unanana and the Elephant**—When Unanana is away, an elephant swallows her children. Brave Unanana acts quickly to save them. She grabs a knife and some food and finds the elephant. Just as Unanana plans, the elephant swallows her. Once inside the elephant, she sees other people and animals as well as her children. She cuts pieces of the elephant's flesh and cooks them. The elephant dies, and Unanana cuts her way out. Her children and the other people and animals are safe and free.

Chapter Quiz

Choose the letter of the correct answer. Rewrite the sentences on a separate sheet of paper.

1. In "The Heroic Fisherman," the great danger that Munjurr and Nurru face is
   a. catching fish.
   b. Walu, the Sun Woman.
   c. the drone pipe.
   d. the whale.

2. Munjurr is a hero because
   a. he is king of his people.
   b. he is a fisherman.
   c. he saves Nurru.
   d. he gets away from the whale.

3. In "Beowulf and the Fire Dragon," Beowulf kills the fire dragon
   a. all alone.
   b. with the help of the gods.
   c. with twelve warriors.
   d. with Wiglaf.

4. Beowulf fights the dragon even though he knows
   a. the battle will be his last.
   b. Wiglaf will die.
   c. all the warriors will die.
   d. the dragon will win.

5. When Unanana in "Unanana and the Elephant" goes to find her children, she takes
   a. a rope and some soup.
   b. cheese and firewood.
   c. a knife and a pot of beans.
   d. food for the elephant.

Thinking and Writing

Write answers to the following questions on a separate sheet of paper.

1. In myths, heroes are often rewarded for their great deeds. What is Munjurr's reward?

2. How do Beowulf's words and actions show that he is a hero?

3. Part of being a hero sometimes means being a little clever. How does Unanana outsmart the elephant?

Unit Two Review

A. The following questions are about some of the selections you read in this unit. Answer each question by writing one or two sentences on a separate sheet of paper.

1. Long ago the women in Cambodia met a challenge. What was it?

2. Sometimes our challenges begin with where we live. In "My Brilliant Career," think about the place where Sybylla lives. What challenges does she face because of her surroundings?

3. Consider the dialogue used in the stories in this unit. What do you learn about the characters from the dialogue? Use examples from two stories in your answer.

B. Choose two of the essay questions below. Answer them on a separate sheet of paper. Write one or two paragraphs for each one.

1. Even though we may not see ourselves as heroes, our actions may show that we are. Think about some of the heroes you read about in this unit. In what ways do their actions show that they are heroes?

2. In "My Brilliant Career" and "The Mountain of the Men and the Mountain of the Women," the main characters hope to make important changes in their lives. Discuss the challenges that they face. Are they able to meet the challenges? Explain your answer.

3. Descriptive details can make us feel that we are a part of what is happening in a story. How are descriptive details used in some of the stories in this unit?

Unit Three

THE NATURAL WORLD

▲ Everything that is loved and feared in nature is part of Rene Magritte's *L'lle aux Tresors.*

Chapter Learning Objectives

- Identify similes in a poem.
- Learn about the use of imagery in a haiku.
- Identify the plot of a story.
- Understand third-person point of view.
- Identify a stanza in a poem.
- Understand the use of rhyme in a poem.

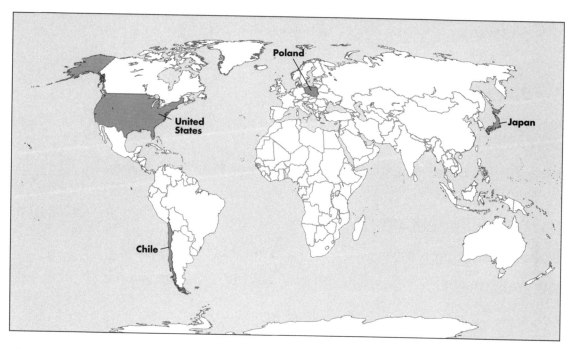

Japan
Four Haiku
haiku by Bashō, Jōsō, Chiyo, and Shiki

Chile
The Horses
a poem by Pablo Neruda

Poland
Zlateh the Goat
an adapted story by Isaac Bashevis Singer

United States
'maggie and milly and molly and may'
a poem by e. e. cummings

Some experiences make us feel closer to the joys of nature. At other times, we are frightened by the things that happen in nature. In this chapter, you will read about people whose experiences carry them through the best and the worst of the natural world.

Four Haiku

haiku by Bashō, Jōsō, Chiyo, and Shiki

Words to Know

LITERARY TERM

imagery words that help the reader to "see" how something looks,
sounds, feels, or tastes

SELECTION VOCABULARY

withered dried up, shriveled

captured caught

remains stays behind

collide crash or bump into

---

*We experience each of the four seasons in different ways.
By noticing the differences, we can better appreciate the
beauty of nature.*

Autumn

A withered branch is
something you might
see in autumn.

On a **withered** branch
　　a crow has settled—
　　　　autumn nightfall.
　　—*Bashō*

Winter

"Nothing" is fitting
imagery for winter.

Mountains and plains,
　　all are **captured** by the snow—
　　　　nothing **remains**.
　　—*Jōsō*

◀ The special quality of each of the four seasons is shown in four plates by Fornasetti Milano.

After a Long Winter

After a long winter, giving
       each other nothing, we **collide**
              with blossoms in our hands.
—*Chiyo*

The image of blossoms creates a picture of spring.

Heat

The summer river:
       although there is a bridge, my horse
              goes through the water.
—*Shiki*

What season is described in "Heat"?

Literature Practice

Answer these questions on a separate sheet of paper.

1. In "Autumn," what kind of branch does the crow settle on?

2. In "Winter," what is captured by the snow?

3. In "After a Long Winter," why do the speaker and her campanion "collide/with blossoms in our hands"?

4. In "Heat," what does the speaker's horse go through?

The Haiku

Haiku is a form of Japanese poetry. Each three line poem contains seventeen syllables. The first line contains five syllables; the second line has seven syllables; and the third, five syllables. Usually, the subject of haiku is nature. A haiku uses one image to suggest the sight or sound of something in nature.

The greatest of the haiku poets is Bashō. Bashō lived in Japan during the 17th century. He wrote the rules for the haiku form and described the kinds of images that could be used in the poems.

The Horses

a poem by Pablo Neruda

Words to Know

LITERARY TERMS

simile a comparison of two things using *like* or *as*

first-person point of view the use of the words *I*, *me*, and *my*, to tell a story

SELECTION VOCABULARY

scarcely just barely, hardly

spumed foamed or frothed

intense extreme in strength or size

vibrant full of energy

Certain scenes or events in nature can leave lasting impressions in our minds. In this poem, the speaker describes ten horses walking in the snow. It is a scene he shall never forget.

From my window I saw the horses.

It was in Berlin, one winter. The light
was without light, there was no sky in the sky.

The air was white like fresh bread.

From my window I saw a kind of circus-ring,
a ring bitten in snow by the teeth of winter.

The speaker uses a simile to describe air. What other similes can you find?

▲ This painting called *Horses* is by Senaka Senanayake.

Suddenly, led out by a man,
ten horses walked out into the snow.

They **scarcely** shook or moved as they came out,
like fire, but to my eyes they filled the world,
which had been empty before. Perfect, flaming,
they were like ten gods with great, clean hooves,
their manes were like a dream of salt-**spumed** waves.

Their rumps were round as worlds or oranges.

Their color was honey, amber, fire.

Their necks were like towers
carved out of stone in pride.

And energy, like a prisoner,
looked out from their furious eyes.

And there in the silence, in the middle of the day,
one dirty, disorganized winter,
those **intense** horses became blood,
became rhythm, became the **vibrant** treasure of life.

The speaker compares how he feels about the horses to how he feels about winter.

I looked at them, looked, and revived!
I hadn't known it, but this was the fountain,
the golden dance, the sky, the fire that lived in beauty!

I have forgotten that dark winter in Berlin.

I shall never forget the light from those horses.

Literature Practice

Answer these questions on a separate sheet of paper.

1. What does the speaker see from his window?
2. Why are the horses "like ten gods"?
3. What effect do the horses have upon the speaker?
4. How does the speaker describe the winter in Berlin?
5. Why does the speaker say that he "shall never forget the light from those horses"? Explain your answer.

Zlateh the Goat

an adapted story by Isaac Bashevis Singer

Words to Know

LITERARY TERMS

plot the action or series of events in a story

third-person point of view someone other than a character is telling the story or poem

SELECTION VOCABULARY

furrier someone who makes and sells clothing made out of furs

numb without feeling, as from cold

innocent free of guilt

udders baglike parts of a cow or goat that holds milk

cocked turned to one side

Friendships with animals can add special meaning to our lives. In the following story, Aaron and his goat Zlateh share a difficult experience that changes their lives and makes their friendship stronger.

Zlateh (ZLAHT-eh)

At Hanukkah, the road from the village is usually covered with snow. But the winter had been mild this year. Hanukkah had almost come, but little snow had fallen.

Hanukkah (HAH-nuh-kuh) is a Jewish festival that lasts eight days. Special candles are lit each day.

For Reuven the **furrier**, it was a bad year. Nobody needed furs when it was so warm. After thinking a long time, he decided to sell Zlateh the goat. She was old and gave little milk. Feivel the butcher said he

Reuven (ROO-ven)

Feivel (FEYE-vuhl)

would pay eight gold coins for her. With the money, the family could buy many things for Hanukkah—candles, potatoes and oil for pancakes, and gifts for the children.

Reuven's decision to sell Zlateh is the first event in the story's plot. Then Reuven tells the family of his decision. Notice other events as you read.

Reuven told his oldest boy, Aaron, to take the goat to Feivel. Aaron knew what this meant, but he had to obey his father.

Aaron's mother, Leah, wiped her eyes when she heard the news. Aaron's younger sisters, Anna and Miriam, cried loudly.

Aaron put on his jacket and took two slices of bread with cheese to eat on the road. He was supposed to take the goat to the butcher's, spend the night, and come back the next day with the money.

The family said goodbye to the goat. Aaron placed a rope around her neck. Zlateh stood patiently as always. She licked Reuven's hand. Zlateh trusted human beings. She knew they always fed her and never hurt her.

This story is told from a third-person point of view. Notice that the narrator tells both the thoughts and actions of all the characters.

When Aaron took Zlateh out on the road, she seemed very surprised. She looked at Aaron as if to say, "Where are you taking me?" But after a while she seemed to realize that goats shouldn't ask questions.

The sun was shining when Aaron left the village. Suddenly the weather changed. A large black cloud with a bluish center spread quickly over the sky. The crows flew low. It began to hail. It was early in the day, but it became as dark as evening. Soon the hail turned to snow.

Aaron was twelve. He had seen all kinds of weather. But he had never seen a snow like this one. It was so thick it shut out the light of day. In a short time, the path was covered. The wind became cold as ice. Aaron could not see through the snow. He no longer knew where he was.

Zlateh was twelve years old, too. She knew what winter meant. But when her legs sank deeper and deeper into the snow, she began to turn her head and

▲ This etching, called *Worry*, is by Albert Abramowitz.
Reuven worries about how he will take care of his family.

Aaron and Zlateh are caught in a terrible storm.

The author uses words that let you feel how cold both Aaron and Zlateh are. What are the words?

give Aaron puzzled looks. Her mild eyes seemed to ask, "Why are we out in such a storm?" Aaron hoped that someone would come along with a cart, but no one passed by.

The snow grew thicker. It fell to the ground in large, whirling flakes. The wind whistled and howled. Aaron felt the softness of a plowed field beneath his boots. He realized he was no longer on the road. He could not figure out which was east or west.

Zlateh stopped. She could walk no longer. Icicles hung from her white beard. Her horns were covered with frost.

Aaron knew if they did not find shelter, they would freeze to death. This was no ordinary storm. This was a mighty blizzard. The snow had reached his knees. His hands were **numb**. He could no longer feel his toes. His nose felt like wood.

Zlateh's bleating began to sound like crying. The humans she trusted so much had dragged her into a trap. Aaron began to pray to God for himself and for the **innocent** animal.

Suddenly he made out the shape of a hill. He wondered what it could be. He moved toward it, dragging Zlateh after him. When he came near it, he realized that it was a large haystack, covered with snow.

Aaron knew they were saved. No matter how cold it is outside, it is always warm in a haystack. Aaron was a village boy, and he knew what to do. He dug through the snow and hay. He dug out a nest for himself and Zlateh.

The snow kept falling. Quickly, it covered the tunnel Aaron had dug. He and Zlateh had hardly any air in their nest. Aaron dug a kind of window through the hay and snow. He was careful to keep the tunnel clear.

Zlateh was happy eating the hay in their nest. She seemed to trust humans once again. Aaron ate his bread and cheese, but he was still hungry. He looked at Zlateh and noticed her **udders** were full. He lay down next to her and squirted her milk into his mouth. It was rich and sweet.

Through the window, Aaron could see a little of the blizzard outside. The wind carried along whole drifts of snow. It was completely dark. Thank God that in that hay it was not cold. The dried hay and grass gave off the warmth of the summer sun. Zlateh ate often. She nibbled from above, below, from the left and right. Her body gave off an animal heat, and Aaron cuddled up to her. He had always loved Zlateh, but now she was like a sister. He was alone, cut off from his family. He wanted to talk.

Aaron said, "Zlateh, what do you think about what has happened to us?"

Zlateh said, "Maaa."

Aaron said, "If we hadn't found this stack of hay, we would be frozen stiff by now."

The goat said, "Maaa."

In many parts of Europe, goats are raised for their milk. Most goat's milk is made into cheese.

◀ For Zlateh and Aaron the snow-filled forest looked like this painting by Victor Charreton. The painting is called *Snow, Winter Landscape.*

Aaron said, "If the snow keeps on falling like this, we may have to stay here for days."

Zlateh said, "Maaa."

Aaron said, "What does 'maaa' mean? You better speak up clearly."

Zlateh tried. She said, "Maaa, maaa."

Aaron said, "Well, let it be 'maaa' then. You can't speak, but I know you understand. I need you, and you need me. Isn't that right?"

"Maaa."

Aaron became sleepy. He made a pillow out of some hay, leaned his head on it, and dozed off. Zlateh fell asleep, too.

When Aaron opened his eyes, he didn't know whether it was morning or night. The snow had blocked up his window. He used his stick to break through to the open air.

It was still dark outside. The snow was still falling. The wind wailed, first with one voice and then with many. Sometimes it had the sound of devilish laughter.

Zlateh woke up. When Aaron said "Hello," she said, "Maaa." Zlateh could only say one word, but it meant many things. Now she was saying, "We must accept all that God gives us — heat, cold, hunger, happiness, light, and darkness."

Aaron was hungry. His food was gone, but Zlateh had plenty of milk.

For three days, Aaron and Zlateh stayed in the haystack. Aaron had always loved Zlateh. But in these three days he loved her more and more. She fed him and helped keep him warm. She comforted him with her patience. He told her many stories, and she always **cocked** her ears and listened. When he patted her, she licked his hand and face. Then she said, "Maaa." Aaron knew she meant, "I love you, too."

The snow fell for three days. Sometimes Aaron felt there had never been summer. It seemed like the

Why do you think Aaron and Zlateh need each other?

Why does Aaron love Zlateh more after three days in the haystack?

◀ Other than the horns, this drawing of a goat might look very much like Zlateh. The artist is unknown.

snow had always fallen, ever since he could remember.

Aaron and Zlateh slept all night and a good part of the day. Aaron's dreams were all about warm weather. He dreamed of green fields, trees covered with blossoms, and singing birds.

By the third night, the snow had stopped. The sky became clear, and the moon shone. The stars were large and close. But Aaron did not dare to find his way home in the darkness.

On the morning of the fourth day, Aaron heard sleigh bells. The man who drove the sleigh told Aaron which way to go back to the village. Aaron was not going to Feivel the butcher. Aaron had decided in the haystack that he would never part with Zlateh.

There was great joy in the family when Aaron and Zlateh returned. Aaron's sisters kissed and hugged Zlateh. Nobody ever again thought of selling her.

Now that the cold weather had finally arrived, Reuven the furrier had plenty of business. When

This is the high point in the action of the plot. The major problem of whether or not to sell Zlateh is solved. Now everything changes.

Hanukkah came, Aaron's mother was able to fry pancakes every evening. Zlateh always had some, too.

Once in a while, Aaron would ask Zlateh, "Zlateh, do you remember the three days we spent together?"

Zlateh would make a single sound. That sound would tell of all her thoughts, and all her love.

Literature Practice

Answer these questions on a separate sheet of paper.

1. Why does Reuven send Aaron and Zlateh to Feivel the butcher?

2. What problem do Aaron and Zlateh face soon after leaving the village?

3. How do Aaron and Zlateh survive?

4. How does the author give information about the characters and their thoughts?

5. How does Aaron solve his problem about selling Zlateh?

'maggie and milly and molly and may'

a poem by e. e. cummings

Words to Know

LITERARY TERMS

stanza a group of lines in poetry

rhyme the repetition of sounds in the words of a poem; words that sound alike

SELECTION VOCABULARY

befriended made friends with

stranded forced onto the shore

rays arms

languid weak or without energy

People relate to nature in different ways. In this poem, four girls spend the day together at the beach. Each girl has her own special experience.

maggie and milly and molly and may
went down to the beach(to play one day)

and maggie discovered a shell that sang
so sweetly she couldn't remember her
troubles,and

milly **befriended** a **stranded** star
whose **rays** five **languid** fingers were;

and molly was chased by a horrible thing
which races sideways while blowing bubbles:and

Cummings has an unusual writing style. None of the words begin with capital letters. Few sentences end with periods. Words and sentences often run together.

▲ The two girls playing on the beach are having as much fun as maggie and milly. The painting by Liddall Armitage is called *When We Were Young*.

may came home with a smooth round stone
as small as a world and as large as alone.

For whatever we lose(like a you or a me)
it's always ourselves we find in the sea

Notice the rhyme pattern. "May" and "day," "stone" and "alone," and "me" and "sea" are words that rhyme.

Literature Practice

Answer these questions on a separate sheet of paper.

1. Why do the girls go to the beach?

2. What does each girl do at the beach?

3. Which girls seem to enjoy their trip to the beach? Explain your answer.

4. What do you think the poet means when he says we always find ourselves in the sea?

Chapter Review

Summaries

- **Four Haiku**—The four seasons are described in a series of haiku.

- **The Horses**—The speaker recalls what he saw one winter night in Berlin. From his window, he sees ten horses walking in the snow. The sight of the horses deeply affects him.

- **Zlateh the Goat**—Aaron must take Zlateh to the butcher. On the way Aaron and Zlateh are caught in a blizzard. Aaron finds shelter for them in a haystack. After the storm, Aaron feels closer to Zlateh and cannot bear to take her to the butcher. The family is happy to see them both return.

- **'maggie and milly and molly and may'**—Four girls go to the beach to play. Maggie finds a shell that makes her forget her problems. Milly finds a starfish. Molly is chased by something horrible. May finds a smooth round stone.

Chapter Quiz

Choose the letter of the correct answer. Rewrite the sentences on a separate sheet of paper.

1. In "The Horses," the speaker sees from his window
   a. a circus.
   b. ten horses.
   c. a dark winter day.
   d. a fire.

2. Aaron and Zlateh spend three days in a haystack because they
   a. are hiding from the butcher.
   b. ran away from home.
   c. must seek shelter from a blizzard.
   d. are playing a game.

3. What do the images in the four haiku stand for?
   a. autumn.
   b. spring and winter.
   c. the four seasons.
   d. summer and fall.

4. The horrible thing that chases Molly on the beach
   a. blows bubbles.
   b. is stranded.
   c. sings sweetly.
   d. is smooth.

Thinking and Writing

Write answers to the following questions on a separate sheet of paper.

1. In "The Horses," the speaker says that the horses "filled the world." What similes are used in the poem to show how they filled the world?

2. In "Zlateh the Goat," Aaron and Zlateh "talk" together. If Zlateh could talk, how might she describe her experience with humans? Use examples from the story to support your answer.

3. In 'maggie and milly and molly and may,' which girl's experience with nature is most like another character's in this chapter? Use examples from the poem and another selection to explain your answer.

▲ An embroidered mantle from Peru during the early 1st century shows three crocodiles. Appreciating animals is one way of enjoying nature.

Chapter Learning Objectives

- Identify metaphors.
- Learn about the speaker in a poem.
- Recognize use of images in a poem.
- Understand alliteration.
- Recognize similes.

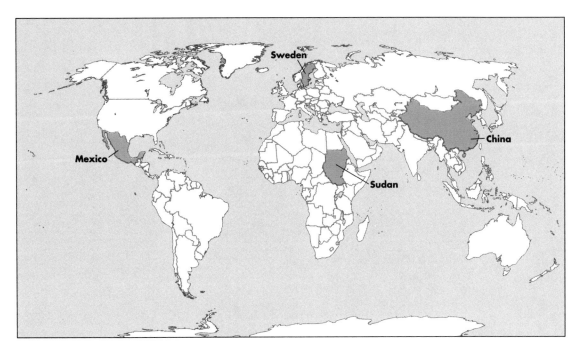

Sweden
The Earthworm
a poem by Harry Edmund Martinson

China
Green Creek
a poem by Wang Wei

Mexico
The Cedar Chest
a poem by Rosario Castellanos

Sudan
The Magnificent Bull
a Dinka traditional poem

The poems in this chapter celebrate the smallest and largest of nature's wonders. They remind us of the respect we should have for nature. The more we respect the natural world, the more we are filled with a sense of peace and pride.

▲ This painting called *Der Macher* by Albin Egger-Leinz shows a farmer working the soil.

The Earthworm
a poem by Harry Edmund Martinson

Words to Know

LITERARY TERM

metaphor a way of comparing two unlike things

SELECTION VOCABULARY

respects has a high opinion of

harvest time of year when ripe crops are gathered

Even some of the smallest animals play important roles in nature. In this poem, the speaker praises a creature that you might not think of as very important. Perhaps the speaker will change your mind!

Who really **respects** the earthworm,
the farmworker far under the grass in the soil.
He keeps the earth always changing.
He works entirely full of soil,
speechless with soil, and blind.

He is the underneath farmer, the underground one,
where the fields are getting on their **harvest** clothes.
Who really respects him,
this deep and calm earth-worker,
this deathless, gray, tiny farmer in the planet's soil.

The poet compares the earthworm to the farmer.

Literature Practice

Answer these questions on a separate sheet of paper.

1. What metaphor does the poet use to describe the earthworm?

2. What does the earthworm have in common with the thing or person it is compared to?

3. What is the speaker's opinion of the earthworm?

4. What do you think the speaker means when he calls the earthworm "deathless"?

Green Creek

a poem by Wang Wei

Words to Know

LITERARY TERMS

speaker the character who tells what happens in a poem

imagery words that help the reader to "see" how something
looks, sounds, feels, or tastes

SELECTION VOCABULARY

bounds moves forward quickly with
leaps and jumps

dense thick or crowded

waterchestnuts water-loving plants
found in Asia and Africa

lucid clear

serene calm and peaceful

loaf to pass the time doing little
or nothing

---

*Nature offers us a place to escape from our worries and to
feel at peace. The speaker in the following poem describes
a place that has special meaning for him.*

To find the meadows by Yellow Flower River
you must follow Green Creek
as it turns endlessly in the mountains
in just a hundred miles.
Water **bounds** noisily over the rocks.
Color softens in the **dense** pines.
Weeds and **waterchestnuts** are drifting.
Lucid water mirrors the reeds.

The phrase "Water
bounds noisily" is one
example of the poem's
imagery. It helps you to
hear the moving water.

This 16th century painting by an unknown artist is called *Scholar Playing the Qin.* ▶

My heart has always been **serene** and lazy
like peaceful Green Creek.
Why not **loaf** on a large flat rock,
dangling my fishhook here forever?

Literature Practice

Answer these questions on a separate sheet of paper.

1. Where is Green Creek?

2. What imagery does the poet use to give you a picture of Green Creek?

3. What feelings does the speaker have about Green Creek?

4. The speaker starts out by giving directions to the meadows by Yellow Flower River. Why do you think the speaker never finishes giving the directions?

▲ It is sometimes hard to imagine that all wood things were once majestic trees. This decorated box was once part of a pine tree.

The Cedar Chest

a poem by Rosario Castellanos

Words to Know

LITERARY TERM

alliteration the repeating of consonant sounds that begin words

SELECTION VOCABULARY

felled cut down

fragrance a sweet or pleasing smell

torso trunk

severed separated, broken apart

routines regular ways or patterns of doing things

Sometimes humans harm or destroy the natural world for their own uses. In this poem, the speaker remembers the beauty of a tree in the forest before it is destroyed.

The ax that **felled**
forever the **fragrance**
and the tree taken
with its **torso severed**.

Now here you are, under a roof,
in the corner of a bedroom
and guests take you for granted
and you, you seem to accept it and to keep still.

There is a repeated *f* sound in "felled forever the fragrance." Look for a repeated *t* sound in the same stanza.

Don't sell away your memory
to sad **routines** and to time.

Do not forget the woods
or the wind or the birds.

Woods and wind pick up
the repeated *w* sound in
the last stanza.

Literature Practice

Answer these questions on a separate sheet of paper.

1. What past event does the speaker describe in the first stanza?

2. Who is the speaker talking to when using the words *you* and *your?*

3. What does the speaker want the cedar chest to remember?

4. How does the poet make the reader aware of what the tree has experienced?

The Magnificent Bull

a Dinka traditional poem

Words to Know

LITERARY TERM

simile a comparison of two things using *like* or *as*

SELECTION VOCABULARY

shimmering shining

resembles looks like

brow forehead

*When we love an animal, we feel proud of it. We will
do anything to protect it. In this poem, the speaker
expresses his feelings about an animal that is very
important to him.*

—⊶⊷—

My bull is white like the silver fish in the river
white like the **shimmering** crane bird on the river bank
white like fresh milk!
His roar is like the thunder to the Turkish cannon on the
    steep shore.
My bull is dark like the raincloud in the storm.
He is like summer and winter.
Half of him is dark like the storm cloud,
half of him is light like sunshine.
His back shines like the morning star.
His **brow** is red like the beak of the Hornbill.
His forehead is like a flag, calling the people from a
    distance.
He **resembles** the rainbow.

During most of the 19th century, Turks and Egyptians ruled the Dinkas's land.

The bull's forehead isn't just red, it is "like a flag." Look for other similes.

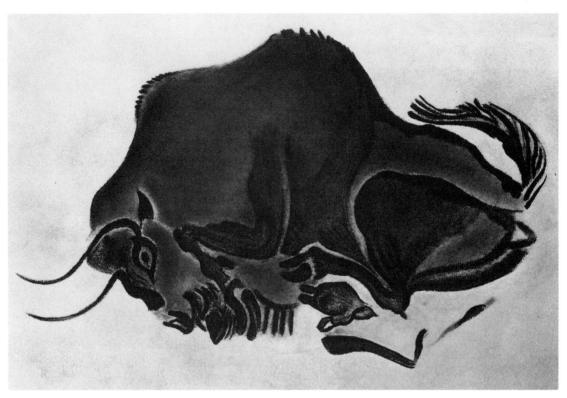

▲ This painting from the
Cave of Altamira is a
curled-up female bison.

I will water him at the river.
With my spear I shall drive my enemies.
Let them water their herds at the well;
the river belongs to me and my bull.
Drink, my bull, from the river; I am here
to guard you with my spear.

Literature Practice

Answer these questions on a separate sheet of paper.

1. What colors or shades does the speaker use to describe his bull?

2. The speaker uses similes to describe the bull. Identify two similes. What items are being compared?

3. What do the bull and a rainbow have in common?

4. What feelings does the speaker have for his bull?

Dinka Cattle Herders

Almost three million Dinka live in southern Sudan in Africa. The smallest villages can be home to about 1,000 people. As many as 30,000 Dinka might live in the largest villages. Most Dinka villages are near swampy parts of the Nile River.

Like the speaker in "The Magnificent Bull," the Dinka are cattle herders. They move their herds during the year according to when the rain falls. It rarely rains from December to April. During this dry season, the Dinka graze their cattle in pastures near the river bank. When the rains come, the Dinka herders return to the savanna where they have their permanent homes. The savanna is a flat, grassy plain where few or no trees grow. While the rain falls, the Dinka can grow crops for food.

Chapter Review

Summaries

- **The Earthworm**—The speaker wonders who respects the earthworm. He calls the earthworm a farmer who always works the soil. The speaker praises the earthworm for its continued work.

- **Green Creek**—The speaker says that the meadows can be found if one follows Green Creek. The creek winds through the mountains. It provides a peaceful place for people to rest.

- **The Cedar Chest**—A cedar tree is chopped down and taken from the woods. The speaker sees a cedar chest in a bedroom. The chest seems to accept its new home. The speaker wants the cedar chest to remember when it was a tree.

- **The Magnificent Bull**—The speaker proudly describes his bull. He compares it to other animals.

Chapter Quiz

Choose the letter of the correct answer. Rewrite the sentences on a separate sheet of paper.

1. The speaker in "The Earthworm" admires the earthworm because the
   a. speaker likes insects.
   b. speaker is a farmer.
   c. earthworm works hard.
   d. earthworm is intelligent.

2. The speaker likes Green Creek because
   a. it is a very sunny place.
   b. it makes him feel peaceful.
   c. many tourists go there.
   d. it is a secret place.

3. The cedar chest stands in
   a. a bedroom.   c. a basement.
   b. an attic.   d. a living room.

4. In "The Magnificent Bull," the speaker compares his bull to everything but
   a. a shimmering crane bird.   c. the rainbow.
   b. the morning star.   d. a mountain.

5. The speaker takes his bull to drink water at the
   a. well.   c. lake.
   b. river.   d. pump.

Thinking and Writing

Write answers to the following questions on a separate sheet of paper.

1. How do the images in "Green Creek" help you understand the speaker's feelings? Use examples from the poem in your answer.

2. How does the speaker in "The Cedar Chest" feel about the natural world and the human-made world? Give examples from the poem to explain your answer.

3. Most of the similes in "The Magnificent Bull" are related to nature. What do these similes tell you about the speaker's feelings for his bull and for nature? Use details from the poem to explain your answer.

4. How do you think the speaker in "The Earthworm" would respond to someone who felt that worms were not important? Support your answer with details from the poem.

Unit Three Review

A. The following questions are about some of the selections you read in this unit. Answer each question by writing one or two sentences on a separate sheet of paper.

1. In "Zlateh the Goat," Aaron was supposed to take Zlateh to the butcher and bring back money for his family. How do you feel about Aaron's decision to choose Zlateh over his family?

2. Why does the poet feel the tree in "The Cedar Chest" is better off in the woods?

3. Does the haiku "After a Long Winter" describe a change in a human relationship? Explain your answer.

4. The speaker in "The Magnificent Bull" will protect the bull from his enemies. How do you think cattle are valued in the speaker's land? Explain your answer.

B. Choose two of the essay questions below. Answer them on a separate sheet of paper. Write one or two paragraphs for each one.

1. In 'maggie and milly and molly and may,' e. e. cummings notes that "it's always ourselves we find in the sea." Use details from two poems in this unit to explain how nature helps us find ourselves.

2. What do each of the haiku suggest about our feelings toward the seasons? Use examples from the haiku to support your answer.

3. Sometimes experiences with nature leave us feeling happy and peaceful. Think about the characters in the stories and poems of this unit. How is each character left with feelings of happiness and respect after an experience with the natural world? Use examples from the selection.

A PLACE IN THE HEART

▲ Sharing with others opens a special place in our hearts. Shah Abbas I and his wife share a special moment in a painting by an unknown artist.

Chapter Learning Objectives

- Learn about myths.
- Identify the hero in a story.
- Learn about folktales.
- Recognize a story-within-a-story.
- Learn about plot.
- Identify internal conflict.
- Learn about resolution of a conflict.

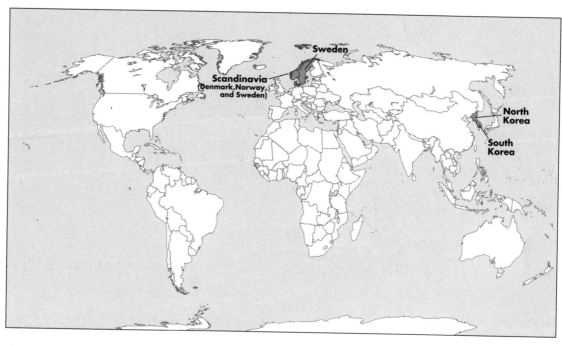

Scandinavia
How Odin Lost His Eye
a myth retold by Catharine F. Sellew

Korea
The Good Brother's Reward
*an adapted folktale retold
by Frances Carpenter*

Sweden
The Rat Trap
an adapted story by Selma Lagerlöf

Good deeds come from open hearts. Often, the kindness of a good deed can change lives. The stories in this chapter are about people whose lives are changed in different ways because of good deeds.

How Odin Lost His Eye

a myth retold by Catharine F. Sellew

Words to Know

LITERARY TERMS

myth a story from the past that explains how things began

hero the main character in a story

SELECTION VOCABULARY

helmet a strong hat that protects the head

perched sat or rested on something

snarling growling angrily with the teeth showing

flit to move about with quick motions

sorrow great sadness

sacrificed given unselfishly

glorious wonderful

Odin, a great king, wants to keep the world safe from the terrible frost giants. Before he can accomplish his goal, he must make an important decision. His good deed can only happen with a great sacrifice.

⊷⊶⊷

Odin (OH-dihn) is the king of the gods in Norse myths. Asgard (AZ-gard) is the home of the Norse gods.

Once when the world was still very young, Odin sat on his throne in the most beautiful palace in Asgard. His throne was so high that he could see over all three parts of the world from where he sat. On his head he wore a **helmet** shaped like an eagle. On his shoulders **perched** two black ravens called Memory and Thought. At his feet crouched two **snarling** wolves.

The great king gazed thoughtfully down on the earth below him. He had made the green land that stretched out before his eyes. With the help of the other gods, he had made men and women who lived on that earth. He felt truly like the All-father he was called.

The fair elves had promised they would help his children of the earth. The elves were the tiny people who lived between heaven and earth. They were so small that they could **flit** about doing their work unseen. Odin knew that they were artists who painted the flowers and made the beds for the streams. They took care of all the bees and the butterflies. It was the elves who brought the gentle rain and sunshine to the earth.

Even the ugly dwarfs, who lived in the heart of the mountains, agreed to help. They forged iron and metals, made tools and weapons. They dug gold and silver and beautiful jewels out of the earth. Sometimes they even cut the grain and ground the flour for the farmers on the earth.

All seemed to be going well. Odin found it hard to think of evil times. But he knew that the frost giants were only waiting for a chance to bring trouble to his children. They were the ones who brought cold and ice to the world and shook the earth in anger. They hated Odin and all the work of the gods.

From high on his throne, Odin looked down beyond the earth, deep into the gloomy land of his enemies. He saw the dark figures of huge men moving about. They looked like evil shadows. He, the king of the gods, must have more wisdom. It was not enough just to see his enemies. He must know more about them.

So Odin wrapped his tall figure in a blue cloak. Down from his throne he climbed. Down the broad rainbow bridge he strode and across the green earth until he came to one of the roots of the great

Odin is the hero of this myth. As you read, look for the qualities that make him a hero.

Everyone helps Odin in making the world a wonderful place. Even the elves and dwarfs have important jobs.

How will knowledge of his enemies help Odin?

evergreen tree. There, close by the tree, was a well full of clear water. Its surface was so still it was like a mirror. In it one could see pictures of things that had happened and things that were going to happen.

Beside the well sat an old man. His face was lined with the troubles of the world. His name was Mimir, which means "memory." No one, not even the great Odin, could see the pictures in the well unless he first drank some of its water. Only Mimir could give the magic drink.

"Aged Mimir," Odin said to the old man, "you who hold the knowledge of the past and future in your

Mimir (MEE-mer) sat by the well. Why do you think the well needed to be guarded in this way?

This is a detail from a 12th century Swedish tapestry of a Norseman going off to war. ▼

magic waters, let me have but one sip. Then I can know enough to protect the men and women of the earth from the hate of the giants."

Mimir looked kindly at Odin, but he did not smile. Although he spoke softly, his voice was so deep it reminded Odin of the distant roar of the ocean.

"The price of one drink from this well is not cheap," Mimir said. "Once you have drunk and gazed into the mirror of life, you may wish you had not. For **sorrow** and death as well as joy are pictured there. Think again before you ask to drink."

But once the king of the gods had made up his mind, nothing could change it. He was not afraid to look upon sorrow and death.

"What is your price, aged Mimir?" Odin asked.

"You are great and good, Odin," answered Mimir. "You have worked hard to make the world. Only those who know hard work may drink from my well. But that is not enough. What have you given up that is very dear to you? What have you **sacrificed**? The price of a drink must be a great sacrifice. Are you still willing to pay the price?"

What could the king of the gods sacrifice? What was most dear to him? Odin thought of his handsome son, Balder, whom he loved most in the world. To give up his son would be like giving up life and all that was wonderful around him. Odin stood silent before Mimir. Indeed that would be a high price! Then Mimir spoke again. He had read Odin's thoughts.

"No, I am not asking for your dear son. The Fates say his life must be short, but he has time yet to live and bring happiness to the gods and the world. I ask for one of your eyes."

Odin put his hands up to his bright blue eyes. Those two eyes had gazed across the world from his high throne in the shining city of the gods. His eyes had taught him what was good and beautiful, what was evil and ugly. But those eyes had also seen his

What do you learn about Odin's character in this part of the story?

The Fates were the goddesses who decided what would happen to people and how long they would live. What do the Fates say will happen to Balder?

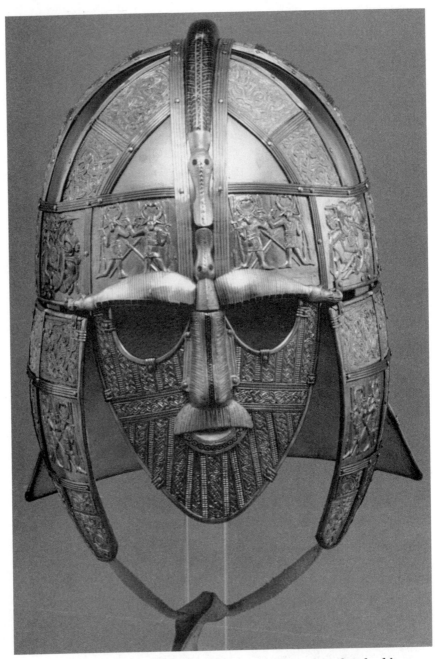

▲ In 1939, the remains of an Anglo-Saxon ship that had been buried for 1,000 years were discovered at Sutton Hoo in England. This helmet was one of the items found.

children, the men and women of the earth, struggling against the hate of the giants. One eye was a small sacrifice to win knowledge of how to help them. Without another thought, Odin plucked out one of his blue eyes and handed it to Mimir.

Then Mimir smiled and gave Odin a horn full of the waters of his well.

"Drink deeply, brave king, so you may see all that you wish in the mirror of life."

Odin lifted the horn to his lips and drank. Then he knelt by the edge of the well and watched the pictures passing across its still and silent surface. When he stood up again, he sighed, for it was as Mimir had said. He had seen sorrow and death as well as joy. It was only the **glorious** promise at the end that gave him courage to go on.

So Odin, the great king of the gods, became one-eyed. If you can find Mimir's well, you will see Odin's blue eye resting on the bottom. It is there to remind men and women of the great sacrifice he made for them.

Literature Practice

Answer these questions on a separate sheet of paper.

1. Who are Odin's children?
2. Why does Odin visit Mimir?
3. What price must Odin pay for the drink at the well?
4. How does Odin feel after he looks into the well?
5. What qualities make Odin a hero?

THE VIKINGS

Odin was the mighty king of the Norse gods. These gods were worshipped by people called Vikings. The Vikings were fierce pirates, fighters, and explorers. They lived in the part of Europe that we now call Sweden, Denmark, and Norway. Together, these countries are called Scandinavia.

One of the greatest Viking explorers was Leif Eriksson. He landed in North America around 1000 A.D. That was nearly 500 years before Christopher Columbus did!

The Vikings could explore lands far away from Europe because of their amazing wooden boats. These boats were called longships. These Viking warships were as much as 75 feet long, but only 17 feet wide.

Viking sailors crossed the Atlantic Ocean in ships with woolen sails. The ocean winds gave power to the ships. Sometimes large black birds called ravens helped lead the ships to land. A raven was released from a ship. Sails were then set in the same direction in which the birds were flying.

The Good Brother's Reward

an adapted folktale retold by Frances Carpenter

Words to Know

LITERARY TERMS

folktale a story handed down for many years among the people of a community or region

story-within-a-story one story within another story; a character from the outer story tells the inner story to another character

plot the action or series of events in a story

SELECTION VOCABULARY

shelter a place to live

huddled crowded close together

porter a person who carries things for other people

sprouted took root, began to grow

gourds fruits that have thick skins or rinds

brim the top edge of a jar or container

In this story, the lives of two brothers are suddenly changed by one act of kindness.

—⟨∞⟩—

Another family had come to join the others who lived in the crowded houses inside the Kim courts. Another brother of the Master had fallen into bad luck. He had brought his wife and many children to seek the **shelter** of these tiled roofs.

▲ This hanging scroll painting is a 19th century work showing San Shin, a Korean Mountain spirit.

"Why do they come to live with us?" Yong Tu asked his grandmother. "Why didn't they stay in their own house?" The boy was not sure he liked having his cousins there. They wanted to spin his tops and fly his kites. There were so many that Yong Tu's own little sister seldom had a turn now on the swing in the Inner Court.

"Bad luck found them, blessed boy," the old woman explained. "Where should they come but to their rich brother? How could he do anything but make them welcome? Our gates are always open to guests. Even a stranger is offered food here. How then could a brother be turned away?

"If this custom is broken, my young dragon, trouble surely would follow. Have I ever told you the tale of the two brothers? One was good, and the other was greedy. Do you know how each was rewarded? No? Then sit down beside me and listen well.

"Once long ago there were two brothers. One was rich. The other, like your uncle, had fallen into the hands of bad luck. When their father died, the oldest son took all the family riches. He kept them for himself. He didn't fill his father's place as the head of the house and look after his younger brother. Instead, he put his brother out of the gate to seek shelter and food and clothes for his family wherever he might.

"To give these brothers names, let's call the older, greedy one Koh Sang Chip. The younger one might have been named Koh Sang Hun. In the fine Koh family houses, Sang Chip lived alone with his wife. No children blessed his selfish days. Sang Hun, on the other hand, lived with his wife and several sons. They shared a little mud hut. Its old grass roof had huge holes in it. The rain fell through the holes and onto the family as if straight from the sky. At night those poor young people slept on their ragged straw mats on a cold dirt floor. They kept warm only by lying **huddled** together.

"By weaving straw shoes and by doing whatever

Yong Tu (YUNG-too) asks his grandmother about his cousins who have come to live with his family. How does Yong Tu feel about his cousins?

The grandmother answers Yong Tu by telling him a story.

The grandmother is telling the folktale. As she tells the story, each paragraph begins with quotation marks to show that she is speaking.

The two brothers in the folktale are Koh Sang Chip (koh SUNG chihp) and Koh Sang Hun (koh SUNG hun). What do you know about each brother?

jobs he could find, Sang Hun barely managed to keep his little family alive. His children often cried out for food. Even the rats complained. They told their neighbors that there was not one grain of rice in the house to steal.

The plot of the story begins with Sang Hun's need to find a way to feed his family.

"'Send our youngest son to ask help from your rich brother,' Sang Hun's wife said one day to her unhappy husband. 'Surely when he sees that small boy's hungry look, he will give us some food. He has so much.'

"But that greedy rich brother turned the boy away from his gate. 'I have food enough only for the people in my house,' he said roughly. 'My rice and my bean flour are both locked up in a storeroom. My bran I shall keep for my own cows. Any extra grain must go to my chickens. If I give you scraps from our table, my dogs will be angry. Go before they bite you!'

Why does the boy lie to his parents?

"'When the little boy returned home, he felt ashamed. He did not want to tell his uncle's cruel words. The boy only said, 'I have brought nothing. My uncle was not at home.'

"'Well,' said his mother, 'I will sell these shoes off my feet. Their straw soles are still good. They will bring enough cash for a little rice. Then we can have supper.'

"But that night luck found its way to the good brother. Sang Hun had been gathering wood on the mountain side. When he returned home, he brought along a rich treasure. This treasure was a plant root. It was from the medicine plant called insam (ginseng). Even the King and Queen drank insam soup in the spring. The medicine sellers paid Sang Hun much money for this root. His wife's shoes could now be bought back. Together with her husband, she could again look for work.

Insam or ginseng is used to make tea, medicine, and other products.

"Sang Hun's wife found a job cleaning rice. The husband worked as a **porter**. With a wooden frame on his back, he carried loads for the rich people of the village. So they got through the winter.

"Spring came, and the swallows flew back from the south. They built their nests under the straw roof of Sang Hun's little house. Soon baby birds filled the nests. One day while Sang Hun was weaving sandals in his yard, he saw a great roof snake. It slid out from below the straw toward the little birds. Before the man could drive the snake away, it had gobbled up all but one of the young birds. That one had fallen out of the nest and onto the hard ground. When the man picked it up, he saw that one of its tiny legs was broken.

"Gently, big-hearted Sang Hun tied up the swallow's leg. He made braces from dried fish skin. The children fed the bird and nursed it until it could hop about once more. Its tiny leg was crooked, but it seemed strong enough. Soon the bird began to fly about, chirping with joy.

"The days began to grow short and the autumn nights began to grow cooler. The little bird with the crooked leg hopped once more across Sang Hun's yard. It was chirping and chirping as if to say good-bye before it flew off to the south.

"The next spring the swallow with the crooked leg came again. It landed on Sang Hun's hand. Into his palm it dropped a strange seed. On one side of the seed the man's name was written in golden brush strokes. On the other side were the words 'Plant me! Water me!'

"This little bird with the crooked leg could not talk. Still, my grandmother always told me that the seed was sent to Sang Hun by the King of the Birds. It was a reward for saving the baby swallow from the roof snake and for healing its broken leg.

"Well, that seed **sprouted** and grew. Its plant climbed high up to the grass roof of that little house. Three huge **gourds** hung upon its thick vine. About the middle of the Ninth Moon, the man spoke to his wife about them. 'We shall cut the gourds down today.

Swallows are small songbirds. They travel many miles every year to spend the winter months in a warm, sunny place.

Sang Hun takes the time to help even a tiny bird. What does this tell you about the kind of person he is?

The moon travels around the earth in about a month. The middle of the Ninth Moon is about the middle of September.

▲ Two Korean dolls (Dong-ja).

We can eat their soft flesh, and we can make water bowls out of their hard shells.'

"When Sang Hun sawed the first gourd open, the couple saw a strange sight. Two servants stepped out of it. They carried a fine table covered with silver bowls and bottles. 'This bottle contains a drink that gives a man long life,' the servants said to Sang Hun. 'This bottle holds a drink that makes the blind see. This one will bring back speech to one who can't talk.'

"The man and his family were silent with wonder as they sawed open the second gourd. At once their yard was filled with shining chests, with rich silks and rolls of shining white linen. Then the third gourd was opened. From it came an army of carpenters with tools and strong pieces of fine wood. Before the stunned man's eyes rose houses with tiled roofs. These were followed by stables for horses and storehouses for grain. Into his gates came a long train of oxen. The animals were loaded with furniture and with rice and other good food. There was enough to fill his storage jars to the **brim**. Servants, horses, and all that a rich man's house holds came to Sang Hun. It all came from these three magic gourds.

"Now, news travels fast. It was not long before Sang Hun's older brother heard of his good fortune. The greedy man came quickly to find out how it had happened. Good Sang Hun told him the story of the swallow with the crooked leg. Sang Chip decided to try the same magic himself.

"With his cane he struck at every little bird he met during his trip home. He killed many, but at last he broke one little sparrow's leg. The cruel man caught it easily. He tied up the sparrow's leg with braces from the dried skin of fish. He kept the bird inside his house until it could hop again. He did just what Sang Hun had done. But there was no kindness in Sang Chip's cruel actions. There was no chirping of thanks when that

As the plot continues, Sang Hun's fortune changes. Imagine how Sang Hun and his wife felt as they watched all of this happen.

Sang Chip's actions are described by the narrator.

sparrow flew away from his courts. I am sure it chirped loudly enough when it told the King of the Birds about cruel Sang Chip, who had broken its leg.

"When this sparrow with the crooked leg came back in the spring, it brought a seed for this brother, too. Greedy Sang Chip watched with joy when the green vine from it began to climb the side of his house. But the plant grew far too fast. It grew and it grew until it choked his entire home. Its great creeping vines pulled loose his roof tiles. Rain poured in upon all his treasures. It cost him a great sum of money to have his roof fixed.

Kimchi (KIM-chee) is a spicy Korean dish. It is prepared in large clay pots made especially for that purpose.

"Instead of three gourds there were twelve on his plant. These were giant balls almost as big as a huge *kimchi* jar. When the Ninth Moon came around, Sang Chip had to pay a carpenter hundreds of dollars to open these gourds.

"Here were troubles indeed. Out of the first gourd stepped a group of traveling dancers. It cost Sang Chip much rice and money before those traveling dancers would leave his courts. Even more money was needed to get rid of the priests who came out of the second gourd. They demanded thousands to rebuild a temple.

The mudang (MOO-dahng) were women who cured sick people in the village.

"Each opened gourd brought fresh demands on Sang Chip's cash chests. A funeral, whose mourners had to be paid. A band of singing girls, whose music and dancing and bright waving flags cost so much. Traveling performers. A clown who needed much money for a long journey. A group of officials wanting their share of his tax money. A band of *mudang* women, who threatened to bring sickness into his house instead of driving it out. All these pests sprang from the gourds to take this greedy man's money. Jugglers, fortune-tellers, and poets had to be paid. Finally, little was left. From the eleventh gourd stepped a great giant. He took the very last coin from Sang Chip.

"'At least we have the twelfth gourd,' Sang Chip's weeping wife cried. 'Surely we have been punished enough. Surely there will be something good inside this last one.'

"But when the carpenters sawed the last gourd in two, smoke and hot flames poured out. They destroyed every house, every stable, and every storehouse inside Sang Chip's walls. His money was gone. His houses were burned to the ground! Where could the selfish man go now to seek shelter?

The bird sitting on the brim of this Makuzu Kozan porcelain dish is a kingfisher. ▼

"'We must ask help from my brother, Sang Hun,' he said to his wife.

"'But will he not turn us away from his gates, as you turned away his hungry child?' the woman asked.

"'I do not think so,' Sang Chip replied. 'Sang Hun has a heart as wide as the sky. He follows the ways of our father, who always gave with a big hand.'

The grandmother finishes the story. She applies the folktale's lessons to Yong Tu's father and uncle.

"Sang Chip was right. His good younger brother opened his gates for them. He gave them tables of food. Just as we give a home to your unlucky uncle, Sang Hun helped his greedy brother. That was as it should be, my dragon. After all, there was plenty of room in the fine houses which the Bird King had given him."

Literature Practice

Answer these questions on a separate sheet of paper.

1. Why does the grandmother tell her grandson the story of the two brothers?

2. What good deed does the good brother do?

3. Why does the greedy brother break the little bird's leg?

4. What is the lesson of the folktale?

Family Life in Korea

Folktales almost never come with dates. But we can figure out when "The Good Brother's Reward" might have been written. Look at what the folktale says about the family.

In the main story, family members come to live with the Kims. Another brother of the Master has bad luck He needs the help of his older brother. In the story told by the grandmother, Sang Chip is the older brother. He is supposed to fill his father's place. He is the head of the household. He must look after his younger brother. All of these details have a basis in fact.

Before the 1900s Korea was a country built on strong family ties. Almost all the people lived in small villages. They worked on farms. Grandparents, parents, and their sons and unmarried daughters lived together. Their sons' wives and children also were part of the family. This is called an extended family. The oldest male served as the head of the family. All members were expected to obey him without question.

The Korean way of life began to change. Japan took control of the country in 1910. The Japanese brought industry to Korean cities. They took much farmland away from the farmers. This meant that many young Koreans moved to the cities to work. This movement weakened Korea's strong family ties.

It is easy to figure out that this folktale was written before Japan took over. The folktale had to have been written at a time when the family was the most important group.

The Rat Trap

an adapted story by Selma Lagerlöf

Words to Know

LITERARY TERMS

internal conflict the struggle a character has in making a difficult decision

resolution the point at which the conflict in a story ends

SELECTION VOCABULARY

peddler a person who sells things

bait something, usually food, that attracts animals to a trap

anvil an iron block where hot pieces of metal are hammered into shape

bellows a hand-operated machine that creates a current of air so a fire will burn

clatter a sharp noise

intruder a person who doesn't belong in a certain place

shabby worn out

wretch a very unhappy person

Sometimes one person's kindness can help another person see the world in a new way. The kindness of a lonely woman during the Christmas season touches the heart of a poor, unhappy man.

People used to sell rat traps for a living.

Once upon a time there was a **peddler** who went around selling wire rat traps. He made his traps from things he got by begging in stores and farms. But the business was not making much money. As a result, he had to beg and steal to keep body and soul together. Even so, his clothes were in rags. His cheeks were sunken, and hunger showed in his eyes.

This man had a sad and lonely life. One day, while he was walking, he thought about his rat traps. Suddenly he was struck by an idea. The whole world, he decided, was nothing but a big rat trap. It only

◄ This *Portrait of Renoir at Cagnes* is by Maurice Denis.

existed to set **bait** for people. It offered riches and joys, a roof and food, heat and clothing. This is like the rat trap's offerings of cheese and pork. As soon as anyone touched the bait, the trap closed on him. Everything came to an end.

The world had never been very kind to him. It gave him unusual joy to think of it in this way.

What does the peddler think of the world?

One dark evening as he walked along the road, he noticed a little gray cottage. He knocked on the door to ask shelter for the night. He was not refused. The owner, an old man without wife or child, was happy to see him. He wanted someone to talk to in his loneliness. Quickly he put the pot on the fire and gave his guest supper. Next he poured them both a cup of hot tea. Finally, he got out an old pack of cards. Together they played cards until bedtime.

The old man told his guest his secrets. The guest was told that in better times his host had rented a small farm from the Ramsjö Ironworks. There he had worked the land. Now he could no longer do such labor. It was his cow that supported him. The cow could give milk for the creamery every day. Last month he had received thirty kronor in payment.

Though this is not a true story, the Ramsjö (ram-shyo) Ironworks might have existed. Sweden had a great many ironworks, factories that made iron products out of iron ore, in the late 1800s.

The guest must have been stunned by what happened next. The old man got up and went to the window. There he took down a leather pouch hanging on a nail by the window. From it he picked out three wrinkled ten-kronor bills. These he held up before the eyes of his guest. Then he stuffed them back into the pouch.

The krona is the money used in Sweden. Several krona are called kronor.

The next day both men got up. The old man was in a hurry to milk his cow. The other man felt he should not stay in bed since his host was up. They left the cottage at the same time. The old man locked the door. He put the key in his pocket. The man with the rat traps said good-bye and thank you. Then each man went his own way.

Half an hour later the rat-trap peddler stood again before the old man's door. He did not try to get in, however. He only went up to the window. Then he smashed a pane and stuck in his hand. Grabbing the pouch, he took the money and shoved it in his pocket. Then he hung the leather pouch carefully back in its place and went away.

Walking along with the money in his pocket, he felt quite pleased. He knew that he could not take the public highway. He had to turn off the road into the woods. At first this caused him no problems. Later in the day, however, it became worse. The forest was big and confusing. The paths twisted back and forth so strangely. He walked and walked without coming out of the woods. Finally, he saw that he had only been walking around in circles. He remembered his thoughts about the world and the rat trap. Now, his own turn had come. He had let himself be fooled by the bait. Now he had been caught. The whole forest closed in on him. It seemed like a tightly locked prison from which he could never escape.

It was late in December. Darkness was already settling over the forest. This added to the danger. It also added to his gloom and loss of hope. Finally, he saw no way out. He sank to the ground. He was very tired. He thought his last moment had come. As he laid his head on the ground, he heard a sound. It was a hard, regular thumping. There was no doubt as to what that was. He raised himself. "Those are the hammer strokes from an iron mill," he thought. "There must be people nearby." With his last bit of strength, he slowly stood up. He walked slowly toward the sound.

The Ramsjö Ironworks is now closed. At one time, however, it was a large plant. It had a huge melting pot, rolling mill, and forge.

On this winter evening just before Christmas, the master smith and his helper sat in the dark forge.

The main character's internal conflict begins. He knows he made a mistake. He feels as if he is in a prison even though he is in a forest.

The author tells the thoughts and feelings of the characters. This helps the reader know what is going on.

The ironworks was a big workshop with a large furnace, or forge. At the anvil, the smith would hammer hot pieces of iron to form tools or horseshoes.

They waited near the furnace for the pig iron in the fire to be ready to put on the **anvil.** Every now and then one man got up to stir the glowing mass with a long iron bar. Returning in a few minutes, he dripped with sweat. As was the custom, he wore nothing but a long shirt and a pair of wooden shoes.

There were always many sounds to be heard in the forge. The big **bellows** groaned. The burning coal cracked. The fire boy shoveled charcoal into the mouth of the furnace with a great deal of **clatter.** Outside the waterfall roared. At the same time, a sharp north wind whipped the rain against the roof.

It was probably because of these noises that the blacksmith did not see the man open the gate and

In *Schmeide* painted by Julius Von Ehren, a blacksmith is shown working at a forge. The forge in the Ramsjö Ironworks was much larger. ▼

enter the forge. When the blacksmith saw the man, he was standing close to the furnace.

Poor tramps often came there to warm themselves in front of the fire. The blacksmith glanced only casually at the **intruder.** He looked like most people of his type. He had a long beard. He was dirty and ragged. He had a bunch of rat traps hanging on his chest.

The rat-trap man asked if he might stay. The blacksmith nodded yes.

The tramp did not say anything else. He had not come there to talk. He wanted only to warm himself and sleep.

In those days the Ramsjö Ironworks was owned by a well-known ironmaster. It was his greatest desire to make good iron for his customers. He watched day and night to see that the work was done well. At this very moment he came into the forge on one of his nightly checks.

Naturally, the first thing he saw was the tramp. By then the tramp was sitting by the furnace. The ironmaster walked up to the tramp. He looked at the man closely. Then he tore off the man's floppy hat to get a better look at his face.

"But of course it is you, Nils Olof!" the ironmaster said. "How you do look!"

Nils Olof (NEYELS O-lohf)

The man with the rat traps had never seen the ironmaster before. He did not even know his name. But he thought if the fine gentleman thought he was an old friend, he might give him a few kronor. He decided to pretend he knew the ironmaster.

"Yes, things have gone downhill with me," he said.

"You should not have left the regiment," said the ironmaster. "That was the mistake. If only I had still been in the service, it never would have happened. Well, now of course you will come home with me."

The tramp did not like this plan.

"No, I could not think of it!" he said, looking quite alarmed.

He thought of the thirty kronor. To go up to the manor house could be like throwing himself into the lion's den. He only wanted to sleep in the forge and then sneak away unnoticed.

The ironmaster believed that he felt uneasy because of his **shabby** clothing.

"Please don't think that I have such a fine home that you cannot be my guest," the ironmaster said. "Elizabeth is dead, as you may have heard. My boys are abroad. There is no one at home except my oldest daughter and me. We were just saying that it was too bad we didn't have company for Christmas. Now, come along with me. Help us make the Christmas food disappear a little faster."

But the stranger said no and no and again no. At last the ironmaster saw that he must give in.

"It looks as though Captain Nils Olof wants to stay with you," he said to the blacksmith. Then he turned away on his heel.

But the ironmaster laughed to himself as he went away. The blacksmith, who knew him, understood that he had not said his last word.

It was not more than half an hour before they heard the sound of a carriage. A new guest came in. This time it was not the ironmaster. He had sent his daughter. He seemingly hoped she might talk the tramp into coming to the house.

She entered followed by a servant. The servant carried a big fur coat on his arm. She was not at all pretty. She seemed modest and shy. The stranger had stretched himself out on the floor in front of the furnace. A piece of pig iron lay under his head. His hat was pulled down over his eyes. As soon as the young girl saw him, she went up and lifted his hat. The man was clearly used to sleeping with one eye open. He jumped up suddenly. He seemed to be quite frightened.

"My name is Edla Willmansson," said the young girl. "My father came home and said that you wanted to sleep here in the forge tonight. I asked if I might come and bring you home to us. I am so sorry, Captain, that you are having such a hard time."

She looked at him kindly. She noticed that the man was afraid. "Either he has stolen something or else he has escaped from jail," she thought. Then she added quickly, "You may be sure, Captain, that you will be allowed to leave as freely as you came. Only please stay with us over Christmas Eve."

She said this in such a friendly manner that the man must have felt he could trust her.

"I never thought that you would bother with me yourself, miss," he said. "I will come at once."

Even though Edla Willmansson feels the peddler may be in trouble, she still invites him into her home.

A woodcut of a wooden mouse trap. ▼

He accepted the fur coat from the servant. Throwing it over his rags, he followed the young lady out to the carriage. He did not give the surprised blacksmith so much as a glance.

But while he was riding up to the house, he had gloomy thoughts about what the future held.

"Why did I take that fellow's money?" he thought. "Now I am sitting in the trap and will never get out of it."

The next day was Christmas Eve. When the ironmaster arrived for breakfast, he was no doubt thinking happily of his old friend. How lucky it was to have run into him.

"First of all we must see to it that he gets a little flesh on his bones," he said. "Then we must see that he gets something else to do. He should not run around the country selling rat traps."

His daughter was busy at the table. "It is odd that things have gone downhill with him as badly as that," said the daughter. "Last night there was nothing to show that he had once been an educated man."

"You must have patience, my little girl," said the father. "As soon as he gets clean and dressed, you will see something different. Last night he was, of course, ashamed. The tramp manners will fall away with the tramp clothes."

Just as he said this the door opened and the stranger came in. Yes, now he was truly clean and well dressed. The servant had bathed him, cut his hair, and shaved him. Moreover, he was dressed in fine clothes owned by the ironmaster. He wore a white shirt with a stiff color and new shoes.

Even though his guest was now groomed, the ironmaster did not seem pleased. He looked at him with a frown. He had only seen the strange fellow in the dim light of the furnace. It was easy to understand how he might have made a mistake. Now with the stranger standing there in broad daylight, it was impossible to mistake him for his old friend.

"What does this mean?" the ironmaster thundered.

The stranger made no effort to carry on the disguise. He saw at once that all the glory had come to an end.

"It is not my fault, sir," he said. "I never tried to be anything but a poor trader. I pleaded and begged to stay in the forge. But no harm has been done. At worst, I can put on my rags again and go away."

"Well," said the ironmaster, slowly. "It was not quite honest, either. You must admit that. I should not be surprised if the sheriff would like to know something of this matter."

The tramp took a step forward. He struck the table with his fist.

"Now, I am going to tell you, Mr. Ironmaster, how things are. This whole world is nothing but a big rat trap. All the good things that are offered you are nothing. They are just cheese rinds and bits of pork set out to drag a poor fellow into trouble. If the sheriff locks me up for this, then you, Mr. Ironmaster, must remember something. A day will come when you may want to get a big piece of pork. Then you too will get caught in the trap."

The ironmaster began to laugh.

"That was not so badly said, my good fellow. Perhaps we should let the sheriff alone on Christmas Eve. But now get out of here as fast as you can," the ironmaster said.

But as the man opened the door, the daughter spoke up. "I think he ought to stay with us today. I don't want him to go." With that she closed the door.

"What in the world are you doing?" said the father.

The daughter stood there feeling quite ashamed. She hardly knew what to answer. That morning she had felt so happy. She thought how homelike and Christmassy she was going to make things for the poor

Why is the ironmaster so angry at the peddler?

hungry **wretch.** She could not give up the idea all at once. That is why she spoke up for the tramp.

"I am thinking of this stranger here," said the young girl. "He walks and walks the whole year long. There is probably not a single place in the whole country where he feels at home. Wherever he turns, he is chased away. Always he is afraid of being arrested and questioned. I should like to have him enjoy a day of peace with us here. It would be just one day in the whole year."

The ironmaster mumbled something in his beard. He could not bring himself to say no.

"It was all a mistake, of course," she continued. "But I don't think we ought to send away someone we have asked to come here. We have promised him Christmas cheer."

"You talk worse than a preacher," said the ironmaster. "I only hope you won't be sorry about this."

The young girl took the stranger by the hand and led him to the table.

"Now sit down and eat," she said. She could see that her father had given in.

The man with the rat traps said not a word. He only sat down and helped himself to the food. Time after time he looked at the young girl who had spoken up for him. Why had she done it? What could the crazy idea be?

After that, Christmas Eve passed just as it always had. The stranger did not cause any trouble. He did nothing but sleep. The whole morning he lay on the sofa in a guest room and slept. At noon they woke him so he could have his share of the good Christmas food and drink. After that, he slept again. It seemed as though for many years he had not been able to sleep as quietly and safely.

In the evening, when the tree was lighted, they woke him again. He stood blinking as though the

▲ This painting by Jacques Callot is called *Beggar*.

candlelight hurt him. After that, he disappeared again. Two hours later he was awakened once more. He then had to go down into the dining room to eat the Christmas supper.

As soon as they got up from the table, he went to each person and said thank you and good-night. When he came to the young girl, she told him that her father wished him to keep the suit he wore. It was to be a Christmas present—he did not have to return it. She further told him if he wanted to spend next Christmas Eve with them, he would be welcomed back again.

The man with the rat traps did not answer. He only stared at the young girl in great amazement.

The next morning the ironmaster and his daughter got up to go to the early Christmas service. Their guest was still asleep. They did not disturb him.

At about ten o'clock, they drove back from church. The young girl sat and hung her head. She was more downcast than usual. At church she learned that one of the old farmers of the ironworks had been robbed by a man who sold rat traps.

"Yes, that was a fine fellow you let into the house," said her father. "I only wonder how many silver spoons are left in the cupboard."

The wagon had hardly stopped at the front steps when the ironmaster questioned the servant. He wanted to know if the stranger was still there. He added that he had heard at church that the man was a thief. The servant answered that the fellow had gone. He further stated that he had not taken anything with him. In fact, quite the opposite was true. He had left behind a little package, a Christmas present for Miss Willmansson.

The young girl opened the package. It was so badly wrapped that she saw at once what was inside. She gave a little cry of joy when she found a small rat trap. In it lay three wrinkled ten-kronor notes. But that was not all. In the rat trap lay also a letter written in large, uneven letters:

Honored and noble Miss:

You have been so nice to me all day long, as if I was a captain. I want to be nice to you in return, as if I was a real captain. I do not want you to be shamed at Christmas by a thief. You can give back the money to the old man on the roadside. He has the money pouch hanging on the window as a bait for poor tramps.
The rat trap is a Christmas present from a rat. This rat would have been caught in this world's rat trap if he had not been raised to captain. As a captain, he got the power to clear himself.

Written with friendship and high regard,

Captain Nils Olof

This is the resolution of the peddler's internal conflict. How does it end?

Literature Practice

Answer these questions on a separate sheet of paper.

1. How does the poor peddler feel about the world?

2. Why does the peddler pretend to know the ironmaster?

3. What kind of person is Edla Willmansson?

4. Why do you think the peddler signs his letter "Captain Nils Olof"?

5. How does Edla Willmansson's act of kindness change her and the peddler as well?

Chapter Review

Summaries

- **How Odin Lost His Eye**—Odin is the mighty king of the Norse gods. He wants to protect his children, the men and women of the earth, from the evil frost giants. Odin asks Mimir to let him drink from his magic well. Just one sip of water will let Odin see the past and future. But first he must sacrifice one of his eyes. The mighty Odin makes the sacrifice to protect his children.

- **The Good Brother's Reward**—A grandmother tells a story to her grandson about two brothers. One brother was poor but kind. The other brother was rich but greedy. After the poor brother helps an injured bird, he is rewarded with many riches. His greedy brother hopes to get the same reward. Instead, he loses his fine home and all his money. His good younger brother takes him in and gives him food and shelter.

- **The Rat Trap**—A poor peddler makes a living by selling rat traps. After stealing money from an old man, the peddler seeks shelter in the ironworks. The owner of the ironworks thinks the peddler is an old friend. He invites the peddler to spend Christmas at his home. When the rich man realizes his mistake, he becomes very angry. But his kind daughter wants the poor peddler to stay in their home. After the man and his daughter return from church, they find the peddler has run away. He has left the stolen money and a letter. In the letter he thanks the young woman for treating him kindly.

Chapter Quiz

Choose the letter of the correct answer. Rewrite the sentences on a separate sheet of paper.

1. The one thing that Odin didn't want to sacrifice is
   a. his beautiful palace.
   b. his son Balder.
   c. his ravens.
   d. his jewels and gold.

2. In "The Good Brother's Reward," the narrator is the
   a. grandson.
   b. greedy brother.
   c. good brother.
   d. grandmother.

3. When the poor brother sends his son to ask for food, the older brother
   a. sends food and money.
   b. will not help.
   c. hurts a small bird.
   d. invites the boy into his big house.

4. In "The Rat Trap," the poor farmer gladly invites the peddler into his house because
   a. he is lonely.
   b. he is greedy.
   c. he is a rich farmer.
   d. he no longer works.

Thinking and Writing

Write answers to the following questions on a separate sheet of paper.

1. What do you think the "glorious promise at the end" that Odin sees in the well is?

2. What lesson does the grandson learn from the grandmother in the "The Good Brother's Reward"?

3. What does the title "The Rat Trap" have do to with the story?

▲ Time shared with friends is very special. In *L'Equipe Au Repos* by Fernand Leger, three friends enjoy the day together.

Chapter Learning Objectives

- Recognize a fable.
- Identify the theme of a story.
- Understand how writers use simile.
- Understand the climax of a story.
- Discover how writers use surprise endings.
- Learn about the use of chronological order in a memoir.

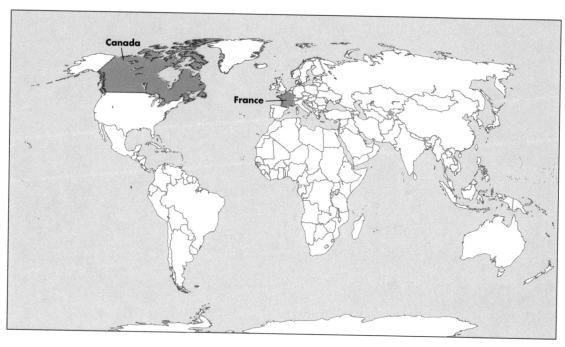

France
**The Lion and the Rat;
The Pigeon and the Ant**
*adapted fables by Jean de
La Fontaine*

Canada
The Friends of Kwan Ming
an adapted story by Paul Yee

France
**Memoirs of Madame Vigée-
Lebrun**
*adapted from the memoirs of
Élisabeth Vigée-Lebrun*

Feelings between friends are special. We open our hearts to our friends. We look to them for comfort, encouragement, advice, and support. The stories in this chapter are reminders of how precious a good friend is.

▲ In *Livre des propriétés des choses: de la propriétes des bétes*, artist Barthelem L'Anglois shows pictures of different animals. Some of them appear in La Fontaine's fables.

The Lion and the Rat;
The Pigeon and the Ant

adapted fables by Jean de La Fontaine

Words to Know

LITERARY TERMS

fable a very short story, usually with animal characters, that teaches a lesson

theme the main idea of a novel, story, poem, or play

SELECTION VOCABULARY

gnawed chewed

blade a single stem of grass

crossbow a weapon like a bow and arrow that was used by people long ago

There is a saying that one good turn deserves another. In the following two fables, a lion and a pigeon are rewarded for their acts of kindness.

———— ✺ ————

The Lion and the Rat

Early one morning the rat popped out of his hole. He did not think about who might be on the ground above him. Unfortunately, it was a lion. The rat popped up right between the lion's paws.

But the king of beasts pulled in his claws. He was not very hungry that morning. He let the rat go.

The lion's kind act did not go to waste. But could a

The lion is called the "king of beasts."

The lion lets the rat go. What does this tell you about the lion?

▲ The illustration *The Maccarte Lion* by an unknown artist shows an angry king of beasts.

rat pay back a debt to a lion? Could that really happen? It did happen.

Several days later that lion got caught in a net on the edge of the jungle. The lion was very angry.

His roars were powerful. But all his roaring could not untangle the net.

The rat heard the lion's angry roars. He ran up to the lion. He got to work with his sharp little teeth. He **gnawed** and gnawed until, bit by bit, he picked the net apart. He paid back his debt to the lion.

The lion was angry and strong. But anger and strength could do nothing. The rat was patient. He did not give up. With a little time, he did more than the lion could do.

What is the theme of this first fable?

◀ The patient and steady gnawing of the black rat, shown in this illustrattion, saved the lion. The artist is unknown.

The Pigeon and the Ant

An ant leaned over the edge of the water. It leaned just a little too far. Suddenly, it lost its balance. The poor ant fell in.

A thirsty pigeon was getting a drink from the water. She saw the ant fall.

To the ant, the water was like a sea. The water was deep and wide. The ant struggled hard, but it began to sink.

The kind pigeon threw the ant a **blade** of grass. The ant used it as a plank. It crawled back to dry land. The ant was wet and tired. But it was safe. The pigeon had saved the ant's life

This is an illustration of *The Wild Pigeon* by an unknown artist. The kind deed of the pigeon saved the life of the ant. ▼

Soon a man from the village walked by. His bare feet made no sound. He happened to have a **crossbow** in his hand.

He saw the pigeon, who is called the bird of Venus. He imagined the pigeon cooking in pot. He thought of how good her meat would taste.

The pigeon never saw the man. But the ant did. Just as the man aimed his crossbow, the ant stung him in the heel.

The man jerked his head. Now the pigeon heard him. She flew up quickly. She was out of range of his crossbow. The man's supper was gone. Because of the ant, there would be no pigeon pie tonight!

What do you think the man uses his crossbow for?

Venus appears in Roman myths. She is the goddess of love and beauty.

The tiny ant rewarded the good deed of the pigeon by saving it from the hunter. Real ants are much smaller than the ant in this illustration by an unknown artist. ▼

Literature Practice

Answer these questions on a separate sheet of paper.

1. What lesson do both fables teach about friendship?

2. How does the rat repay the lion's kind act?

3. How does the ant help the pigeon?

4. What personal quality of the rat helps him to save the lion?

The Fable: The First Short Story

Fables have been told for 2,000 years. They are still popular. They offer advice that everyone can use.

The fable is like a short story. It has a plot and a conflict. The characters are animals. They talk and act like people. They show the good and bad side of human nature. The fable ends with a moral. It is a helpful lesson about the best way to act.

Writers from many different times have written fables. Aesop was the first person to write them. He lived in Greece around 600 B.C. His stories are known and loved by people of all ages. Jean de La Fontaine is the author of "The Lion and the Rat" and "The Pigeon and the Ant." He retold Aesop's fables in poetry during the 17th century. His fables are still taught in French schools. Today, James Thurber writes fables for our time. His simple, funny stories often have surprise endings.

The Friends of Kwan Ming

an adapted story by Paul Yee

Words to Know

LITERARY TERMS

simile a comparison of two things using *like* or *as*

climax the most exciting part of a story that comes near the end

surprise ending an ending of a story that is not expected

SELECTION VOCABULARY

warehouse a place where food or other products are stored before they are taken to stores or markets

apprentice a person who works for an experienced worker to learn a skill

houseboy a boy or man hired to do housework

mansion large house

stingy unwilling to spend money

scuffed scratched or scraped

stale not fresh; tasteless

tantrum a display of bad temper or anger

True friends never let each other down in times of trouble. Kwan Ming has three special friends who help him outsmart a mean boss.

———— ✸ ————

When his father died, Kwan Ming had to sell the house and his little rice field to pay for the burial.

Kwan Ming (KWAHN-mihng)

During the mid-1800s, ships carried thousands of people from Europe and Asia to America. The ships were often overcrowded and travel was uncomfortable. Imagine traveling in the bottom of a ship for six weeks!

After the funeral, Kwan Ming looked around his village. He saw that he owned nothing—not even one roof tile. He had just enough money to buy a ticket on a ship to America. He had heard there were plenty of jobs there.

Kwan Ming told his mother, "I can start a new life in America. I will send money home."

The trip lasted six weeks. Kwan Ming sat in the bottom of the ship with hundreds of other Chinese. He became good friends with three men from nearby villages: Chew Lap, Tam Yim, and Wong Foon. Together the four men ate, told jokes, and shared their dreams for the future.

When they arrived in New York, everyone went off to different places to look for work. Kwan Ming hurried to the **warehouse** district, the train station, and the waterfront. But doors slammed in his face because he was Chinese. So he went to every store and laundry in Chinatown. But there were no jobs to be found anywhere. There were too many men looking for work in a country that was too young.

Kwan Ming cannot find a job. What do you think he will do?

Every night, Kwan Ming went back to the inn where he was staying with his three friends. Like Kwan Ming, his friends had found no work. Every night the men ate their small bit of rice dotted with soy sauce. They talked about the places they had visited and the people they had met.

Every night, Kwan Ming worried more and about his mother. He wondered how she was doing. His friends had worries, too.

One evening, Chew Lap said, "If I don't find work soon, I'm going back to China."

Tam Yim said, "What for, you fool? Things are worse there!"

Chew Lap said, "But at least I will be with my family!"

Wong Foon means to be helpful. How might he have hurt Chew Lap's feelings?

Wong Foon said, "Your family needs money for food

more than they need your company. Don't forget that."
Then there was a knock at the door. The innkeeper
pushed his way into their tiny room.

The innkeeper said, "Good news! I have found a job
for each of you!"

The men jumped to their feet.

The innkeeper said, "Three of the jobs are good,
and they pay well. But the fourth job is, well…." The
innkeeper coughed sadly.

For the first time, the four men gave each other
unfriendly looks. They were like four hungry cats
about to pounce on a bird.

The innkeeper said, "The biggest bakery in
Chinatown needs a worker. You'll always be warm next
to the oven. Who will go?"

This is a 19th century
painting showing
six young Chinese
men. The artist is
unknown. ▼

As you continue to read, you will learn why each man left China.

Kwan Ming said, "You go, Chew Lap. Your parents are sick. They need money for medicine."

The innkeeper said, "The finest tailor in Chinatown wants an **apprentice**. The man who takes this job will be able to throw away the rags he is wearing."

Kwan Ming said, "That's the job for you, Tam Yim. You have four little ones waiting for food in China."

The innkeeper said, "The best shoemaker in Chinatown needs a helper. He pays well. Who wants to cut leather and stitch boots?"

Kwan Ming said, "You go, Wong Foon. You said the roof of your house in China needs to be fixed. Better get new roof tiles before the rainy season starts."

The innkeeper shook his head and said, "The last job is for a **houseboy**. The boss owns the biggest **mansion** in town. But he is also the most **stingy** man around!"

Kwan Ming had no choice. He knew his mother needed money very badly. So off he went.

The boss was fatter than a cast-iron stove. He was as cruel as a blizzard at midnight. Kwan Ming's room was next to the furnace. Black soot and coal dust covered his pillow and blankets. It was hard to save money. For food, he had only leftovers.

Every day, Kwan Ming swept and washed every floor in the mansion. He moved the heavy oak tables. He rolled up the carpets. The house was huge. When Kwan Ming had finished cleaning the last room, the first one was dirty all over again.

One afternoon, Kwan Ming was mopping the front porch. His boss came running out in a hurry and slipped. He crashed down the stairs. Kwan Ming ran over to help. But the fat man turned on him.

The boss's neck turned purple as he screamed at Kwan Ming, "You turtle! You lazy oaf! You doorknob! You rock brain! You're fired!"

Think about what Kwan Ming is doing for his friends. What does this tell you about the kind of person he is?

What do you see in your mind when you read that the boss was "as cruel as a blizzard at midnight"?

What do the boss's actions and words tell you about the kind of person he is?

Kwan Ming said, "Please sir, give me another chance. I will work even harder if you let me stay."

The boss said, "Very well, Kwan Ming, I won't fire you. But I will have to punish you. You have ruined this suit. Because of you, I have **scuffed** my boots. You also made me miss my dinner."

The boss went on, "You have three days to find me the following things. Bring me a fine wool suit that will never tear. Bring me a pair of leather boots that will never wear out. Bring me forty loaves of bread that will never go **stale**. If you can't, you're fired. I will see that you never find another job!"

Kwan Ming ran off. What the boss wanted seemed impossible. Where would he ever find such things? He walked through the streets of Chinatown. He sat down on the wooden sidewalk.

Suddenly, he heard the familiar voices of his friends. Kwan Ming told them about the three things he had to bring to his boss.

Tam Yim said, "Don't worry! I'll make the wool suit you need."

Wong Foon said, "I'll make the boots."

Chew Lap said, "I'll make the bread."

Three days later, the friends brought the goods they had promised. The boss's eyes lit up when he saw them. He put on the suit. He was surprised at how well it fit. He sat down and tried on the boots. They slid onto his feet as if they had been buttered.

Then the boss started eating the bread. It was so soft, so sweet, that he couldn't stop eating. He ate twelve loaves, then thirteen, then twenty.

The boss's stomach swelled like a circus tent. But his well-made suit and strong boots held him tight like a huge sausage. He shouted for help. He tried to stand up, but he couldn't. He kicked his feet like a baby having a **tantrum**.

This is an important point in the plot. Kwan Ming may or may not lose his job. His friends may or may not be able to help. The story could go in almost any direction.

This is the climax of the story. The conflict between Kwan Ming and his boss is about to be solved.

This is the surprise ending of the story. Describe how this surprise ending made you feel.

Before anyone could do a thing, there was a great *Bang*!

Kwan Ming stared at the chair and blinked his eyes. There was nothing left of his boss.

He had exploded into a million little pieces.

This is a picture of Chinese passengers arriving in San Francisco. They are being met by friends. Kwan Ming and his friends also traveled to America on a very crowded ship. ▼

Literature Practice

Answer these questions on a separate sheet of paper.

1. Why did the four men leave their villages in China?
2. Why did Kwan Ming's friends help him?
3. What happens in the climax of this story?
4. How would you describe Kwan Ming's character?

Memoirs of Madame Vigée-Lebrun

adapted from the memoirs of Élisabeth Vigée-Lebrun

Words to Know

LITERARY TERMS

chronological order the order in which events happen

memoir a true story about events that an author has lived through

SELECTION VOCABULARY

nobility high social class

splendor grandness

satin a smooth, shiny material

superior as if of greater importance or value

exhibit show of art work

rabble a noisy crowd of people that is hard to control

It is rare to have a friendship with a famous person. In this memoir, Madame Vigée-Lebrun describes her experience as a portrait painter for Marie Antoinette, the Queen of France. The two women soon form a special bond.

Most memoirs are organized in chronological order because they tell about real events in people's lives.

It was in the year 1779 that I painted the Queen, Marie Antoinette, for the first time. She was at the peak of her youth and beauty. She was tall and pleasantly built. Her arms were superb. Her hands, small and perfectly formed. Her feet, charming. She had the best walk of any woman in France. She carried herself with much pride. It marked her as the queen.

The Queen had both grace and **nobility.** Her features were not regular. She had a long, narrow face. Her eyes were not large. They were almost blue and at the same time merry and kind. Her nose was slender and pretty. Her mouth was not too large. The most striking thing about her face was the tone of her skin. I have never seen skin so brilliant. I could never show the clearness of her skin as I wished. I had no colors to paint such freshness. Such fine shades were hers

◀ This portrait of *Marie Antoinette* was painted by Madame Élisabeth Vigée-Lebrun.

Why do you think the narrator was uncomfortable around the Queen?

alone. I had never seen them in any other woman.

At the first sitting, the **splendor** of the Queen frightened me greatly. But Her Majesty spoke to me very pleasantly. I felt better. It was at that sitting that I began the picture showing her with a large basket. She wore a **satin** dress and held a rose. This portrait was for her brother, Emperor Joseph II. The Queen ordered two more copies. One was for the Empress of Russia, the other for her palace rooms.

I painted various pictures of the Queen. In one I did her wearing a pale red dress. She stood before a table arranging flowers in a vase. I liked to paint her in a plain gown without a wide skirt. She usually gave these portraits to friends or foreign officials. One shows her wearing a straw hat and a plain cotton dress. When this work was viewed, cruel people remarked that the Queen had been painted in her underclothes. Even so, the portraits were very successful.

I was fortunate to be a friend of the Queen. She heard I had a fair voice. After that, we rarely had a sitting without singing. The Queen was very fond of music. But she did not sing very well.

Marie Antoinette was wonderful to talk with. She never missed a chance to praise others. The kindness she showed to me has been one of my sweetest memories.

One day I missed the time she had given me for a sitting. I had suddenly become ill. The next day I hurried to Versailles to offer my excuses. The Queen was not expecting me. Her horses had been harnessed for a drive. Her carriage was the first thing I saw in the palace yard. Even so, I went to speak with the officials on duty. One received me with a stiff, **superior** manner. Then he bellowed at me in a loud voice, "It was yesterday, madame, that Her Majesty expected you." Then he added, "I am sure she is going out driving. I am also very sure she will give you no sitting today!"

Versailles is a city located in France. It is famous for the palace and gardens built there during the time Louis XIV ruled France.

I replied that I had only come to set another day. With that, he went to the Queen. She at once had me brought to her room. She had just finished dressing. In her hand she held a book while she listened to her daughter say her lessons. My heart was beating wildly, for I knew I was wrong. But the Queen looked up and said most kindly, "I was waiting for you yesterday. What happened?"

"I am sorry, Your Majesty," I replied. "I was so ill that I was unable to obey your commands. I came to receive more now. Then I will leave without delay."

"No, no! Do not go!" exclaimed the queen. "I do not want you to have made your journey for nothing!" She canceled her carriage and gave me a sitting. In my confusion, I eagerly opened my box. I was so excited I spilled my brushes on the floor. I stooped down to pick them up. "Never mind, never mind," said the Queen. In spite of all I said, she picked them all up herself.

The Queen overlooked nothing to teach her children the polite manner which made her so beloved to all. I once saw her make her little daughter dine with a country girl. The Queen saw to it that the little visitor was served first. She told her daughter, "You must do the honors."

The last sitting I had with Her Majesty was at Trianon. I did her hair for a large picture of her with her children. After doing the Queen's hair, I did separate paintings of the children. Then I busied myself with my large picture. I gave it great importance and had it ready to **exhibit** in 1788. The frame, which had been sent ahead, caused many hateful remarks. "That's how the money goes," the people said.

At last I sent my picture. However, I could not find the courage to follow it. I was afraid it would be badly received. In fact, I became quite ill with fright. I shut myself in my room. There I prayed for the success of

Notice how the narrator describes the Queen. What event in the story shows the Queen's kind, thoughtful nature?

At this time in French history, a revolution against the wealthy ruling class was forming. The French Revolution began in 1789 and lasted for ten years.

▲ This painting, *Marie Antoinette with Her Children*, is the work of Madame Élisabeth Vigée-Lebrun.

my "Royal Family." Suddenly my brother and a group of friends burst in. They told me my picture had received the highest praise. After the exhibit, the King had the picture moved to the palace. A minister presented me to the King. Louis XVI kindly agreed to talk to me at length. He told me he was very pleased. Then, looking at my work, he added, "I know nothing about painting, but you make me like it."

The picture was placed in one of the rooms in the palace. The Queen passed it going to and from mass. After the death of her son early in 1789, the picture reminded her of her painful loss. She could not go through the room without tears. The Queen ordered the picture taken away. With her usual thoughtfulness, she told me of her reasons for removing the picture. It is because of the Queen's tender feelings that my picture was saved. The common **rabble** who soon came to the palace would have destroyed it.

Literature Practice

Answer these questions on a separate sheet of paper.

1. Why does Madame Vigée-Lebrun visit the Queen?

2. What physical features does Madame Vigée-Lebrun most admire in the Queen?

3. How does the Queen treat Madame Vigée-Lebrun?

4. What feelings does the artist have toward the Queen?

5. How does the use of chronological order help readers understand the events in the memoir?

Chapter Review

Summaries

- **The Lion and the Rat**—One day a rat pops up from a hole in the ground between a lion's paws. Surprisingly, the lion doesn't kill the rat. Later, when the lion is caught in a net, the rat saves his life.

- **The Pigeon and the Ant**—A pigeon is drinking water from a brook. An ant falls in the water and starts to sink. The pigeon saves it. When a hunter is about to shoot the pigeon, the ant stings him. The pigeon is able to fly away.

- **The Friends of Kwan Ming**—Four Chinese men set sail for America. They become good friends. When they reach their new home, they all look for work. Kwan Ming lets his friends take the best jobs. He ends up working for a mean boss who wants to fire him. However, Kwan Ming's friends help him save his job. When the mean boss eats twenty loaves of bread, his body swells and he explodes.

- **Memoirs of Madame Vigée-Lebrun**—Madame Vigée-Lebrun tells about her experiences painting portraits of the Queen of France. Over the years, the artist grows to admire the Queen for her kindness. The artist paints her last portrait of Marie Antoinette shortly before the French Revolution.

Chapter Quiz

Choose the letter of the correct answer. Rewrite the sentences on a separate sheet of paper.

1. The rat saves the lion's life by
   a. biting the man who trapped him.
   b. gnawing through the net.
   c. getting help.
   d. taking him home.

2. Kwan Ming's boss wants to fire him because
   a. he falls down the stairs that Kwan Ming mops.
   b. he is a lazy worker.
   c. he didn't follow his orders.
   d. he couldn't bake bread.

3. Madame Vigée-Lebrun recalls her first sitting with the Queen and feeling
   a. uncomfortable.
   b. scared.
   c. nervous.
   d. clumsy.

4. One of Madame Vigée-Lebrun's sweetest memories is
   a. visiting the Palace at Versailles.
   b. meeting King Louis XVI.
   c. painting the Queen's portrait.
   d. the Queen's kindness toward her.

Thinking and Writing

Write answers to the following questions on a separate sheet of paper.

1. Why do you think La Fontaine uses animals to teach lessons in his fables?

2. Do you think "The Friends of Kwan Ming" is a good title for this story? Explain your answer.

3. When Élisabeth Vigée-Lebrun first meets the Queen, she does not know what to expect. How is Lebrun's first portrait sitting with the Queen different from the last sitting?

Unit Four Review

A. The following questions are about some of the selections you read in this unit. Answer each question by writing one or two sentences on a separate sheet of paper.

1. In "The Good Brother's Reward," the poor brother helps a bird and is rewarded. The older brother helps a bird but is not rewarded. Why?

2. Why does the peddler in "The Rat Trap" return the money he stole?

3. In "How Odin Lost His Eye," what conflict does Odin face?

4. What do the animal characters in "The Lion and the Rat" and "The Pigeon and the Ant" learn about friendship and being kind to one another?

B. Choose two of the essay questions below. Answer them on a separate sheet of paper. Write one or two paragraphs for each one.

1. When put to the test, both Odin in "How Odin Lost His Eye" and Kwan Ming in "The Friends of Kwan Ming" are willing to make sacrifices. How are Odin and Kwan rewarded? Use examples from the stories to support your answer.

2. In her memoir, Élisabeth Vigée-Lebrun says that some people do not like the Queen. How do you think Lebrun might describe the Queen to those people?

3. In "The Good Brother's Reward," Yong Tu is unhappy about his cousins moving in with his family. What do you think the peddler in "The Rat Trap" might teach the boy about being kind to others? Use examples from the story to explain your answer.

FAMILY MATTERS

▲ As we grow up, we learn many things about ourselves. Some of what we learn comes from our family. This is a family of four African statues by an unknown artist.

Chapter Learning Objectives

- Recognize the speaker in a poem.
- Identify rhyme in a poem.
- Identify a stanza in a poem.
- Learn about nonfiction.
- Recognize the tone of a story.
- Understand character motivation.
- Learn how authors use dialogue in a story.

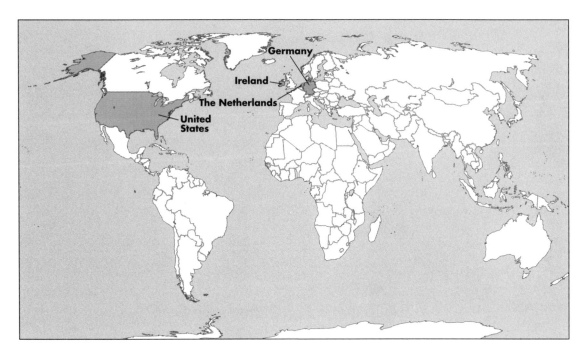

United States
Manners
a poem by Elizabeth Bishop

The Netherlands
Anne Frank Remembered: The Story of the Woman Who Helped to Hide the Frank Family
adapted from the autobiography of Miep Gies (with Alison Leslie Gold)

Germany
Anne Frank: The Diary of a Young Girl
adapted from the diary of Anne Frank

Ireland
The Trout
an adapted story by Sean O'Faolain

Some experiences are part of growing up for almost anyone. For example, we all learn from our families. We all learn to put aside most of our fears. We all do many things for the first time. The characters in these selections all experience the joys and pains of growing up. You might recognize something about your own "growing up" as you read.

Manners

a poem by Elizabeth Bishop

Words to Know

LITERARY TERMS

speaker the character who tells what happens in a poem

rhyme the repetition of sounds in the words of a poem; words that sound alike

stanza a group of lines in poetry

SELECTION VOCABULARY

overtook caught up with and passed, as in a race

mare a female horse

Sometimes the things we learn from older relatives stay with us forever. The speaker in this poem learns, from a caring grandfather, how to treat others.

The speaker in this poem uses *my*, *me*, and *I*.

My grandfather said to me
as we sat on the wagon seat,
'Be sure to remember to always
speak to everyone you meet.'

We met a stranger on foot.
My grandfather's whip tapped his hat.
'Good day, sir. Good day. A fine day.'
And I said it and bowed where I sat.

▲ This painting by Helen Bradley is called *Bonnie Warfe Brings Us Home.*

There is a rhyme pattern in every stanza. *Seat* and *meet* rhyme in the first stanza. What other patterns can you find?

Then we **overtook** a boy we knew
with his big pet crow on his shoulder.
'Always offer everyone a ride;
don't forget that when you get older,'

my grandfather said. So Willy
climbed up with us, but the crow
gave a 'Caw!' and flew off.   I was worried.
How would he know where to go?

But he flew a little way at a time
from fence post to fence post, ahead;
and when Willy whistled he answered.
'A fine bird,' my grandfather said,

'and he's well brought up. See, he answers
nicely when he's spoken to.
Man or beast, that's good manners.
Be sure that you both always do.'

When automobiles went by,
the dust hid the people's faces,
but we shouted "Good day! Good day!
Fine day!' at the top of our voices.

When we came to Hustler Hill,
he said that the **mare** was tired,
so we all got down and walked,
as our good manners required.

Literature Practice

Answer these questions on a separate sheet of paper.

1. What are the grandfather and grandchild doing in the poem?
2. Why does the grandfather think that the crow is a "fine bird"?
3. What three pieces of advice does the grandfather give?
4. How does the grandfather show his good manners?
5. What do you think the grandchild can learn from the grandfather's advice?

Mind Your Manners

Adults play an important role in teaching us what we need to know. Most likely, a parent or a grandparent may have taught you about manners.

Manners are important because they help us to get along with one another. However, manners are always changing. What was proper one hundred years ago may not be proper today. Here are a few rules of modern manners. As you read the list, think about how many you actually use.

- The flavor of a birthday cake should please the guest of honor.

- Keep your elbows off the table when eating.

- When sending a thank-you note for a gift of money, do not mention the amount.

- Forks go to the left of a plate when setting a table.

- Always apologize when you dial a wrong number.

- Always hold the door for someone if he or she is coming behind you.

Anne Frank Remembered: The Story of the Woman Who Helped to Hide the Frank Family

adapted from the autobiography of Miep Gies
(with Alison Leslie Gold)

Words to Know

LITERARY TERM

nonfiction a story that is about real places, people, and events

SELECTION VOCABULARY

brigade a group of people organized for a specific purpose

lodger a person who rents a room

reassure to make a person feel confident

The word "family" sometimes refers to people who are not related. Friends who make special efforts to help each other might be as close as family members. The woman who wrote this biography was like a family member to the people she helped.

———◦◦◦———

Hitler's army killed six million European Jews as well as five million other people.

During World War II, the leader of Germany, Adolf Hitler, wanted to remove all Jews from Europe. Thousands of Jews left Europe. Many others went into hiding. Jews who were in hiding often had helpers. These non-Jewish people provided food and other necessary items for the people in hiding.

Miep Gies worked for Anne Frank's father, Otto. Later, Miep and her husband, Henk, helped hide the Frank family, Mr. and Mrs. Van Daan and their son Peter, and a dentist named Dussel. For more than two years, Miep scraped together enough food to feed all eight people in hiding. Following is Miep's account of the day Anne Frank, her sister Margot, and her parents went into hiding.

Anne Frank Remembered

It was the first Sunday in July. The night was warm. Henk and I had eaten our dinner. Suddenly, the doorbell rang.

A ringing doorbell could mean trouble. We became very nervous. Our eyes darted to one another. Quickly, Henk went to the door. I followed him. There stood Herman Van Daan. He was very upset.

Van Daan said, "Please come right away. Margot Frank just got a postcard. She is being ordered to report for a forced labor **brigade**. The Franks cannot let this happen. They have decided to go into hiding right away. Can you come right now? Can you take a few things they'll need?"

Henk said, "We will come."

We put on our raincoats. We could not be seen carrying bags and packages. It would be too dangerous. We could hide many things under our baggy old raincoats. It might seem odd to be wearing raincoats on a dry night in summer, but it was better than carrying bags.

Henk and I left with Mr. Van Daan. When Mr. Frank had told me the plan for his family to go into hiding, I told Henk about it. Henk and I did not need to talk it over. He said right away he would help the Frank family as much as he could. But Henk and I didn't know the Franks would go into hiding this soon.

Herman Van Daan works for Mr. Frank. The Van Daan family later joins the Franks in hiding.

Van Daan said, "The Franks are having a hard time. There is so much to do, and so little time. Also, their **lodger** keeps hanging around, so it is very difficult to get anything done."

As we walked to the Frank's apartment, I worried for them. I thought of the postcard Margot had received. Now the Germans were sending sixteen-year-old girls into forced labor. This was a new horror for the Jews. How many young girls like Margot had gotten such a postcard? What if they had no father like Mr. Frank? What if they had no place to hide? Those girls must be horribly afraid tonight. I had to force myself not to run to the Frank's apartment.

When we got to the Frank's apartment, we spoke little. There was a feeling of near-panic in the air. I could see that they had much to do, and many things to prepare. It was all too terrible. Mrs. Frank handed us piles of things. They felt like children's clothes and shoes. I was so nervous and scared I didn't look at what she was giving me.

I hid the bunches of things under my coat, in my pockets, under Henk's coat, in his pockets. The plan was I would take these things to the hiding place some time after the Franks had moved in.

Our coats were bursting. Henk and I went back to our place. We quickly unloaded what we had under our coats. We put it all under our bed. When our coats were empty again, we hurried back to the Frank's apartment for another load.

We had to keep everything secret from the Frank's lodger. Everyone tried to seem normal. We did not run. We did not raise our voices. The Franks handed us more things. Mrs. Frank put things in bundles. She sorted through things quickly. She gave them to us and again we took and took. Her hair was falling from her tight bun into her eyes. Anne came in. She brought too many things. Mrs. Frank told her to take them back. Anne's eyes were like saucers. They were a mixture of excitement and terrible fear.

Henk and I took as much as we could and quickly left.

The next day was Monday. I woke to the sound of rain. We had planned what to do the night before. I rode my bicycle to the Frank's apartment. Margot's bike was standing outside. She had been ordered to hand it in, but she had not done so.

Margot came out the apartment door. Mr. and Mrs. Frank were inside. Anne hung back inside the doorway. Her eyes were wide.

I could tell that Margot was wearing layers of clothing. Mr. and Mrs. Frank looked at me. Their eyes pierced mine.

I tried to **reassure** them. I said, "Don't worry. The rain is very heavy. Even the Green Police won't want to go out in it." Mr. Frank looked up and down the street. He said to Margot and me, "Go. Anne and Edith and I will come later in the morning. Go now."

Margot and I pushed our bicycles onto the street. Quickly, we pedaled away, but not too fast. We wanted to look like two everyday working girls on their way to work on a Monday morning.

Not one Green Policeman was out in the rain. I took the big crowded streets. All the way, Margot and I did not speak. We knew that from the moment we had gotten on our bicycles, we had become criminals. There we were, a Christian and a Jew. She was a Jew without a yellow star, riding an illegal bicycle. This Jew was ordered to report for a forced-labor brigade. She had been about to leave for some unknown place in Hitler's Germany. Margot's face showed no fear. She showed nothing of what she was feeling inside. Suddenly, Margot and I were two allies against the strength of the German beast.

We arrived at the office building and carried our bicycles into the storeroom. All at once I could see that Margot was about to crumble.

The Germans ordered all Jews to turn in their bicycles in June of 1942.

The German soldiers were called "Green Police" because of their green uniforms.

All Jews were required to wear yellow stars sewn onto their clothing. This German order helped separate the Jews.

I took Margot's arm and led her past Mr. Frank's office. Then we went up the stairway to the hiding place. By now it was time for the office to open. I was afraid that people would be coming to work, but I kept silent.

Margot was like someone stunned, in shock. I held her arm to give her courage. Still, we said nothing. She disappeared behind the door to the hiding place. I went to the front office and sat down at my desk.

My heart was thumping. I wondered how I could get my mind onto my work.

Later that morning, the moment I had been waiting for finally came. I heard Mr. and Mrs. Frank and Anne coming through the office door. I quickly joined them. I hurried them through the office and up the stairway to the door of the hiding place.

In the afternoon, when no one was around, I went to the hiding place myself. I closed the door tight behind me. I had never been there before. Sacks and boxes and things were piled everywhere.

The author describes the hiding place. Try to imagine living in this place with seven other people for two years and not being allowed to go outside.

On the first floor were two very small rooms and a toilet. One room was shaped like a rectangle with a window. The other room was long and thin. It also had a window. The wallpaper was old, yellow, and peeling. Upstairs there was a large room with a sink and stove and cabinets. In this room the windows were covered with curtains. Then there was another stairway. This led to an attic and storage area.

Mrs. Frank and Margot were like lost people. The blood seemed drained from them. Anne and her father were trying to do something with all the boxes and sacks. They were pushing, carrying, clearing. I asked Mrs. Frank, "What can I do?"

Mrs. Frank shook her head.

I said, "Let me bring you some food?"

She gave in to me. "A few things only, Miep. Maybe some bread, a little butter. Maybe milk?"

The situation upset me. I wanted to leave the family

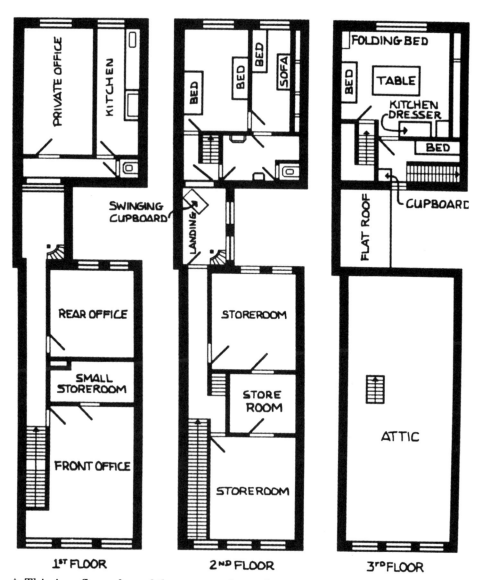

PRIVATE OFFICE

KITCHEN

SWINGING CUPBOARD

LANDING

REAR OFFICE

SMALL STOREROOM

FRONT OFFICE

1ST FLOOR

BED

BED

BED

SOFA

STOREROOM

STORE ROOM

STOREROOM

2ND FLOOR

FOLDING BED

BED

TABLE

KITCHEN DRESSER

BED

CUPBOARD

FLAT ROOF

ATTIC

3RD FLOOR

▲ This is a floor plan of the rooms where the Frank family lived for two years.

alone together. I couldn't begin to imagine what they must be feeling. They had walked away from everything they owned in the world. They left behind their home, a lifetime of possessions they had gathered, Anne's little cat, Moortje, keepsakes from the past, and friends.

They had simply closed the door of their lives. They had disappeared from Amsterdam. Mrs. Frank's face said it all. Quickly, I left them.

Literature Practice

Answer these questions on a separate sheet of paper.

1. What is Miep Gies's relationship to the Frank family?

2. What causes the Frank family to go into hiding on this day?

3. Why is Miep surprised when she first goes up to the hiding place?

4. How is Miep Gies like a member of the Frank family?

Anne Frank: The Diary of a Young Girl

adapted from the diary of Anne Frank

Words to Know

LITERARY TERM

tone the feeling the author shows toward the subject of the story

SELECTION VOCABULARY

mischief action that bothers or
annoys others

failings faults or weaknesses

reserves extra supplies

forbid to order not to do something

Children grow up, even under difficult conditions. These entries from a young girl's diary show that even during war, teenagers are teenagers. This young girl worries about her family relationships and about how other people think of her. In her diary entries, we see that she learns about herself and other people in spite of the war.

On June 12, 1942, Anne Frank celebrated her 13th birthday. She received a diary from her father. She thought of the diary as a friend and named the diary "Kitty." A little less than a month later, Anne's family went into hiding. Anne told all her feelings, fears, and thoughts to her diary.

On August 4, 1944, the Green Police arrested Anne Frank and the other seven people in hiding. Someone had given their hiding place away to the Germans. Sometime in March of 1945, Anne and her sister died at Bergen-Belsen, one of Hitler's work camps in Germany. Otto Frank was the only one of the eight who survived. Miep Gies had collected Anne's writings from the hiding place after the arrest. She gave the diaries and papers to Mr. Frank on the day they learned that Anne was not coming back.

Monday, 21 September, 1942

Dear Kitty,

I can't stand Mrs. Van Daan. I get nothing but blow-ups from her. She thinks I talk too much. Now she's making up excuses to get out of washing the pans when it's her turn.

I'm busy with Daddy working out his family tree. As we go along, he tells me a little about everyone. It's most interesting. Mr. Koophuis brings a few special books for me every other week.

School time has begun again. My favorite subject is history. We brought a lot of school books and supplies with us. I'm working hard at my French. Peter sighs and groans over his English.

The adults were talking about me. They decided that I wasn't completely stupid after all. Of course, that made me work extra hard the next day.

I was just writing something about Mrs. Van Daan when in she came. Slap! I closed the book. She wanted to take a peek anyway, but I wouldn't let her. It gave me quite a shock!

Sunday, 27 September, 1942

Dear Kitty,

Just had another big blow-up with Mother. We just don't get along these days. It's not going too well between Margot and me, either. We usually don't yell much in our family, but lately Margot and Mother are getting on my nerves.

Anne expresses her feelings about Mrs. Van Daan, her father, and her studies. These feelings make up the tone of Anne's writing.

The Franks have been in hiding for about three months. Think of reasons why they might be getting on each others' nerves.

The Van Daans love to talk about other people's children. Margot doesn't mind; she is such a goody-goody. I, however, seem to have enough **mischief** in me for two. The Van Daans think I'm spoiled. They are always quick to let Mother and Daddy know it. My parents always defend me. But they do tell me I shouldn't talk so much or poke my nose into everything. If Daddy weren't so sweet, I'd be afraid I was a disappointment to them.

Monday, 28, September, 1942

Dear Kitty,

Why do grown-ups quarrel so much, and over the stupidest things? I used to think it was only children who had quarrels. Of course grown-ups call them "discussions." I suppose I should get used to it. But I can't, not as long as nearly every discussion is about me! Nothing about me is right. They talk about the way I look, my character, my manners. I'm just supposed to take it and keep quiet. But I can't! I'll show them! Maybe they'll keep their mouths shut when I start educating them. I am amazed at their awful manners and especially by Mrs. Van Daan's stupidity.

Kitty, if only you knew how angry they make me! I shall just explode one day!

Tuesday, 7 November, 1942

Dear Kitty,

Mother is in a bad mood. That always means problems for me. Is it just chance that she and Daddy never scold Margot and always dump on me for everything? Just last evening I picked up a book Margot had been reading. When Margot came back into the room, she had this look. She asked for "her" book back. Just because I wanted to look at it a little while longer, she got angry. Then Mother jumped in. "Give the book to Margot; she was reading it," she said. Then Daddy came in. He didn't even know what it was about, but he took Margot's side. I put the book down and left the room. They thought I was angry, but it was only that my feelings were hurt.

I knew Mother would stick up for Margot. She always takes her side. I'm so used to it that I don't care any more. I love them, but only because they are my mother and sister.

With Daddy, it's different. He's the one I look up to. He doesn't notice that he treats Margot differently from me. I have always been second-best. I have always had to pay double for anything I did wrong. First, I am scolded and then my feelings get hurt. I won't take it any more. I want something from Daddy that he is not able to give me.

I'm not jealous of Margot. It's only that I long for Daddy's real love. I don't want him to love me just as his child, but as Anne, myself.

Only through Daddy can I feel the least bit of family feeling. He doesn't like it when I talk about Mother's failings. He doesn't want to hear about it. Just the same, I find her **failings** harder to take than anything else. I don't like always having to call attention to how mean and sloppy she is. But I just can't keep it all to myself. I wish I could only see Mother's good side. But it doesn't work. Neither she nor Daddy understands this empty space in my life. I wonder if parents can ever make their children happy.

Sometimes I think that God wants to test me. I must become good on my own, with no one to be an example for me. Then later on it will make me stronger. From whom but myself will I get comfort? I need comforting. My faults are too great. I know this, and every day I try to make myself better.

The way they treat me changes so much. One day they think I'm grown up. The next day I hear that Anne

Anne feels that her parents are unfair.

Anne is upset with herself because she is not able to see the good side of her mother.

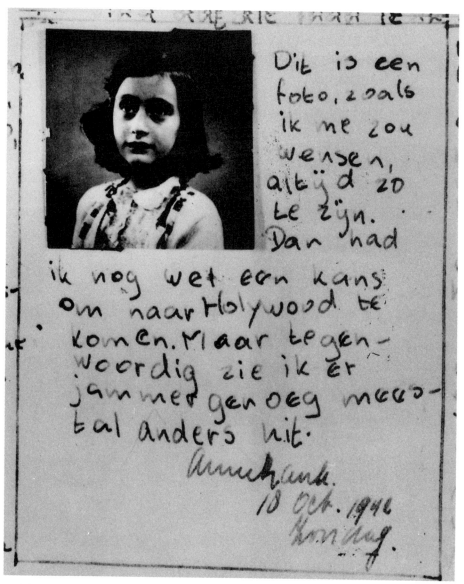

▲ This is a picture of Anne Frank from a page of her diary.

is just a silly little goat. She doesn't know anything. I'm not a baby any more. I'm not to be laughed at. I have my own plans and ideas, even though I can't put them into words yet. I'm tired of having no one who understands me. That is why in the end I always come back to my diary, because Kitty is always patient. I'll promise her that I'll be strong. I'll find my own way through it all, without crying. I only wish I could sometimes hear a kind word from someone who loves me.

When Anne speaks of her "friend" Kitty, the tone is warm and comforting.

Tuesday, 15 June, 1943

Dear Kitty,

June 12th, 1943, was Anne's 14th birthday.

Daddy wrote me a sweet poem for my birthday. I got some lovely things. One was a fat book on my favorite subject—the myths of Greece and Rome. There were also a lot of sweets. Everyone broke into their last **reserves**. As the youngest of our family in hiding, I am more honored than I deserve.

We must hand in our radio next month. Koophuis has a small, secret one at home that he will let us use. It is a shame to have to hand in our big one, but one can't take any chances of getting caught. The radio has been our source of courage. It helps us say, "Chin up. Better times will come."

Sunday, 11 July, 1943

Dear Kitty,

We are back on the "upbringing" theme again. I really am trying to be helpful and polite. It is very hard to be on such good behavior with people you can't stand. But I really do see that I get along better by pretending a little.

Margot and I have been studying shorthand. Now I have to let it go a bit. I need more time for my other

▲ Anne Frank signed the autograph book of her childhood friend, Henny.

subjects, and I am also having trouble with my eyes. I have needed glasses for a long time. (Yuck, I would look like an owl!) Yesterday Mother talked about sending me to the eye doctor with Mrs. Koophuis. Imagine it! Going outside on the street! But I don't think it will happen. Now that the British have landed in Sicily, Daddy is hoping for a "quick finish."

Elli gives Margot and me a lot of office work. It makes us both feel very useful, and it is a big help to her. We take special care to do a good job.

Miep is just like a pack mule. Almost every day she finds some vegetables for us. She brings them on her bicycle. We long for Saturdays, when our books come. It's just like getting a present. People outside don't know what books mean to us. Reading, learning, and the radio are our fun.

Elli works in the office downstairs. She leaves work for the girls to do at night. Going downstairs at night is the only "freedom" the girls have.

Dear Kitty,

Daddy is not happy with me. He thought that after our talk on Sunday I wouldn't go upstairs every evening. He is making it very hard for me. I will talk to him today. This is roughly what I want to say:

"I believe, Daddy, that you are not happy with me. I suppose you want me to be just as a 14-year-old should be. But that's where you're wrong.

"Since we came here, I have not had an easy time. If you knew how unhappy I felt, how lonely, you would understand that I want to be with Peter!

"I am now able to live on my own, without Mother's help or yours. You can laugh at me and not believe me, but that can't hurt me. I am only telling you this because I thought that otherwise you might think I was being sneaky. I don't have to explain what I do to anyone but myself.

"When I had problems, none of you helped me. You only scolded me about being so loud and foolish. I acted that way only so that I wouldn't be hurting all the time. Now the battle is over. I have won! I am free. I don't need a mother any more. This battle has made me strong.

"And now I will go my own way. You must not see me as 14, for all these troubles have made me older. I will not be sorry for what I do. I will act as I think I must. Either **forbid** me to go upstairs, or trust me. Then leave me in peace!"

Sunday, 7 May, 1944

Dear Kitty,

Daddy and I had a long talk yesterday. I cried a lot, and he joined in. On Friday I wrote what I explained to you in a letter. I put it in his pocket before supper. Margot told me that he was very upset for the rest of the evening. (I was upstairs doing the dishes.)

Anne and Peter Van Daan have become good friends. Anne seems to think she is the only one who has "not had an easy time" since they went into hiding.

Anne's tone in the later entries is different. She is learning how to handle problems.

Yesterday he told me that I had done him a great wrong. "You, Anne, who have received such love from your parents, can you say we have not helped you? We have always been ready to help you. We have always defended you. How can you talk of feeling no responsibility to us? Maybe you didn't mean it that way, but that is what you wrote."

Oh, this is the worst thing I have ever done! I was only showing off. I was just trying to appear big so that he would respect me. Certainly I have had problems. But to accuse Daddy, who has done so much for me—no, that was too low for words.

It's right that my pride has been shaken. I was becoming much too taken up with myself again. The way Daddy has forgiven me makes me feel ashamed of myself. No, Anne, you still have much to learn.

I want to start over with him. That can't be hard, now that I have Peter. With him to help me, I can and will!

Anne felt that she needed to act grown up to win her father's love and respect. She learns an important lesson.

Literature Practice

Answer these questions on a separate sheet of paper.

1. What complaints does Anne have about Mrs. Van Daan?

2. What is the tone of Anne's writing when she writes about her father?

3. Anne's father is hurt by a note she writes. How does Anne respond to this?

4. What signs are there in these entries that Anne grows up?

The Diary: Life and Times

A diary is a daily account of personal experience. In it, people write about what they do and see. They write about reactions to things. They keep this record for many reasons. The diary may help them think about their life. It may help them keep track of changes.

Very few people think their diary will be published. This makes the diary much more personal than an autobiography. People who write their autobiography pick and choose what they want others to know about them. But diary writers often reveal their true thoughts, feelings, and opinions. This gives readers a special kind of understanding. They see an honest record of the events and customs of a time period.

Anne Frank wrote her diary for herself. "Kitty" was a place to record her thoughts and feelings about growing up. She never thought about other people reading it. She never thought of publishing it as a book. But Anne Frank's diary became a best-seller. People liked reading the words of a lively teenager. They were curious about Jewish people having to hide from the Nazis. *Anne Frank: The Diary of a Young Girl* has remained popular. Even today, readers are moved by Anne's hopes for a peaceful world. Even today, people read the diary as a historical description of World War II.

The Trout

an adapted story by Sean O'Faolain

Words to Know

LITERARY TERMS

dialogue the words spoken between two or more characters in a story

symbol a thing that stands for something else

SELECTION VOCABULARY

sneer an expression that shows dislike

panting breathing rapidly in short gasps

reel a spool attached to a fishing rod on which the fishing line is wound

scuttling running in a hurry

slimy slippery, wet, and smooth

lashed moved or waved suddenly and violently

ooze soft mud at the edge of a body of water

superior as if of greater importance or value

There are certain moments in growing up that are filled with meaning. They become the memories of childhood that we keep as we grow old. In this story, a young girl sees something she's never seen before. It bothers her. Finally, she decides to do something about it.

————— ⁂ —————

One of the first places Julia went was The Dark Walk. It is a very old, tree-lined walk. It rose like a large, dark tunnel with smooth, strong branches. Underfoot the tough brown leaves never crackle.

The author describes The Dark Walk. The words used can help you see how the setting looks.

Julia raced right into it. For the first few yards, she could still remember the sun behind her. Then she felt the end of the day fading around her. It made her scream with pleasure. She would race to the light at the far end of the walk. The end was always just a little too long in coming. So, she always came out gasping, laughing, clasping her hands, and drinking in the sun. When she was warmed by the light, she would turn around. For a moment she would think about doing it again.

This year she had the added joy of showing her game to her small brother. She could terrify him as well as herself. For him the fear lasted longer because his legs were so short. She had gone out the far end while he was still screaming and racing.

When they had done this many times, they came back to the house. There they could tell everybody about their game. They began to argue.

"Cry baby!" Julia said to her brother.

"You were afraid yourself, so there!" he shot back.

"I won't take you anymore," she threatened.

"You're a big pig," her brother said.

"I hate you," she shouted back.

Tears were threatening to fall. Then someone said, "Did you see the well?"

Julia held up her long lovely neck. Julia was suspicious. How could there be a well in The Dark Walk? She knew the Walk. She had visited it year after year. With a **sneer** she said, "Nonsense."

But she went back to The Dark Walk. She acted as if she were going somewhere else. Once there she found a hole scooped in the rock at the side of the walk. It was choked with damp leaves. It took her a while to uncover the hole. At the back of this small hole there was about a quart of water. In the water she suddenly saw a trout breathing heavily. She rushed for Stephen and dragged him to see it. They were both so excited that they were no longer afraid of the darkness

Notice the dialogue here between Julia and her brother. What does the dialogue tell you about their relationship?

▲ This painting by Thomas Bewick is called *Golden Carp*. Both carp and trout live in the waters of North America.

as they hunched over the hole. There they saw the fish **panting** in his tiny prison. His silver stomach went up and down like an engine.

Nobody knew how the trout got there. Even old Martin in the kitchen garden laughed. He would not believe that it was there. At least he pretended not to believe, until she made him come down and see. Kneeling and pushing back his ragged cap, he looked in.

"You're right. How did that fella get there?" Martin asked.

Julia stared at him. There was doubt in her eyes. "You knew?" she asked.

But Martin said, "No, I didn't know." He reached down to lift it out. Julia stopped him. If she had found it, then it was her trout.

Her mother suggested that a bird had carried the egg. Her father thought a small stream might have carried it down there as a baby. It may have happened in the winter when it was safe. But in the summer the water began to dry up. She said, "I see."

Julia feels the trout belongs to her. Start thinking about the reasons why Julia feels and acts this way.

Julia's parents try to explain why the trout is in the tiny hole.

She went back to look again and think about it alone. Her brother stayed behind. He wanted to hear the whole story of the trout. He was not really interested in the story his mummy began to make up for him. She began her story with, "So one day Daddy Trout and Mummy Trout . . . ." When he retold the story to his sister, she said, "Pooh."

It troubled her that the trout was always in the same place. He had no room to turn. All the time the silver belly went up and down. Otherwise he never moved. She wondered what he ate. Between visits to Joey Pony and the boat and a cool bath, she thought of his hunger. She brought him down bits of dough. Once she brought a worm. The trout never gave the least thought to the food. He just went on panting. Hunched over him she thought how all the winter, he had been in there. All day, all night, he floated around alone in The Dark Walk. She was still thinking of it as she lay in bed.

How does Julia feel about the fish?

It was late June, the longest days of the year. The sun had sat still for a week, burning up the world. Although it was after ten o'clock, it was still bright and still hot. She lay on her back under a single sheet, trying to keep cool. She could see the half moon through the trees. Before they went to bed her mummy had told Stephen the story of the trout again. She, in her bed, however, had purposely turned her back to them and read a book. But she had kept one ear turned to the story.

"So, in the end, this naughty fish who would not stay at home got bigger and bigger and bigger. The water got smaller and smaller. . . ."

With great passion, she cried, "Mummy, don't make it a horrible old story that teaches us some lesson!"

Her mummy had brought in a fairy godmother then. The fairy godmother sent lots of rain and filled the hole. A stream poured out of the hole. The trout floated down to the river. Staring at the moon, she

▲ In *The Water Girl* by William A. Bouguereau,
a girl carries a water jar.

knew that there are no such things as godmothers. She also knew that down in The Dark Walk the trout was panting like an engine. She heard somebody unwind a fishing **reel.** Would the beasts fish him out?

She sat up. Stephen was a hot lump of sleep, lazy thing. She leaped up and looked out the window. Somehow she did not feel as lively now that she saw the dim mountains and the black trees. The land seemed to breathe as she heard a dog bark. Quietly she lifted the pitcher of water and climbed out the window. **Scuttling** along the cool gravel, she reached the open mouth of the tunnel. Her night clothes were very short so that when she splashed water, it wet her ankles. She gazed into the tunnel. Something alive rustled inside there. She raced in. She cried aloud, "Oh, gosh, I can't find it." Then at last she did. Kneeling down in the damp she put her hand into the **slimy** hole. When the body **lashed** out, they were both mad with fright. But she gripped him. She shoved him into the pitcher. With her teeth ground, she raced out of the tunnel and down the steep paths to the river's edge.

All the time she could feel him lashing his tail against the side of the pitcher. She was afraid he would jump right out. The gravel cut her feet until she came to the cool **ooze** of the river bank. She poured the water out. She watched the fish until he plopped. For a second he could be seen in the water. She hoped he was not dizzy. Then all she saw was the glimmer of the moon in the silent-flowing river.

She scuttled up the hill, climbed through the window, plonked down the pitcher, and flew through the air like a bird into bed. The dog barked. She hugged herself and giggled. Like a river of joy, her holiday spread before her.

In the morning Stephen rushed to her, shouting that "he" was gone. He wanted to know "where" and "how." Lifting her nose in the air, she said in a

Imagine how frightened Julia feels, thinking that her fish might be caught!

superior voice, "Fairy godmother, I suppose?" She strolled away patting the palms of her hands.

Literature Practice

Answer these questions on a separate sheet of paper.

1. What changes Julia's fear of The Dark Walk?

2. Why doesn't Julia like her mother's story about the trout?

3. How does Julia grow up in this story?

4. What reason can you give for Julia letting the trout go?

Chapter Review

Summaries

- **Manners**—The speaker recalls a wagon trip with a grandfather. The grandfather offers advice about what he considers good manners. In the end of this poem, they even use good manners with the tired horse!

- **Anne Frank Remembered**—A woman helps a Jewish family named Frank during World War II. The young woman tells how she helps on the day the family must go into hiding.

- **Anne Frank: The Diary of a Young Girl**—A 13-year-old girl shares her thoughts and feelings with her diary. Her Jewish family is in hiding. Young Anne writes about how she feels about herself and how other people feel about her.

- **The Trout**—Julia often visits a dark, tree-lined walk and likes to scare her little brother while they run through it together. They discover a trout trapped in a small well. Julia claims the fish as her own and decides what shall become of it. In the process, she saves the life of the trout.

Chapter Quiz

Choose the letter of the correct answer. Rewrite the sentences on a separate sheet of paper.

1. One piece of advice the grandfather gives in "Manners" is
   a. "Give money to the poor."   c. "Speak to everyone you meet."
   b. "Don't trust crows."   d. "Don't give rides to strangers."

2. In *Anne Frank Remembered,* Miep Gies helps the Frank family
   a. find jobs.   c. obey the German laws.
   b. go into hiding.   d. pretend not to be Jewish.

3. In her diary, Anne Frank says the happiest times are
   a. when the Van Daans are not arguing.
   c. when Elli leaves.
   b. when their friends bring books and food.
   d. when Peter tells stories.

4. In "The Trout," the fish
   a. swims back and forth and breathes heavily.
   c. jumps out of the well.
   b. swims happily in the well.
   d. plays with other trout.

5. In the end, the trout
   a. dies in the well.
   b. is caught by Martin.
   c. becomes Julia's pet.
   d. swims away into the river.

Thinking and Writing

Write answers to the following questions on a separate sheet of paper.

1. Julia in "The Trout" and Miep Gies in *Anne Frank Remembered* must deal with fear. How do they face their fears? Use examples from the selections to support your answer.

2. Sometimes part of what we learn as we grow up comes from our grandparents. What is the relationship between grandparent and grandchild in "Manners"? Use examples from the poem to support your answer.

3. *Anne Frank Remembered* and *Anne Frank: The Diary of a Young Girl* are both nonfiction. Miep Gies and Anne Frank both write about real people and real feelings. What do you learn about the woman and the girl from the memoir and the diary? Use examples from the selections to support your answer.

▲ Three generations are visible in this Chinese carving.

Chapter Learning Objectives

- Identify the theme of a story.
- Recognize autobiography.
- Understand the use of a flashback in a story.
- Learn about repetition in poetry.
- Identify imagery in poetry.
- Recognize the use of free verse in a poem.
- Identify simile.

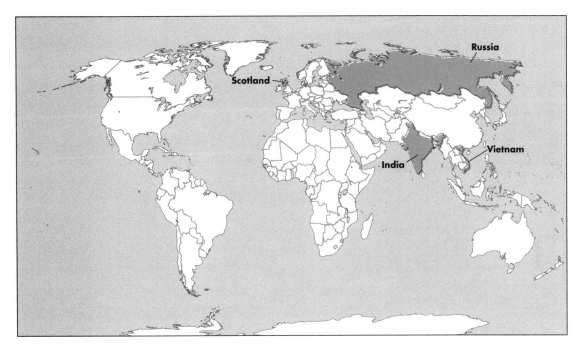

Russia
The Old Grandfather and His Little Grandson
an adapted folktale by Leo Tolstoy

Vietnam
When Heaven and Earth Changed Places
adapted from the autobiography of Le Ly Hayslip

Scotland
Aunt Julia
a poem by Norman MacCaig

India
Grandfather's Photograph
a poem by Mangalesh Dabral

Families are made up of people of many ages who play various roles. As we get older, the roles change. Children become parents. Parents become grandparents. In the process, many things are passed from generation to generation. The stories and poems in this chapter are about the special things that live on from generation to generation.

The Old Grandfather and His Little Grandson

an adapted folktale by Leo Tolstoy

Words to Know

LITERARY TERM

theme the main idea of a novel, story, poem, or play

SELECTION VOCABULARY

scolded told someone angrily what he or she did wrong

ashamed feeling guilty or sorry for something done wrong

Usually, parents teach their children. In this short tale, however, it's the child who teaches his parents a valuable lesson.

The grandfather is old, but he still deserves respect.

The grandfather had become very old. His legs would not carry him. His eyes could not see and his ears could not hear. He had no teeth. Sometimes when he ate, bits of food dropped out of his mouth. His son and his son's wife no longer let him eat with them at the table. He had to eat his meals in the corner near the stove.

One day they gave the grandfather his food in a bowl. He tried to move the bowl closer. It fell to the floor and broke. His daughter-in-law **scolded** him. She told him that he spoiled everything in the house and broke their dishes. She said that from now on, he would get his food in a wooden dish. The old man sighed and said nothing.

A few days later, the old man's son and his wife were in their hut, resting. They watched their little boy

▲ This painting is called *Portrait of The Old Guy* by Thomas
Hart Benton.

playing on the floor. He was making something out of small pieces of wood. His father said, "What are you making, Misha?"

The little grandson said, "I'm making a wooden bucket. When you and Mamma get old, I'll feed you out of this wooden dish."

The young man and his wife looked at each other. Tears filled their eyes. They were **ashamed** they had treated the old grandfather so badly. From that day on, they let the old man eat at the table with them, and they took better care of him.

The theme of this folktale is the lesson the little boy teaches his parents.

Gramercy Park by Norman Rockwell shows a grandfather and grandson spending time together. ▶

Literature Practice

Answer these questions on a separate sheet of paper.

1. Why do the son and his wife make the grandfather eat in the corner?

2. What happens when the grandfather's bowl falls and breaks?

3. What does the little boy learn from his parents?

4. What do the parents learn from their son?

Tracing Your Family History

There are three generations living together in the folktale "The Old Grandfather and His Little Grandson." If any family member wanted to know more about the family background, he or she might research the history of the family. Researching your family history is called genealogy. Genealogy tells you about your family history and gives you a closer look at who you are.

A genealogist can help you find out about your family history. A genealogist begins with a family tree. This tree shows three generations.

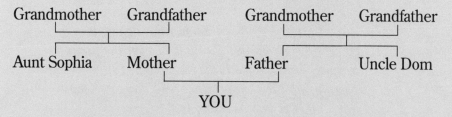

Grandmother   Grandfather   Grandmother   Grandfather

Aunt Sophia   Mother   Father   Uncle Dom

YOU

The genealogist will find out information about each person on the family tree. The information will include each person's date and place of birth, date and place of marriage, and date and place of death. These facts are called vital statistics. Each state in the United States has a Bureau of Vital Statistics that records information for people in that state.

When Heaven and Earth Changed Places

adapted from the autobiography of Le Ly Hayslip

Words to Know

LITERARY TERMS

autobiography a story of a person's life written by the person

flashback a scene or story that takes place before the main events
of the larger story

SELECTION VOCABULARY

solid strong, not thin or skinny

soy a salty brown sauce made
from soybeans

flexible easy to bend

worthy having value or honor

dowry money or belongings that
a woman brings to a marriage

savage wild, cruel, very unkind

shriveled wrinkled, often from
being in water

shrine a place where people pay
respect to a god

---

*Many things are passed down from generation to
generation. From our families, we get the language
we speak and the foods we like to eat. In this story, the
relationship between a father and daughter shows that
much more is passed down to us.*

———— ⊗⊗⊗ ————

The author of this story
has written about her life.

My father had a **solid** build for a Vietnamese man.
This meant he probably had come from a family of
well-fed, noble people. Many people said he had the
body of a natural warrior. He was a year younger and
an inch shorter than my mother. Still, he was just as

good-looking. His face was round and his skin was brown as **soy** from working outdoors all his life. He took life easy and seldom hurried. Seldom, too, did he say no to a request from his children or his neighbors. Although he was relaxed, he was a hard worker. Even on holidays, he was always fixing things or taking care of our house and animals. He would not wait to be asked for help if he saw someone in trouble. Likewise, he also said what he thought. Like most honest men, though, he knew when to keep silent. Because of his honesty and his feelings for others, he understood life deeply. Perhaps that is why he was so calm.

As a parent, my father was less strict than our mother. We sometimes ran to him for help when she was angry. Most of the time it didn't work. He would just rub our heads as we were dragged off to be spanked. The village saying went: "A naughty child learns more from a whipping stick than a sweet stick." We children were never quite sure about that. Still, we agreed the whipping stick was a powerful teacher. When he just had to punish us himself, he didn't waste time. Without a word, he would find a long, **flexible** bamboo stick. Then he would let us have it behind our thighs. It stung, but he could have whipped us harder. I think seeing the pain in his face hurt more than feeling his half-hearted blows. Because of that, we seldom did anything to merit a father's spanking. That was the highest penalty in our family. Violence in any form bothered him. For this reason, I think, he grew old before his time.

Once, when I was the only child at home, my mother went to Da Nang to visit Uncle Nhu. My father had to take care of me. I woke up from my nap in the empty house. I began to cry for my mother. My father came in from the yard and comforted me. Still, I was cranky and kept on crying. Finally, he gave me a rice cookie to shut me up. Needless to say, this was an approach my mother never used.

> Le Ly describes her father. According to Le Ly, what kind of man is her father?

> Da Nang is a city in Vietnam.

▲ This painting is called *Chinese Girl* by Emil Orlik.

The next afternoon I woke up again. Though I was not feeling cranky, I thought a rice cookie would be nice. I cried a fake cry. My father came running in.

"What's this?" he asked with a worried face. "Little Bay Ly doesn't want a cookie?"

I was confused.

"Look under your pillow," he said with a smile.

I twisted around. Then I saw that, while I was sleeping, he had placed a rice cookie under my pillow. We both laughed. He picked me up like a sack of rice and carried me outside. All the while I gobbled the cookie.

In the yard, he plunked me down. He told me stories. After that, he got some scraps of wood and showed me how to make things. We made a doorstop for my mother and a toy duck for me. This was unheard of—a father doing these things with a daughter! My mother would teach me about cooking and cleaning. She would tell stories about brides. My father showed me the mystery of hammers. He explained the ways of our people.

He had much knowledge about the Vietnamese. His knowledge reached back to the Chinese Wars in ancient times. I learned about one of my distant ancestors, a woman named Phung Thi Chinh. She led Vietnamese fighters against the Han. In one battle, she was about to have a baby. She was surrounded by Chinese. Even so, she delivered the baby and tied it to her back. Then she cut her way to safety, waving a sword in each hand. I was amazed at this warrior's bravery. I was proud to be of her family. Even more, I was amazed by my father's pride in her great deeds. He believed that I was **worthy** of her example. "Follow in her footsteps," he said. Only later would I learn what he truly meant.

Never again did I cry after my nap. Phung Thi women were too strong for that. Besides, I was my father's daughter, and we had many things to do together.

"Little Bay Ly" is the nickname Le Ly's father gives her.

Phung Thi Chinh (fung teye chihn)

The father is very proud of Phung Thi Chinh. He wants Le Ly to be strong and brave like Phung Thi Chinh.

On the eve of my mother's return, my father cooked a feast. He made roast duck. When we sat down to eat it, I felt guilty. My feelings showed on my face. He asked why I acted so sad.

"You've killed one of mother's ducks," I said. "One of the fat kind she sells at the market. She says the money buys gold. She saves this for her daughters' weddings. Without gold for a **dowry,** I will never marry."

My father looked properly moved at first. Then he brightened. "Well, Bay Ly," he said, "if you can't get married, you will just have to stay at home with me!"

I clapped my hands at the happy possibility.

My father cut into the rich, juicy bird. He said, "Even so, let's not tell your mother about the duck, okay?"

I giggled and swore to keep the secret.

The next day I took some water out to him in the fields. My mother was due home any time. I used every chance to step outside and watch for her. My father stopped working and drank gratefully. Then he took my hand and led me to the top of a nearby hill. It had a good view. I could see the village and the land beyond it, almost to the ocean. I thought he was going to show me my mother coming back. In fact, he had something else in mind.

He said, "Bay Ly, you see all this here? This is the Vietnam we have been talking about. You know that a country is more than dirt, rivers, and forests, don't you?"

I said, "Yes, I understand." We had learned in school that one's country is as sacred as a father's grave.

"Good. You know, some of these lands are battlefields. Your brothers and cousins are fighting there. They may never come back. Even your sisters have all left home looking for a better life. You are the only one left in my house. If the enemy comes back,

Le Ly's father feels deeply about Vietnam. His statement shows that he feels that his country is part of who he is. For him, a country is a place that people honor, love, and fight for if necessary.

◀ This painting by Fu Baoshi is called *Figures in a Landscape.*

you must be both a daughter and a son. I told you how the Chinese used to rule our land. People in this village had to risk their lives diving in the ocean. They took the risk just to find pearls for the Chinese emperor's gown. They had to risk tigers and snakes in the jungle just to find herbs for his table. For this they got a bowl of rice and another day of life. That is why Phung Thi Chinh fought so hard to rid us of the Chinese. When the French came, it was the same old story. Your mother and I were taken to Da Nang. We had to build a runway for their airplanes.

We worked from sunup to well after dark. If we stopped to rest, a Moroccan would whip us. Our reward was a bowl of rice and another day of life. Freedom is never a gift, Bay Ly. It must be won and won again. Do you understand?"

I said that I did.

"Good." He moved his finger from the brown dikes. Finally he pointed to our house near the village. "This land here belongs to me. Do you know how I got it?"

I thought a moment, trying to remember my mother's stories. Then I said honestly, "I can't remember."

He squeezed me lovingly. "I got it from your mother."

"What? That can't be true!" I said. Everyone in the family knew my mother was poor and my father's family was wealthy. Her parents were dead. She had to work like a slave for her mother-in-law to prove herself worthy. Such women don't have land to give away.

"It's true." My father's smile widened. "When I was a young man, my parents needed someone to look after their lands. They had to be very careful about whom they chose as wives for their three sons. In the village, your mother was known as the hardest worker of all. She raised herself and her brothers without parents. At the same time, I noticed a beautiful woman working in the fields. Then my mother said she was going to talk to the matchmaker about this hard-working village girl she'd heard about. My heart sank. I was attracted to this mysterious, tall woman I had seen in the rice paddies. Imagine my surprise when I learned the girl my mother heard about and the woman I admired were the same.

"Well, we were married, and my mother tested your mother harshly. She had to cook and clean and know everything about children. She had to be able to manage several farms and know when and how to take the extra crops to the market. Of course, she was testing her other daughters-in-law as well. When my

In this flashback, the father remembers meeting Le Ly's mother.

parents died, they divided their many farms among their sons. You know what? They gave your mother and me the biggest share. They knew we would take care of it best. That's why I say the land came from her. Because in fact it did."

I suddenly missed my mother very much. I looked down the road to the south, hoping to see her. My father noticed my sad face.

"Hey." He poked me in the ribs. "Are you getting hungry for lunch?"

"No. I want to learn how to take care of the farm. What happens if the soldiers come back? What did you and Mother do when the soldiers came?" I asked my father.

My father squatted on the dusty hilltop. He wiped the sweat from his face. "The first thing I did was to tell myself that it was my duty to survive. I had to take care of my family and my farm. That is a tricky job in a war. It's as hard as being a soldier. The Moroccans were very **savage.** One day the rumor passed that they were coming to destroy the village. You may remember that night. I sent you and your brothers and sisters away with your mother to Da Nang."

"You didn't go with us!" My voice still held the horror of that night. I thought I had lost my father.

"Right! I stayed near the village—right on this hill. I had to keep an eye on the enemy and on our house. If they really wanted to destroy the village, I would save some of our things. That way, we could start over. Sure enough, that was their plan.

"The real problem was to keep things safe and keep from being captured. Their patrols were everywhere. Sometimes I went so deep in the forest that I feared I would get lost. All I had to do, though, was follow the smoke from the burning huts. Then I could find my way back.

"Once, I was trapped between two patrols. They had camped on both sides of a river. I had to wait in

What do you think the father means when he says that taking care of his farm was as hard as being a soldier?

This painting, *Girl With Cormorants*, is by Lin Fengman. ▶

the water for two days before one of them moved on. When I got out, my skin was **shriveled** like an old melon's. I was so cold I could hardly move. From the waist down, my body was black with leeches. But it was worth all the pain. When your mother came back, we still had some furniture and tools to work the earth. Many people lost everything. Yes, we were very lucky."

My father drew me out to arm's length and looked me squarely in the eye. "Now, Bay Ly, do you understand what your job is?"

I squared my shoulders and put on a soldier's face. "My job is to get even for my family's sufferings. To protect my farm by killing the enemy. I must become a woman warrior like Phung Thi Chinh!"

My father laughed and pulled me close. "No, little peach blossom. Your job is to stay alive. You must keep an eye on things. Your job is to find a husband and have babies and tell the story of what you've seen to your children. Tell it to anyone else who'll listen. Most of all, your job is to live in peace and tend the **shrine** of our ancestors. Do these things well, Bay Ly, and you will be worth more than any soldier who ever took up a sword."

The father tells Le Ly that her job is to have babies and tell stories. Why is this so important to the father?

Literature Practice

Answer these questions on a separate sheet of paper.

1. What qualities does Le Ly Hayslip admire in her father?

2. Why does the father say that he got his land from his wife?

3. Why is Phung Thi Chinh important to the writer?

4. How would you describe Le Ly Hayslip's relationship with her father?

Vietnam: What's for Dinner?

It's not surprising that Le Ly's father gives a rice cookie to his daughter. Vietnam is one of the top five rice-producing countries on Earth. Heavy rains and a hot climate make it perfect for growing rice. It's common for all family members to help plant, weed, fertilize, and harvest this important crop. When rice is harvested, almost nothing is wasted. After the grains of rice are removed, the rest of the plant is used for animal feed, for making grass mats, and for fertilizer.

Although rice is served at nearly every meal, the Vietnamese diet is full of variety. Fish, eggs, frogs, and eels are main sources of protein. Other kinds of meat are not common. It is too expensive for most people to afford. Farmers raise chickens, pigs, and ducks, but these animals are eaten only on special occasions, such as festivals or weddings.

Fruits and vegetables are the most important ingredients in the Vietnamese diet. They grow in small gardens near family homes. Onions, bamboo shoots, sugarcane, soybeans, and yams are plentiful. Banana and coconut trees often grow near houses. These trees are valued not only for their delicious fruits, but also for their shade and privacy.

Aunt Julia

a poem by Norman MacCaig

Words to Know

LITERARY TERM

repetition using a word or phrase more than once

SELECTION VOCABULARY

Gaelic a language once widely spoken in Ireland and Scotland

peat a dirt-like substance that is dug up, dried, and burned as fuel

treadle a pedal pushed by the foot to operate a machine

flouncing moving in big, jerking motions

threepennybits coins used in Great Britain

Some relatives make strong impressions on us as we grow up. Perhaps, as in the case of this speaker, we wish we knew more about them when they were alive.

Aunt Julia spoke **Gaelic**
very loud and very fast.
I could not answer her–
I could not understand her.
She wore men's boots
when she wore any.
–I can see her strong foot,
stained with **peat,**
paddling the **treadle** of the spinning wheel
while her right hand drew yarn

The speaker uses the word *I* to let readers know that he actually knew Aunt Julia.

The first image of Aunt Julia describes how she speaks. The images here describe how she looks. Look for other imagery in the poem.

A young woman is peeling onions in Elizabeth Adela Forbe's painting, *Peeling Onions.* ▶

marvellously out of the air.
Hers was the only house
where I lay at night
in the absolute darkness
of the box bed, listening to
crickets being friendly.

She was buckets
and water **flouncing** into them.
She was winds pouring wetly
round house-ends.
She was brown eggs, black skirts
and a keeper of **threepennybits**
in a teapot.
Aunt Julia spoke Gaelic
very loud and very fast.
By the time I had learned
a little, she lay
silenced in the absolute black
of a sandy grave
at Luskentyre.
But I hear her still, welcoming me
with a seagull's voice
across a hundred yards
of peatscapes and lazybeds
and getting angry, getting angry
with so many questions
unanswered.

The poet repeats the phrase *she was*. This makes you aware of how alive Aunt Julia once was. Her memory is important to the poet.

Luskentyre (LUHS-kihn-teyer)

Literature Practice

Answer these questions on a separate sheet of paper.

1. What three things did Aunt Julia do?

2. What problem did the poet have with Aunt Julia when she was alive?

3. How does the imagery in the poem help you to see Aunt Julia?

4. How does the speaker feel about Aunt Julia now?

Grandfather's Photograph

a poem by Mangalesh Dabral

Words to Know

LITERARY TERMS

free verse poetry that is without regular rhyme or meter

simile a comparison of two things using *like* or *as*

SELECTION VOCABULARY

discolored stained, spoiled in color

composed calm, peaceful

alms money given to help the poor

ordinariness the state of being common

Many of us have photographs of relatives who look just like us. In the next poem, a young man discovers a photograph of his grandfather. The young man sees too much of himself in the photograph.

———

Grandfather wasn't fond of being photographed
or didn't find time perhaps
There's just one picture of him
hanging on an old **discolored** wall
He sits serious and **composed**
like a cloud heavy with water

In this simile, what picture do you get of how the grandfather looks?

▲ *Rack Picture for William Malcolm Bunn* is by
John Frederick Peto.

The poet does not use punctuation. Capital letters show where sentences begin. That is part of free verse poetry.

What kind of man is the grandfather?

All we know of Grandfather is
that he gave **alms** to beggars
tossed restlessly in sleep
and made his bed neatly every morning
I was just a kid then
and never saw his anger or
his **ordinariness**
Pictures never show someone's helpless side
Mother used to tell us that
when we fell asleep surrounded

This is a painting of *Akbar and One of His Sons or Grandsons*. The artist of the painting is unknown. ▶

by strange creatures of the night
Grandfather would stay awake inside the picture

I didn't grow as tall as Grandfather
not as composed or as serious
Still something in me resembles him
An anger like his
an ordinariness
I too walk with my head bent down
and every day see myself
sitting in an empty
picture frame.

In what ways does the speaker think he is like his grandfather?

Literature Practice

Answer these questions on a separate sheet of paper.

1. How did the grandfather feel about having his picture taken?

2. What does the grandson know about his grandfather?

3. What did the speaker's mother say about Grandfather's picture?

4. How does the speaker resemble his Grandfather?

Chapter Review

Summaries

- **The Old Grandfather and His Little Grandson**—Two parents begin to mistreat an old grandfather. When their son suggests that he will someday treat them the same way, they see their mistake.

- **When Heaven and Earth Changed Places**—Le Ly Hayslip lovingly describes memories of her father in Vietnam. She shows how he cared for her in her mother's absence. His stories of their ancestors and the way he protected his family from the horrors of war help Le Ly understand what is important for her to do.

- **Aunt Julia**—The speaker fondly recalls Aunt Julia's mysterious, fascinating, and dramatic ways. Even though she is now dead, her memory and her influence stretch across a generation.

- **Grandfather's Photograph**—A single photograph is all the speaker has of his grandfather. It's enough, however, to make the speaker feel a strong connection.

Chapter Quiz

Choose the letter of the correct answer. Rewrite the sentences on a separate sheet of paper.

1. In "The Old Grandfather and His Little Grandson," the grandson
   a. breaks his grandfather's bowl.
   b. hides the bowl from his parents.
   c. fills the bowl with rice.
   d. copies his grandfather's wooden bowl.

2. When the soldiers came in "When Heaven and Earth Changed Places," Le Ly Hayslip's father
   a. sent his family away and protected his home.
   b. joined the army and died.
   c. killed a duck and offered it to the soldiers.
   d. hid everyone at home.

3. Le Ly Hayslip's father tells her to
   a. become a warrior.
   b. tell stories to her children.
   c. buy a sword.
   d. forget about her past.

4. One memory the speaker has of Aunt Julia is that she
   a. spoke only Gaelic.
   b. wore fancy slippers.
   c. was very wealthy.
   d. had 13 children.

5. One memory the speaker has of his grandfather in "Grandfather's Photograph" is that he
   a. made his bed every morning.
   b always told jokes.
   c. was a good photographer.
   d. was a wonderful musician.

Thinking and Writing

Write answers to the following questions on a separate sheet of paper.

1. What do you think life is like for the grandfather in "The Old Grandfather and His Little Grandson" a month later? Write your version of the next part of the story.

2. Think about the way Aunt Julia and the grandfather in "Grandfather's Photograph" are described. How are they different from one another?

3. Do you think Le Ly in "When Heaven and Earth Changed Places" followed her father's advice? Explain your answer.

4. Why do you think the grandson in "Grandfather's Photograph" sees himself sitting in an empty picture frame?

Unit Five Review

A. The following questions are about some of the selections you read in this unit. Write one- or two-sentence answers on a separate sheet of paper.

1. In "When Heaven and Earth Changed Places," why does the father feel that telling stories to Le Ly is important?

2. Why is the wooden bowl important in "The Old Grandfather and His Little Grandson"?

3. How is Miep Gies like a member of the Frank family?

4. What are some of the rules for living that the grandfather in "Manners" passes on to his grandchild?

B. Choose two of the essay questions below. Answer them on a separate sheet of paper. Write one or two paragraphs for each one.

1. How we see ourselves is shaped by the values passed from one generation to the next. What values are taught in some of the stories and poems in this unit? Include one story and one poem in your answer.

2. As we grow up, our relationship with our parents is very important. What are the relationships between parents and children like in the stories in this unit? Choose two stories to discuss in your answer.

3. Consider the poems and stories you have read in this unit. What image from a story or poem do you remember most? Explain why you think it is so important.

Unit Six

SELF-DISCOVERY

Chapter 11 Relationships

▲ This painting by Inatace Alphonse is called *Landscape with Farmers.* It shows a peaceful community of people living and working together.

Chapter Learning Objectives

• Learn about the use of dialogue in a story.
• Learn how conflict is used in a story.
• Discover how a surprise ending adds to a story.
• Learn to identify clues about character.
• Learn about the climax of a story.
• Learn to identify the speaker in a poem.
• Understand the use of theme in an essay.

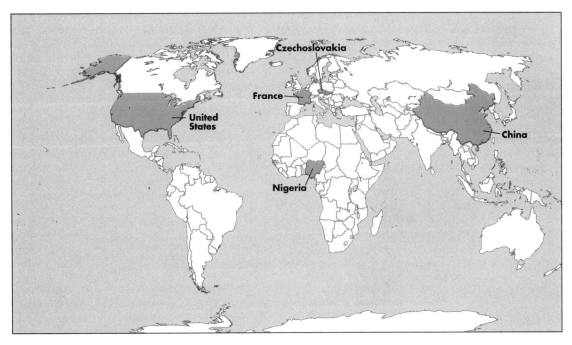

Czechoslovakia
Clever Manka
an adapted folktale retold by Parker Filmore

France
A Piece of String
an adapted story by Guy de Maupassant

Nigeria
Dead Men's Path
an adapted story by Chinua Achebe

China
Bitter Cold, Living in the Village
a poem by Po Chü-i

United States
Young Hunger
an adapted essay by M.F.K. Fisher

Our relationships with our families, friends, and neighbors help us to discover ourselves. Each relationship allows us to see ourselves differently. We have a chance to explore the many sides of who we are and who we might become. In this chapter, you will read about people whose lives are forever changed because of their relationships.

Clever Manka

an adapted folktale retold by Parker Filmore

Words to Know

LITERARY TERMS

dialogue the words spoken between two or more characters in a story

plot the action, or series of events, in a story

SELECTION VOCABULARY

dishonest untruthful

swiftest fastest

cottage a small house in the country

sneering raising one corner of the upper lip in an unpleasant way

meddle to step into another person's business

quarrel an argument

judgment decision

We must respect other people if we wish others to respect us. The mayor in this folktale learns an important lesson about respecting others.

This folktale starts out like a fairy tale. What do you think will happen to the farmer?

There was once a rich farmer who was greedy and **dishonest**. He always cheated his poor neighbors. One neighbor, a simple shepherd, was to receive a cow for work he had done for this farmer. When the payment was due, however, the farmer would not give up the cow. The shepherd took the matter to the mayor. The mayor, a young man with little experience, listened to both sides. After some thought, he said, "I will not decide this case. Instead, I will give you both a riddle.

The man who gives the best answer will have the cow. Do you agree?"

The farmer and the shepherd agreed. Then the mayor said, "Well, then, here is my riddle: What is the **swiftest** thing in the world? What is the sweetest thing? What is the richest? Think about your answers and bring them to me at this time tomorrow."

The farmer went home angry.

"What kind of mayor is this young man!" he growled. "If he had let me keep the cow, I'd have sent him a basket of pears. But now I'm in danger of losing my cow. I can't think of any answer to his foolish riddle."

Explain why you think the farmer is angry.

"What is the matter, husband?" his wife asked.

"It's the new mayor. The old one would have given me the cow without delay. This young man decides the case by asking riddles."

Then he told his wife the riddle. She cheered him quickly by saying she knew the answers at once.

"Why husband," she said, "our gray mare must be the swiftest thing in the world. You know nothing passes us on the road. As for the sweetest, did you ever taste honey sweeter than ours? I'm also sure there is nothing richer than our chest of gold coins. You have been saving them for forty years."

The farmer was thrilled.

"You're right, wife, you're right! That cow stays with us!"

The shepherd arrived home. He was very sad. He had a clever daughter named Manka. She met him at the door of his **cottage** and asked, "What is it, father? What did the mayor say?"

The shepherd sighed.

"I am afraid I've lost the cow. The mayor gave us a riddle, and I know I shall never guess it," the shepherd said.

"Perhaps I can help you," Manka said. "What is it?"

The shepherd told her the riddle. The next day as he left to see the mayor, Manka told him how to answer the riddle.

When he reached the mayor's house, the farmer was already there. He was rubbing his hands. He was extremely happy.

The mayor again stated the riddle. First he asked the farmer for his answers.

The farmer cleared his throat and with a superior look began, "The swiftest thing in the world? Why, my dear sir, that's my gray mare, of course. No other horse ever passes us on the road. The sweetest? Honey from my beehives, to be sure. The richest? What can be richer than my chest of gold coins!"

The farmer pulled his shoulders back and gave them a **sneering,** satisfied smile.

"H'mm," said the young mayor. Then he asked, "What answers does the shepherd give?"

The shepherd bowed politely and said, "The swiftest thing in the world is thought. Thought can run

You learn about the farmer from his dialogue. His answer to the riddle shows that he thinks he is very important.

This painting is *l'Entellement* by Marc Chagall. Chagall used details such as a mule-drawn cart and a street lantern to show a country town. ▼

any distance in the blink of an eye. The sweetest thing of all is sleep. When a person is tired and sad, what can be sweeter? The richest thing is the earth, for out of the earth come all the riches of the world."

"Good!" the mayor cried. "Good! The cow goes to the shepherd!"

Later the mayor said to the shepherd, "Tell me now, who gave you those answers? I'm sure they never came from your head."

At first the shepherd tried not to tell. But when the mayor pressed him, he confessed. The answers came from his daughter, Manka. The mayor, who decided to test Manka's cleverness again, sent for ten eggs. He gave the eggs to the shepherd and said, "Take these eggs to Manka. Tell her to have them hatched by tomorrow and to bring me the chicks."

When the shepherd got home, he gave Manka the mayor's message. Manka laughed and said, "Take a handful of seeds and go right back to the mayor. Say to him, 'My daughter sends you these seeds. She says that if you plant them, grow them, and have them harvested by tomorrow, she'll bring you the ten chicks. You can feed them the ripe grain.' "

When the mayor heard this, he laughed heartily.

"That's a clever girl of yours," he told the shepherd. "If she is as lovely as she is clever, I think I'd like to marry her. Tell her to come to see me. However, she must come neither by day nor by night, neither riding nor walking, neither dressed nor undressed."

When Manka received this message, she waited until the next dawn. Night was not yet gone and day had not arrived. Then she wrapped herself in a fish net and threw one leg over a goat's back, keeping one foot on the ground. In this manner she went off to the mayor's house.

Now I ask you: did she go dressed? No, she wasn't dressed. A fish net isn't clothing. Did she go

Why do you think the mayor wants to test Manka's cleverness again?

undressed? Of course not, for wasn't she covered with a fish net? Did she walk to the mayor's? No, she didn't walk, for she went with one leg over a goat. Then did she ride? Of course she didn't ride, for wasn't she walking on one foot?

When she reached the mayor's house she called out, "Here I am, Mr. Mayor. I have come neither by day nor by night, neither riding nor walking, neither dressed nor undressed."

The young mayor was delighted with Manka's cleverness and lovely appearance. He asked to marry her at once, and in a short time they were married.

"But you must know this, my dear Manka," he said. "You are not to use your cleverness against me. I won't have you **meddle** in my cases. In fact, if ever you advise anyone who comes to me, I will turn you out of my house. I will send you home to your father."

All went well for a time. Manka was busy with her housework. She was careful not to meddle in any of the mayor's cases.

Then one day two farmers came to the mayor with a **quarrel**. One of the farmers owned a mare that had given birth to a colt in the marketplace. The colt had run under the wagon of the other farmer. The owner of the wagon, therefore, claimed the colt was his.

The mayor was thinking of something else when the case was being presented. He said carelessly, "The man who found the colt under his wagon is, of course, the owner of the colt."

As the owner of the mare was leaving the mayor's house, he met Manka. He stopped to tell her about the case. Manka was ashamed of her husband for making such a foolish **judgment.** She said to the farmer, "Come back this afternoon with a fishing net and stretch it across the dusty road. When the mayor sees you, he will come out and ask you what you are doing. Say to him that you're catching fish. He will

▲ This painting is full of activity. Each scene tells part of a story. Some parts of the story in the painting are similar to Manka's story. The artist, Marc Chagall, called it *Autour d'Elle*.

ask you how you expect to catch fish on a dusty road. Tell him it's just as easy for you to catch fish in a dusty road as it is for a wagon to give birth to a colt. Then he will see the unfairness of his judgment and have the colt returned to you. But remember one thing: you mustn't let him find out that it was I who told you to do this."

That afternoon the mayor happened to look out the window and saw a man stretching a fish net across the dusty road. He went out to him and asked, "What are you doing?"

"Fishing," the man answered.

"Fishing in a dusty road? Are you mad?" the mayor asked.

"Well," the man said, "it's as easy for me to catch fish in a dusty road as it is for a wagon to give birth to a colt."

Then the mayor saw that this was the man who owned the mare. The mayor had to admit that what the man said was true.

"Of course, the colt belongs to your mare and must be returned to you. But tell me," he said, "who put you up to this? You did not think of it yourself."

The farmer did not want to tell, but the mayor questioned him until he found out that Manka was at the bottom of it. This made him very angry. He went into the house and called his wife.

"Manka," he said, "did you forget what I told you would happen if you meddled in any of my cases? Home you go this very day. I don't care to hear any excuses. The matter is settled. You may take with you the one thing you like best in the house. I won't have people saying that I treated you badly."

Manka made no complaint.

"Very well, my dear husband, I shall do as you say. I shall go home to my father's cottage. I will take with me the one thing I like best in your house. But don't make me go until after supper. We have been very

What do you think Manka will choose to take with her to her father's house?

happy together, and I should like to eat one last meal with you. Let us have no more words but be kind to each other as we've always been. Then we will part as friends."

The mayor agreed to this, and Manka prepared a fine supper. She made all the dishes her husband loved. The mayor wished Manka good health, then sat down. The supper was so good that he ate and ate and ate. The more he ate, the more tired he became until he fell sound asleep in his chair. Then without waking him, Manka had him carried to the wagon that was waiting to take her home.

The next morning, when the mayor opened his eyes, he found himself in the shepherd's cottage.

"What does this mean?" he roared out.

"Nothing, dear husband, nothing!" Manka said. "You know you told me I might take the one thing I liked best in your house. So I took you! That's all."

For a moment, the mayor rubbed his eyes in shock. Then he laughed loud and heartily at how clever Manka was.

"Manka," he said, "you're too clever for me. Come on, my dear, let's go home."

So, they climbed back into the wagon and drove home.

The mayor never again scolded his wife. But whenever a very difficult case came up, he always said, "I think we had better ask my wife. You know she's a very clever woman."

"The next morning" is another phrase that helps the reader understand the order of events.

Manka teaches her husband a lesson. What do you think he learns?

Literature Practice

Answer these questions on a separate sheet of paper.

1. How does the mayor decide the case between the farmer and the shepherd?

2. What does the dialogue tell about Manka's personality?

3. Why does the mayor want to meet Manka?

4. How does the mayor test Manka's cleverness?

5. Is the mayor more clever than Manka? Explain your answer.

Who Told the First Riddle?

Riddles are as old as ancient history. The Sphinx of ancient Greece asked the riddle: "What creature walks on four feet in the morning, on two at noon, and on three in the evening?" A smart young man named Oedipus answered correctly. He said, "Man. In childhood he crawls on hands and feet. In manhood he walks on both feet. In old age he leans on a staff."

There are two main types of riddles. One kind centers on the way something looks. For example, "What grows bigger and bigger the more you take from it?" The answer is "a hole." The mayor in "Clever Manka" likes the other type of riddle. These are witty riddles that need clever answers. The mayor would enjoy the ancient Greek riddle "What is the strongest of all things?" This ancient riddle has been asked for centuries. The answer is, "The strongest of all things is love. Iron is strong, but the blacksmith is stronger. Love can even control the blacksmith."

A Piece of String

an adapted story by Guy de Maupassant

Words to Know

LITERARY TERMS

conflict a struggle between two or more characters; the problem that needs to be solved in a story

surprise ending an ending of a story that is not expected

SELECTION VOCABULARY

thrifty not wasteful, economical

harness the leather straps and metal pieces used to attach a horse to a plow

grudge a strong, continuing feeling of hatred or ill will against someone

solemnly seriously

squabbled quarreled noisily over a small matter

oaths promises that one will speak the truth

innocence being free of guilt

How we get along with the people in our community is important. We like to think our neighbors trust and respect us. Maître Hauchecome is visiting the small French village of Goderville. His story describes what happens to a person who does not have strong relationships in a community.

Maître Hauchecome
(MAY-trah OSH-kum)

———— ⬦ ————

Along all the roads around Goderville, peasants and their wives were walking toward the village. It was market day. The men moved with slow steps. Their whole bodies bent forward at each movement of their

This painting by Pieter Brueghel is called *A Peasant Holding a Staff.* In 17th and 18th century France, most peasants lived in small villages and farmed for a living. ▶

long, twisted legs. Their legs were twisted from the hard work of pulling heavy plows and using heavy tools. Loose clothes puffed about their thin bodies. Each man looked like a balloon ready to fly away. From each, a head, two arms, and two feet stuck out.

Some led a cow or calf by a rope. The wives walked behind whipping the animal with a branch to hurry it along. They carried large baskets on their arms. From some baskets, chickens and ducks poked out their heads. The wives walked more quickly and with a livelier step than their husbands. Their lean, straight frames were wrapped in thin shawls pinned in the front. Their heads were wrapped in white cloths, then held in place by caps.

In the public square of Goderville, there was a crowd of people and animals mixed together. The horns of cattle and the hats of the peasants rose above the crowd. Loud, sharp voices could be heard. Sometimes the rough sound of a countryman's laugh or the moo of a cow could be heard above all the noise. Everything carried the odor of the dirt, hay, and sweat of men and animals.

Maître Hauchecome of Breaute had just arrived in Goderville. He was walking toward the public square when he noted a little piece of string on the ground. Being a **thrifty** man, he thought that everything useful should be picked up. He bent painfully to pick it up. He suffered from rheumatism. He took the bit of thin string from the ground and rolled it carefully. As he did this, he saw Maître Malandain, looking at him from his doorway. Malandain was the **harness**-maker. The two men were angry with each other over a business deal. Both were good at holding a **grudge.** Maître Hauchecome was ashamed to be seen picking up a string out of the dirt. He therefore quickly hid his "find" in his pocket. For a time, he pretended to be looking for something on the ground that he could not find. Then he continued his slow, painful trip to the square.

There he was soon lost in the dealings of the noisy crowd. Peasants came and went, troubled and always in fear of being cheated. During the bargaining, they watched for tricks or flaws in the goods. The women placed their great baskets on the ground. They lay terrified chickens and ducks on the ground, their legs tied together. They listened to offers and gave their prices. Suddenly agreeing to a price, they might shout: "All right, I'll give it to you for that."

Then little by little, the square emptied. At Jourdain's, the great room was soon filled with people eating. The flames from the huge fireplace warmed the backs of the diners. Over the fire, chickens, pigeons, and legs of lamb

A public square is a place where people go to buy and sell goods.

Breaute (Broht).

Rheumatism makes muscles and joints stiff and painful.

The conflict between Malandain (Ma-law-DAIN) and Hauchecome will be important later in the story.

Jourdain's (Joor-DAINZ) is a restaurant.

turned slowly. The smell of roast meat and gravy rose from the hearth, making everybody's spirits rise and their mouths water. The wealthier farmers ate at Maître Jourdain's. He was a tavern keeper and horse dealer. He was a man who had money.

Plates of food and jugs of yellow cider were passed and emptied. Everyone talked of what he bought or sold, of crops, or of the weather. Suddenly, a drum beat sounded outside the inn. Most of the diners rose and ran to the door or the windows. Their mouths were full, and napkins were still in their hands.

After the town crier stopped his drum-beating, he called out slowly: "Let it be known that there was lost this morning a black leather purse. This purse held five hundred francs and some business papers. The finder is asked to return it to Maître Houlbreque or to the mayor's office. There will be twenty francs reward."

Most 19th century villages and towns had a town crier to spread the news.

Francs are the French form of money.

Father Courbet's Apple Tree Garden in Ornans, painted by Gustave Courbet, shows the beautiful countryside of 19th century France. ▶

Then the town crier went away. His drum and voice were heard again in the distance. Then the talk turned to Maître Houlbreque's chances of finding or not finding his purse. As the meal ended, the chief of police came to the door.

He asked, "Is Maître Hauchecome here?"

Maître Hauchecome answered, "Here I am."

The officer replied, "Maître Hauchecome, will you kindly come with me to the mayor's office? The mayor would like to talk to you."

The peasant was surprised and shaken. He rose painfully to his feet. The first steps after a rest were especially painful. Then he moved forward saying, "Here I am, here I am."

The mayor was waiting for him in his armchair. He was a large, serious man who spoke **solemnly.** "Maître Hauchecome," he said, "you were seen this morning picking up Maître Houlbreque's purse."

Maître Hauchecome was stunned. He looked at the mayor, terrified by his words. Why was he being blamed?

"Me? Me? Me pick up the purse?"

"Yes, you, yourself."

"On my word, I never saw it."

"But you were seen."

"I was seen, me? Who says he saw me?"

"Maître Malandain, the harness-maker."

The old man remembered and understood. His face became red with anger.

"Ah, he saw me pick up this string." He reached in his pocket and drew out the little piece of string.

But the mayor shook his head with doubt.

"Maître Malandain is an honest man. You want me to believe he thought a string was a purse?"

The peasant was furious. "It is God's truth, Maître Mayor! I swear by my soul!"

The mayor went on. "You picked up the purse and

Maître Houlbreque (MAY-trah Ool-BREK)

The mayor knows Malandain. They live in the same village. The mayor believes what Malandain says about Hauchecome.

stood looking for a long while in the mud to see if any piece of money had fallen out."

The good old man choked with fear and rage. "How anyone can tell—how anyone can tell—such lies. Lies to ruin my good name! How can anyone—"

It was no use. Nobody believed him. Maître Malandain arrived and repeated the charge. The two men **squabbled** for an hour. Maître Hauchecome asked to be searched. Nothing was found on him.

Finally, the mayor, very much puzzled, let Maître Hauchecome leave.

This is the beginning of Hauchecome's conflict with the people in the village.

The news had spread. As he left the mayor's office, the old man was surrounded and questioned. He retold the story of the string. No one believed him. They laughed at him.

He stopped his friends, endlessly telling his story. He turned his pockets inside out to prove he had nothing. Still no one believed him. He grew angry and hot at not being believed.

The people in his own village do not believe him. Why do you think his neighbors treat Hauchecome this way?

Night came. He must leave. He started on his way with three neighbors. He pointed to the place where he had found the bit of string. All along the road, he spoke of his adventure. In the evening, he walked around his own village of Breaute. He told the people of Breaute his story. Again, no one believed him. It made him ill all night.

Ymanville (Ih-MAW-vihl)

The next day, a hired man from Ymanville returned the purse and its contents to Maître Houlbreque. He claimed he found the purse in the road. Not knowing how to read, he took it to his employer, Maître Breton.

Maître Breton (MAY-trah Bruh-TON)

The news spread through the town. Maître Hauchecome soon heard it and was filled with joy.

"What hurt me so much was not the thing itself, as the lying. Nothing is so shameful as being ruined by a lie."

Hauchecome talked of his adventure all day long. He told it on the highway to people who passed by. He told people in shops and people coming out of church

◀ Pieter Brueghel's painting of *A Peasant Seated on a Stool* shows another scene of peasant life in a small French village.

the following Sunday. He stopped strangers to tell them about it. He was calm now, but something still bothered him. He didn't know what exactly it was, though. People appeared to be joking while they listened. They did not seem to believe him. He thought that they were making comments about him behind his back.

On Tuesday of the next week, he went to the market at Goderville. His only reason was the need he felt to discuss his story.

Malandain was standing at his door. He began laughing when he saw the old man pass.

Then he spoke to a farmer from Crequetot, but the farmer would not let him finish. He poked the old man's stomach and said: "You big rascal." Then he turned his back on him.

Crequetot (crehk-eh-TOH)

Maître Hauchecome was confused. He had no idea why he was being called a big rascal.

At Jourdain's, he began to explain his story. A horse dealer called to him. "Come, come, that's an old trick. I know all about your piece of string!"

Hauchecome stammered, "But the purse was found."

Another man said, "Shut up, papa. One man finds, and another man returns. At any rate, you are mixed up in it."

The peasant stood choking. He understood. They thought he had a partner who returned the purse. He tried to explain. All the table began to laugh. He could not finish his dinner. He left to the sound of people laughing.

Hauchecome's pride is hurt. He wants his neighbors to respect him.

At home he felt ashamed and upset. It was impossible to prove he did not find the purse since he was known to be quite clever. The thought that people did not believe him hurt him deeply.

Then he began telling his story again and again. Each time the story got longer. New reasons were added. More solemn **oaths** and stronger protests were made. His whole mind was given to the story of the string. Yet the more he explained, the less he was believed.

"Those are lies," they said behind his back.

The old man wore himself out over it and wasted away before their eyes. Some made him tell about the string for their amusement. His mind, touched deeply, began to weaken.

Toward the end of December, he took to his bed.

Here is the surprise ending. Did you expect that Hauchecome would die over such a small matter as a piece of string?

He died in the first days of January. Until his death, he claimed his **innocence** and said again and again:

"A piece of string. A piece of string—look—here it is, M'sieu' Mayor."

Literature Practice

Answer these questions on a separate sheet of paper.

1. What conflict does Maître Hauchecome have with the people of Goderville?

2. What does Maître Hauchecome do to try to make the people in the village believe him?

3. How do Maître Hauchecome and Maître Malandain feel about each other? Explain your answer.

4. What does the ending of the story tell you about Maître Hauchecome?

Peasant Life in 19th Century France

If you lived in a French village like Goderville during the 1800s, your family would probably live by farming. Without television, radio, magazines, or CDs for entertainment, the highlight of your week would be market day. Just like the peasants in "A Piece of String," you would bring your extra crops or livestock to the village. You would sell or trade them for whatever else your family needed. On market day, you would catch up on all the news about the villagers and people on nearby farms.

Since most people lived their whole lives in the same village, everyone knew everyone else. Villages were like a giant family. A person like Maître Hauchecome, who came from a different village, would be treated as an outsider. Most people would never trust an outsider's word over the word of a fellow villager. Villagers knew they needed to stick together to get through the hard times that came with peasant life.

Dead Men's Path

an adapted story by Chinua Achebe

Words to Know

LITERARY TERMS

clues about character thoughts, actions, and words in a story that help the reader find out what a character is like

climax the most exciting part of a story that comes near the end

SELECTION VOCABULARY

headmaster school principal

proper correct

hobble to walk with a limp

shrine a place where people pay respect to a god

pagan not religious

ancestors the family or group a person comes from

sacrifices offerings of valued objects

misplaced wrongly placed

In a community, we have relationships with our neighbors. Part of our relationship is learning to respect the ways our neighbors are different from us. In this story a young teacher learns too late the importance of respecting the different ways of his neighbors.

Ndume (n-DOO-muh)

Michael Obi's hopes came true much sooner than he thought. He was appointed **headmaster** of Ndume Central School in January 1949. It had always been a backward school. For this reason those in charge decided to send a young, eager man to run it. Obi took the job with great excitement. He had many wonderful ideas. This was the chance to put them to work. He had had a **proper** education which earned him the title "master teacher." This set him apart from the other headmasters. He spoke out often against the narrow views of the older, less-educated ones.

"We shall make a good job of it, don't you think?" he asked his young wife when they heard the news.

"We shall do our best," she replied. "We shall have such beautiful gardens. Everything will be modern and delightful . . . . " They had been married two years. In that time, she had become completely taken by her husband's passion for "modern ways." Like him, she mocked "these old useless teachers." They would be better off as traders in the market. She began to see herself as the honored wife of the headmaster. She would be the queen of the school.

The wives of the other teachers would envy her. She would set the style in everything . . . . Then, suddenly, she thought there might not be other wives. Torn between hope and fear, she anxiously asked her husband.

"All our teachers are young and unmarried," he said happily. For once, his wife did not share his feelings. "It's a good thing," he went on.

"Why?" his wife asked.

"Why? They will give all their time and energy to the school," her husband answered.

Nancy was sad. She was not sure about the new school. But this lasted only a few minutes. Her personal bad luck could not blind her. This was her husband's great chance. She looked at him as he sat folded up in a chair. His back was bent, and he looked weak. But he sometimes surprised people with sudden bursts of energy. Now his strength seemed to be resting behind his deep-set eyes. They gave him a rare, piercing power. He was only twenty-six, but looked thirty or more. On the whole, he was fairly handsome.

The author gives clues about the kind of person Michael Obi is.

The author describes Mr. Obi's young wife, Nancy. What do you learn about her?

▲ This bronze sculpture
is from Benin in
western Africa. It shows
the journey of an
important chief. He
listens to music and is
sheltered from the sun.

The conflict of the story
is introduced when Mr.
Obi sees an old woman
walking on a path that
cuts through the school
grounds.

"A penny for your thoughts, Mike," said Nancy
after a while. She sounded like the women's magazines
she read.

"I was thinking about the grand opportunity we
have. At last we can show these people how a school
should be run."

Ndume School was backward in every way. Mr. Obi
put his whole life into the work. His wife did too. He
had two aims. First, the teaching had to be of the
highest quality. Second, the school grounds were to
become a place of beauty. Nancy's dream gardens
came to life with the rains. Beautiful flowers and
hedges of bright red and yellow set the school gardens
apart from the untended neighborhood plants.

One evening Obi was admiring his work. He was
horrified to see an old woman from the village **hobble**
across the school grounds. She went right through a
flower-bed and some hedges. On going there he found
the faint signs of an old path. It went from the village
across the school grounds. This little-used path ended
in the bushes on the other side of the school.

"It amazes me," said Obi to a teacher who had been there three years. "You allowed the villagers to use this path. It is simply beyond belief." He shook his head.

"The path," said the teacher, "seems to be very important to them. It's hardly used, but it connects the village **shrine** with their place of burial."

"What has that got to do with the school?" asked the headmaster.

"Well, I don't know," said the other teacher with a shrug of the shoulders. "But I remember there was a big quarrel some time ago. It happened when we tried to close the path."

"That was some time ago. But it will not be used now," said Obi as he walked away. "What will the Government Officer think? He comes to inspect the school next week. The villagers might, for all I know, decide to do something else. Perhaps they will use a schoolroom for a **pagan** ritual during the inspection."

Heavy sticks were planted across the path at two places. Some were placed where the path entered the school grounds. The others were placed where it left the grounds. Both were wrapped with barbed wire.

By blocking the path with sticks, Mr. Obi thinks he is solving the problem. What do you think will happen next?

Three days later the village priest called on the headmaster. The priest was an old man and walked with a slight stoop. In his hand he carried a thick walking stick. He often tapped it on the floor to mark the importance of what he said.

"I have heard," he said after a few pleasant words, "that our ancient path has been closed. . . . "

"Yes," replied Mr. Obi. "We cannot let people make a road of our school grounds."

"Look here, my son," said the priest bringing down his stick. "This path was here before you were born. It was here before your father was born. The whole life of the village depends on it. Our dead depart by it and our **ancestors** visit us by it. But most important, it is the path of children coming in to be born . . . ."

Compare what you know about Mr. Obi with what you know about the village priest.

Mr. Obi listened with a satisfied smile on his face.

"The whole purpose of our school is to erase such beliefs," he said at last. "Dead men do not need paths. The whole idea is ridiculous. Our duty is to teach your children to laugh at such ideas."

"What you say may be true," replied the priest. "But we follow the ways of our fathers. If you open the path, we shall have no quarrel. What I always say is: let the hawk perch and let the eagle perch." He rose to go.

"I am sorry," said the young headmaster. "But the school grounds cannot be a highway. It is against our rules. I suggest you build another path around our grounds. We can even get our boys to help you build it. I don't think your ancestors will find the extra distance a hardship."

"I have no more words to say," said the old priest, already outside.

Two days later a young woman in the village died giving birth. A wise man was immediately called. He ordered heavy **sacrifices** to satisfy the ancestors angered by the fence.

"Let the hawk perch and let the eagle perch" is a proverb, or saying, about life. What do you think the priest means?

The priest's visit and his final words are the climax of the story.

This scene shows a traditional village like the one Mr. Obi has moved to. It is called *Day's End* and was painted by Abdim Dr No from Somalia. ▶

Obi woke up the next morning among the ruins of his work. The beautiful hedges were torn up. Not only near the path but all around the school, flowers were trampled to death. One of the school buildings had also been pulled down. . . . That day the inspector came to see the school and wrote a nasty report on the appearance of the school grounds. More serious, however, was his damaging report on the war between the school and the village. A war, he said, that was caused in part by the **misplaced** eagerness of the new headmaster.

Mr. Obi failed to build a good relationship between the school and the village. What should he have done differently?

Literature Practice

Answer these questions on a separate sheet of paper.

1. What kind of person is Mr. Obi?
2. What is the conflict in the story?
3. What kind of person is the village priest?
4. Why is the path important to the villagers?
5. What is the climax of this story? Explain your answer.

Bitter Cold, Living in the Village

a poem by Po Chü-i

Words to Know

LITERARY TERM

speaker the character who speaks in a poem

SELECTION VOCABULARY

bamboos woody grasses

cypress a kind of evergreen tree or shrub

perished died

homespun loosely woven home-made cloth

brambles prickly bushes

thatched covered with straw or grass

Caring about other people can help us feel better about ourselves. The speaker in this poem learns an important lesson about caring for and helping other people.

The speaker remembers one very cold winter in his village.

In the twelfth month of this Eighth Year,
On the fifth day, a heavy snow fell.
Bamboos and **cypress** all **perished** from the freeze.
How much worse for people without warm clothes!

As I looked around the village,
Of ten families, eight or nine were in need.
The north wind was sharper than the sword,
And **homespun** cloth could hardly cover one's body.
Only **brambles** were burnt for firewood,
And sadly people sat at night to wait for dawn.

From this I know that when winter is harsh,
The farmers suffer most.
Looking at myself, during these days—
How I'd shut tight the gate of my **thatched** hall,
Cover myself with fur, wool, and silk,
Sitting or lying down, I had ample warmth.
I was lucky to be spared cold or hunger,
Neither did I have to labor in the field.

Thinking of that, how can I not feel ashamed?
I ask myself what kind of man am I.

This painting, *Snowy Landscape* by Nien-Tsu Hu, shows the cold, frozen land of the winter. Most likely, this is the way Po Chü-i's village looked during the bitter winter he describes in his poem. ▼

Literature Practice

Answer these questions on a separate sheet of paper.

1. What event in the past does the speaker remember?

2. How do the village families try to survive the harsh winter?

3. Does the speaker help those families in need? Why or why not?

4. How is the life of the speaker different from the lives of the other villagers?

5. Why do you think the speaker feels ashamed?

Young Hunger

an adapted essay by M.F.K. Fisher

Words to Know

LITERARY TERMS

theme the main idea of a story, poem, or essay

essay a brief piece of writing that develops a single idea

SELECTION VOCABULARY

wince to draw back in pain or distress

despair sadness

godparents people who sponsor, or agree to be partly responsible for, a child at its baptism

inactive not active

hesitate to pause

appetite desire for food

Our families have many lessons to teach us. The narrator in this essay remembers a visit with her godparents, who lived in England, when she was eighteen years old. She once thought they were unkind. Now she knows they had only forgotten what it was like to be young.

⸺ ❧ ⸺

The essay begins with a clear statement of the theme.

It is very hard for people over fifty to remember the hunger of the young. They forget their own youth when dealing with the young people around them. I have seen older people helpless with anger over finding an empty cupboard or refrigerator. All because the cupboard was stripped by one, two, or three youths who could have eaten their fill at dinner.

I am not too old to remember how it feels to be young and hungry. I understand when I see a fifteen-year-old boy **wince** at the thought of waiting hours for food. His guts howl for meat — bread — candy— fruit — cheese — milk — ANYTHING TO EAT.

I remember my own **despair** when I was about eighteen. I was staying overnight with my elderly **godparents.** I had come home alone from France through a cruel storm. It had made me hollow with hunger. The night on the train seemed even rougher than the one on the ship. By the time I reached my godparents' home I was faint.

I got there just in time for lunch. It is as clear as ice in my mind. Before me were a little cup of weak broth, a cracker, and a half piece of thin toast. Then, ah then, came a whole waffle, crisp and brown. A piece of butter melted in its middle. The maid skillfully cut it into four pieces! She put one on my godmother's plate. The next two, after a nod from my godmother, she put on mine. My godfather ate the fourth.

There was a tiny pot of honey. I dutifully put a dab of it on my piggish serving. We all nibbled away and drank a cup apiece of tea with lemon. Both of my godparents left part of their waffles.

It was simply that they were old and **inactive.** They were quite out of the habit of eating a big meal with younger people. It was a good thing for them, but not for me. I did not have the sense to explain how starved I was. I would not **hesitate** doing so now. Instead, I prowled around my bedroom while everyone else in the house took an afternoon nap. Dare I sneak into the strange kitchen for something, anything, to eat! I would rather die than meet the maid or my godmother.

Later we walked slowly down to the village. All the while I was thinking passionately of double ice-cream sodas at the corner store. However, there was no possibility of such heaven. Back at the quiet house,

The narrator develops the theme with examples from her own personal experience. In an essay, the narrator is usually the author.

The narrator describes the portions of food. These details make the narrator's hunger seem more real.

The author's godparents may look like the people in this painting. The painting is called *Le goûter* and was painted by Jean Francois Raffaelli. ▶

the maid brought my godfather a tall glass of rich milk. On the saucer was a handful of dried fruit because he had been ill. We sat and watched him unwillingly eat it. His wife said softly that it was a short time until dinner. She was sure I did not want to spoil my **appetite.** I agreed with her because I was young and shy.

The author compares her hip bones to two bricks. This comparison creates a strong picture in the mind of the reader.

When I dressed, I noticed my hip bones. They stuck out like two bricks under my skirt. I looked like a scarecrow.

Dinner was very long. All I can remember, though, is the main course. It was half of the tiny boiled chicken that made the broth for lunch. My godmother carved it carefully. We each got part of the breast. I, as the guest, should have the leg. First a bit had to be sliced off for her husband. He liked dark meat too.

There were hot biscuits, yes, the smallest I have ever seen. There were two apiece under a napkin on a silver dish. Because of them we had no dessert. It would be too rich, my godmother said.

We drank little cups of coffee on the porch in the hot night. When I went up to my room, I saw a large glass of malted milk beside my poor godfather's bed.

My train would leave before five in the morning. I slept little and sadly. I dreamed of the breakfast I would order. Of course, when I saw it twinkling on the silver dishes, I could eat very little. I was too hungry and too angry.

What do you think the narrator dreams of ordering for breakfast?

I felt my godparents had been very rude to me. They had been selfish and stupid. Now I know they were none of these things. They had just forgotten about any but their own shrinking need for food. They had forgotten about being hungry, being young, being . . . .

Literature Practice

Answer these questions on a separate sheet of paper.

1. What is the theme of the essay?

2. To what does the narrator compare her hip bones? Why?

3. What kind of examples are used to develop the theme?

4. What does the narrator describe in careful detail?

5. How do the narrator's feelings toward her godparents change?

Chapter Review

Summaries

- **Clever Manka**—The new mayor decides his court cases by asking riddles. During one case, a shepherd gives clever answers to the mayor's riddles. The shepherd admits that his daughter, Manka, gave him the answers. The mayor tests Manka to find out how clever she is. After the mayor and Manka marry, she uses one of her husband's riddles to teach him a lesson.

- **A Piece of String**—Maître Hauchecome visits the village of Goderville. In the public square, he picks up a piece of string from the ground. Maître Malandain sees him pick it up. Later, Maître Hauchecome is accused of finding and keeping a purse. He tells everyone that he is innocent and shows them the piece of string he picked up. Even after the purse is found, the villagers do not believe Maître Hauchecome.

- **Dead Men's Path**—Mr. Obi is a young teacher who believes in modern ways of learning. Mr. Obi closes a path through the school yard that is important to the villagers. The village priest explains to Mr. Obi the importance of the path. But Mr. Obi does not respect the beliefs of others.

- **Bitter Cold, Living in the Village**—The speaker recalls a very harsh winter. Many people in the village struggled to survive. The speaker is a wealthy man, but he does not help his neighbors. He is later ashamed of his behavior.

- **Young Hunger**—The narrator remembers what it means to be young and hungry. During a visit to her godparents, she is fed only tiny bits of food. She spends the visit thinking only of how hungry she is.

Chapter Quiz

Choose the letter of the correct answer. Rewrite the sentences on a separate sheet of paper.

1. The one thing in her home that Manka likes best is
   a. clever wit.   c. good food.
   b. her kitchen.   d. her husband.

2. In "A Piece of String," Maître Hauchecome picks up a thin piece of string from the ground because
   a. he is a thrifty person.   c. he collects string.
   b. he is angry.   d. he will give it to a neighbor.

3. In "Dead Men's Path," a conflict occurs between
   a. old ways and modern ways.   c. the villagers and the priest.
   b. Mr. Obi and his wife.   d. Mr. Obi and a friend.

4. The narrator in "Young Hunger" describes her godparents as
   a. young and jolly.   c. angry and stingy.
   b. old and inactive.   d. revolting and piggish.

Thinking and Writing

Write answers to the following questions on a separate sheet of paper.

1. Choose a relationship between two characters that you read about in this chapter. How does the relationship help the characters understand themselves or each other? Give examples from the story to explain your answer.

2. In "Bitter Cold, Living in the Village," do you think the speaker will change his way of life? Explain your answer.

3. Why does the narrator in "Young Hunger" say that older people forget their own youth? Explain your answer.

▲ This painting *Este Depertar Creciente* by Alfredo Castaneda shows a long path of trees. The path you take in life will be one of the many choices you must make.

Chapter Learning Objectives

- Understand foreshadowing in a story.
- Recognize the role of the narrator in an autobiography.
- Learn how authors use symbols in a story.
- Understand the use of concrete words in a poem.

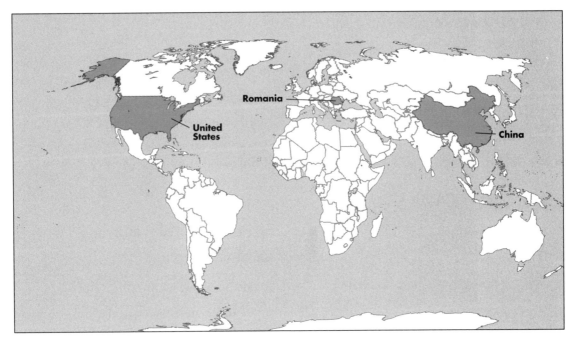

China
The Story of Washing Horse Pond
*an adapted folktale translated
by He Liyi*

United States
Things I Forgot Today
a poem by Martha B. Malavansky

Romania
The Watch
*adapted from the autobiography
of Elie Wiesel*

During our lives we make many choices. These choices affect who we are.
Some of our choices are big. Some are small. Some choices are harder than
others. The characters in these selections discover many things about
themselves through the choices they make.

The Story of Washing Horse Pond

an adapted folktale translated by He Liyi

Words to Know

LITERARY TERM

foreshadowing clues that suggest what will happen later in a story

SELECTION VOCABULARY

drought a long time without rain

thrive grow

spring a source of water

withered dried up

furiously fiercely, angrily

parched very dry

misery great pain, suffering

priceless of great worth

Our choices can affect other people. In this story, Akui chooses to help his neighbors. His choice comes at the cost of his own life.

——— ✸ ———

In the first paragraph, the last two sentences foreshadow what might happen to a young man named Akui (a-KWEE).

One of the most beautiful of Dali's nineteen peaks is called the Treasure Peak. There is a clean pond at the top of the peak. Pure water flows from it all year round. The pond is surrounded by trees and flowers, and is known as Washing Horse Pond. Next to the pond stands a large stone about the size of a man. People say that this stone is the statue of a brave young man called Akui. He lived a long time ago.

Once in Dali there was a terrible **drought.** For three whole years there had not been a single drop of rain. All the pools and ditches had dried up. Even huge Dali Lake had lost its fresh color and shrunk to a muddy hole.

There were no more colorful flowers on the mountain slopes, and no birds sang. The crops wouldn't grow, and the cattle wouldn't **thrive.** All the beautiful mountains were sadly changed. People lived without hope.

Under one of those nineteen peaks was the village of Boluo. There lived a man by the name of Akui. His parents were old and weak. Because of the three-year drought, they could grow no food. Akui had to scrape out a living by looking for firewood in the hills. His parents just got older and weaker. A doctor was called, but there was nothing he could do. It was the drought. Many people could do nothing except wait to die. Akui's parents had no money to buy medicine or food. Very soon they died, one after the other. Akui was very sad.

All the neighbors came to say how sorry they were. They too were suffering. Some of the men talked of a **spring** that never failed. It was supposed to be somewhere at the top of the mountain peaks, but none of them knew where. Akui made up his mind to look for that spring. He took a hoe, a bow, some arrows, and some food. Then he set off for the peak above the village. The villagers watched him go. All their hopes and worries went with him.

For nine days and ten nights he climbed. He climbed over four huge peaks and four dry river beds, until he reached the top of the highest peak. It was a place called the Peak of Horses and Dragons. After his long journey, Akui was so tired that he fell asleep as soon as he lay down.

The day was just dawning when he awoke. As he looked around, all he could see was dry grass and **withered** trees. There was no water in the streams. There was no water anywhere. He searched all day but found nothing. That night he could not sleep. He just stared at the sky all night. Suddenly he saw something shining in the dark sky. It was way to the south. Then the shiny thing passed over his head and landed on

Boluo (boo-LOO-oh)

Akui's life changed because of the drought. How would your life change if you did not have water?

▲ This painting of *Pegasus* by Odillon Redon shows a winged horse. Such a horse might have enjoyed the cool water of Washing Horse Pond.

another peak. Akui was amazed at the sight. He set out immediately for the other peak.

Dawn had come when Akui got there. Looking all around, he found everything just as dried up as everywhere else. Yet, there was one pine tree under a large rock. Its branches were green, and the needles were lush. Akui thought: Water! A tree lives on water. There must be water under the tree.

Lifting his hoe, he dug **furiously** until late that night. He dug until his hands were stained with blood, and his **parched** lips split. His throat was a burning fire. Still he found no trace of water.

That evening, to be safe from wild beasts, Akui climbed up the tree. He was so tired after digging all day that he soon fell asleep. At midnight he was awakened by a sudden flash of light. Looking up in the sky, he saw a number of winged horses flying to a large rock. The leading horse was as white as snow and larger than the rest. It stretched out its leg and struck the rock three times. The rock opened, just like a gate. Within the rock was a real pond of pure water.

The flying horses drank and splashed. They didn't leave until day was about to break. The rock closed again behind them.

Akui jumped down from the tree and ran toward the rock. He hit it three times with his hoe. Slowly the stone gate opened. He went inside and found a lovely pool of rippling water. Grass and flowers grew on its banks. On a stone were carved the words "Washing Horse Pond."

Akui knelt to drink. The water tasted very cool. He was too excited to drink as much as he wished to. He was thinking of his fellow villagers. They were depending on him in their hour of need. They were suffering. So he started to dig a ditch right away.

In a wink, a stream of white smoke came out of the ground. In front of Akui stood a white-haired, old man,

The description of Akui's blood-stained hands helps you understand how furiously he dug for water. What do the details of Akui's parched lips and burning throat help you understand?

Even as he drinks, Akui thinks of his fellow villagers. What does this tell you about Akui?

who said, "Young man, this water must not be touched. This is the only pond where the flying horses come to drink and swim. I am the God of this mountain peak, and this pond is in my care."

Akui told him all about the **misery** caused by the drought. He told him of the people's suffering. As he told the god about the death of his parents, he couldn't hold back the tears.

The God of Treasure Peak understands Akui's sadness and the suffering of the villagers.

The God of Treasure Peak was very much moved by Akui's true story. He said, "Young fellow, let me tell you the truth. The one who frees the water of this magic pond will turn into a piece of rock. You are so young. Don't you think it a pity to become a stone? Go down and tell them to send up an old man instead. It is asking too much of you. It is more than enough for you to have found the water for everybody."

Akui paused for a while after hearing this. He replied, "My honored uncle, I thank you for your kindness. But there must be no delay. This water will save thousands of lives. I'd rather be stone than go back now. You needn't worry about me."

Uncle is used here as a title of respect.

He began to dig again.

Soon Akui had dug out a trench, down which the pure water rushed. All along its path, the trees began to shoot green leaves and the birds sang. All the mountain flowers began to bloom.

Akui shouted for joy. He tried to walk out and watch the world come back to life, but alas! he couldn't find his feet. Looking down, he saw that his two feet had turned into a pair of stone feet. He tried to shout aloud, but his lungs were turned to stone. All his body was turning to stone. Akui knew now he could never return to his village; but he heard the water gurgling by. He knew it would go there for him. He was satisfied. He let his mouth set into a happy, loving, stone smile.

Akui turns to stone. What clues in the story foreshadowed this event?

The villagers were full of joy when the water from Washing Horse Pond reached them. The once dry land was turning green as the water passed. Everyone knew

▲ This painting by Xu Beihong is called *Horse Drinking from a Pond.*

Akui must have found the water. They climbed up to the pond to look for him, but where had he gone? They couldn't find even Akui's shadow. They called and called at the tops of their voices, but nobody answered. Finally they saw the standing stone. The more they looked at it, the more it looked like Akui. A hoe was lying by, with mossy grass still sticking to it. From this more than anything, the people knew that Akui had become a stone.

From that time on, men and women from the villages near the mountain often came up to visit Akui. He was a hero who had given up his life for them. They made Washing Horse Pond a place of beauty, and it still is. Flowering shrubs are everywhere. The trees are thick and green, and the smell of flowers is delightful. It is said that the ancient kings of Dali used to spend their summer days by its banks. Even now, Akui stands stone still beside the **priceless** water.

Literature Practice

Answer these questions on a separate sheet of paper.

1. What causes the people to suffer in the village?

2. What does Akui search for in the mountains?

3. What creatures drink from the magic pond?

4. Why does Akui refuse to take the God of Treasure Peak's advice?

5. What event is foreshadowed in the story?

The Watch

adapted from the autobiography of Elie Wiesel

Words to Know

LITERARY TERM

symbol a thing that stands for itself and something else

SELECTION VOCABULARY

bar mitzvah a ceremony celebrating the beginning of adulthood for a thirteen-year-old Jewish boy

Torah a book that contains Jewish law and literature

cemetery a place for burying the dead

Shabbat the period from Friday evening to Saturday evening, a time of rest and worship for Jews

rabbi the leader of a Jewish house of worship

looter someone who steals openly

Holocaust the killing of European Jews and others by the Nazis during World War II

Talmud a collection of ancient writings that form the basis of Judaism

Hasidim a group of Jewish people who follow strict teachings of Judaism

---

Our choices sometimes result in important discoveries. Elie Wiesel tells a true story about his experience as a young Jewish boy during World War II. The story centers on the gift of a watch. As a boy, Wiesel makes one decision about the watch. Twenty years later, he makes another.

For my **bar mitzvah,** I remember, I had received a splendid gold watch. It was the usual gift for this event.

bar mitzvah (bahr MIHTS-vuh)

The watch was meant to remind each boy that he was now an adult. From now on, he would have to answer for his acts before the **Torah** and its timeless laws.

But I could not keep my gift. I had to part with it the day my town became the pride of Hungary. This was the day it chased from its borders every single Jew. The glorious masters of our city were thrilled. They were rid of us. There would be no more strangely dressed people on the streets.

The time was late April, 1944.

The early morning hours followed a sleepless night. On that day the Jewish part of the city changed into a **cemetery.** Those who lived there became gravediggers. We were digging wildly in the yard, the garden, and the cellar. We were giving all we had left to the earth for just a time, we thought.

My father took care of the jewelry and important papers. His head bowed, he was silently digging near the barn. Not far away, my mother stooped on the damp ground. She was burying the silver candle holder she used only on **Shabbat** eve. She was moaning softly. I avoided her with my eyes. My sisters dug near the cellar. The youngest, Tziporah, had chosen the garden, like me. Thoughtfully shoveling, she turned down my help. What did she have to hide? Her toys? Her school notebooks? As for me, my only belonging was my watch. It meant a lot to me.
I decided to bury it in a dark, deep hole, three steps from the fence. The thick leaves of a tree seemed to offer a safe cover.

All of us planned to get back our treasure. On our return, the earth would give them back. Until then, they would be safe.

Twenty years later, I am standing in our garden. It is the middle of the night. I remember the first and last gift I ever received from my parents. I need to see it. I want to see if it was still here in the same spot.

World War II lasted from 1939 to 1945. During the war, millions of Jewish people were killed.

Tziporah (tsee-PAW-rah)

The watch is the last gift the narrator received from his parents.

▲ In his painting of *Schoolboy with Slate,* Albert Anker
catches the quiet, thoughtful mood of a young scholar.

I want to see if it has by some luck survived. I only think of this. I do not think of my father's money or my mother's candle holder. All that matters is my watch.

In spite of the darkness, I easily find my way to the garden. Once more I am the bar mitzvah child. Here is the barn, the fence, the tree. Nothing has changed. To my left, the path to the Slotvino **Rabbi's** house. The Rabbi, though, had changed.

But I mustn't think of him, not now. The watch, I must think of the watch. Maybe it was saved. Let's see, three steps to the right. Stop. Two forward. I know the place. Automatically, I get ready to act out the scene I recall. I fall on my knees. What can I use to dig? There is a shovel in the barn. Its door is never locked. But by fumbling around in the dark, I risk stumbling and waking the people in the house. They would think I was a **looter,** a thief. They would hand me over to the police. They might even kill me. Never mind, I'll have to get along without a shovel or any other tool. I'll use my hands, my nails. But it is difficult. The ground is so hard and frozen. It is as if it did not want anyone to know its secret. Too bad, I'll punish it by being the stronger.

Emotionally, wildly, my hands claw the earth. I do not feel the cold. I do not feel tired. I do not feel pain. One scratch, then another. No matter. Continue. My nails inch ahead. My fingers dig in. I bear down. My every muscle shares in the task. Little by little the hole deepens. I must hurry. My head touches the ground. Almost. I break out in a cold sweat. I am soaked, dazed. Faster, faster. I shall rip the earth from end to end, but I must know. Nothing can stop or frighten me.

What time is it? How long have I been here? Five minutes, five hours? Twenty years. This night is timeless. I am digging for the watch. I am also digging to bring back the time that has passed. I was working to dig up not an object but time itself.

Suddenly a chill goes through me. A sharp feeling, like a bite. My fingers touch something hard.

The Rabbi did not live through the war.

The narrator builds suspense by telling readers he may be caught as a thief. He also builds suspense by wondering if the watch is still there.

The watch is now a symbol. What does it represent to the narrator?

It is metal and has four sides. So I have not been digging for nothing. The garden is spinning around me. I stand up to catch my breath. A moment later, I'm on my knees again. Carefully, gently I take the box from its tomb. Here it is, in the palm of my hand. I am holding the only remaining symbol of everything I have loved. A voice inside me says: "Don't open it. It contains nothing but emptiness. Throw it away and run." I cannot obey the warning. It is too late to turn back. I need to know, either way. A slight push of my thumb and the box opens. I hold back the cry rising in my throat. The watch is there. Quick, a match. And another. Briefly, I catch a glimpse of it. The pain is blinding. Could this thing, this object, be my gift, my pride? My past? It is covered with dirt and rust. It is crawling with worms. I sit there staring at it. I begin to feel deep pity. The watch, too, lived through the war and **Holocaust.** In its way, the watch is also a survivor. It also has old memories. Suddenly I feel the urge to carry it to my lips, dirty as it is. I want to kiss and comfort it with my tears.

I touch it. I stroke it. I feel thankful. The people I expected to live forever are gone. My teachers, my friends, my guides had all left me. Only this lifeless thing had survived. Its only purpose was to welcome me on my return and to give a final chapter to my childhood. I feel a need to tell it about myself. In turn I would listen to its story.

It is growing late. The eastern sky is turning a deep red. I must go. The people in the house will be waking. They will come down to the well for water. No time to lose. I stuff the watch into my pocket and cross the garden. I enter the courtyard. From under the porch a dog barks. Then he stops. The dog knows I am not a thief. I open the gate. Halfway down the street I feel a great deal of sadness. I have just committed my first theft.

I turn around. I go back through the courtyard and

The narrator explains why the watch means so much to him. How do you think it would feel to lose all the people you love?

the garden. Once again I kneel beneath the poplar tree. Holding my breath, my eyes refuse to cry. I place the watch back into its box and close the cover. My first gift once more finds safety deep inside the hole. Using both hands, I smoothly fill in the earth.

Breathless and with pounding heart, I reach the still empty street. I stop and ask myself about the meaning of what I have just done. I find I cannot explain it.

Looking back, I tell myself that probably I simply wanted to leave behind something to show that I had been there. One day, a child would play in the garden. The child would dig near a tree, and stumble upon a metal box. He would learn that his parents had taken what was not theirs. He would learn that Jews and Jewish children once lived in this town. The Jewish children were robbed of their future.

Talmud (TAHL-mood)
Hasidim (hah-SIHD-eem)

The sun was rising. I was still walking through the empty streets. For a moment I thought I heard the singing of schoolboys studying **Talmud.** I also thought I heard the prayers of **Hasidim** reading morning prayers in thirty-three places at once. Yet above all these chants, I heard clearly the tick-tock of the watch. The sound seemed far away. I had just buried it according to Jewish custom. It was, after all, the very first gift a Jewish child had once been given for his very first celebration.

Since that day, the town of my childhood has stopped being just another town. It has become the face of a watch.

Literature Practice

Answer these questions on a separate sheet of paper.

1. Why are the narrator and his family forced to leave their home?

2. Where does the narrator hide the watch?

3. How has the watch changed in twenty years?

4. What is the watch a symbol of?

5. What does the narrator learn about himself as he searches for the watch?

The Holocaust

The Holocaust took place between 1933 and 1945. Adolf Hitler was in power in Germany. Hitler hated many groups of people, especially Jews. In fact, in 1933 he made it a crime to be Jewish in Germany.

Thousands of German Jews left their homes and went to other countries. Jewish families that stayed in Germany had to go to concentration camps. Many people were separated from their families. All their belongings were taken away from them.

In the concentration camps, Jews suffered greatly. Many were forced to work long hours. Many others were starved.

In 1939 Hitler attacked Poland. This started World War II. Hitler's troops also took over other countries. As Germany began to lose the war, Hitler ordered Jews at the camps to be killed. Jewish men, women, and children were lined up and shot. Others were driven into huge rooms and then sprayed with poison gas. In all, about six million Jews died in the Holocaust. Some, like Elie Wiesel, survived the camps. Their survival reminds us of what happened.

▲ This painting by Emiliano Di Cavalcanti is called *Moca Pensando.*

Things I Forgot Today

a poem by Martha B. Malavansky

Words to Know

LITERARY TERM

concrete words words that describe things that the reader
can see, hear, feel, smell, or taste

SELECTION VOCABULARY

milky like milk in color or form

crackles makes a crisp snapping sound

---

*Sometimes we do the same things day after day without
thinking. The speaker in this poem tells about the different
kinds of things she and a friend chose to do one day. The
speaker understands that her friend did important things.
Maybe the speaker misses doing them herself.*

I sat across from her
She talked of little things
like the fox she had fed today
She said it had been around
for some time

"Did you see the stars tonight
I whistled to see
if they would dance
They were **milky**

Fox is a concrete word. What other concrete words can you find?

The quotation marks show that someone other than the speaker is talking.

▲ In this fine leaded and plated glass window, a woman appreciates the beauty of the rising sun.

"Did you hear the snow
It's so cold
that when you walk
it **crackles**"

I didn't see the stars
hear the snow
feed a fox
I fed my kids
washed dishes
typed reports
did my homework

My days are full
but let me write these in
fox feeding
star watching
and walking

The narrator realizes that her friend has done simple but important things. She makes a note to remind herself about simple pleasures.

Literature Practice

Answer these questions on a separate sheet of paper.

1. How does the speaker spend her day?

2. What does the other woman do when she sees the stars?

3. What does the speaker in the poem forget to do?

4. What do the other woman's choices tell about who she is?

Chapter Review

Summaries

- **The Story of Washing Horse Pond**—For three years the village of Boluo has been without rain. The people in the village suffer. Crops cannot grow. A young man named Akui decides to search for a hidden spring. He finds the magic source for the water. Akui chooses to give his life so that others may have water.

- **The Watch**—Elie Wiesel tells the true story of his return home after twenty years. He looks for a watch he buried in the backyard in 1944. The watch is a gift from his parents. On that night long ago, Wiesel and his family were forced to leave their home in Hungary. As he searches for the watch, Wiesel learns about himself and about what the watch means to him.

- **Things I Forgot Today**—The speaker in the poem tells about her full days. She feeds her kids, washes dishes, and does her homework. Her friend tells about what she did today. She fed a fox, watched the stars, and listened to the snow crackle. The speaker is reminded that it is also important to do simple things.

Chapter Quiz

Choose the letter of the correct answer. Rewrite the sentences on a separate sheet of paper.

1. Next to Washing Horse Pond stands
   a. the village of Boluo.   c. a large stone statue.
   b. a mountain peak.   d. a winged horse.

2. For three years the villagers of Boluo were without
   a. medicine.   c. firewood.
   b. money.   d. rain.

3. In "The Watch," the narrator returns to his home to look for
   a. his gold watch.   c. his father's money.
   b. his mother's candle holder.   d. his sister's toys.

4. In "Things I Forgot Today," the narrator forgets
   a. to feed her daughter.   c. her homework.
   b. simple pleasures.   d. to wash the dishes.

Thinking and Writing

Write answers to the following questions on a separate sheet of paper.

1. In "The Story of Washing Horse Pond," Akui gives his life so that other people may have water. What does Akui's choice tell you about the kind of person he is? Use examples from the story to explain your answer.

2. The narrator in "The Watch" chooses to put back the watch he had hidden twenty years before. Would you have kept the watch or put it back? Explain your answer.

3. What message do you think the poem "Things I Forgot Today" teaches about the choices we make? Explain your answer.

Unit Six Review

A. The following questions are about some of the selections you read in this unit. Answer each question by writing one or two sentences on a separate sheet of paper.

1. In the story "A Piece of String," what destroys Maître Hauchecome?

2. Why do the villagers in "Dead Men's Path" destroy the school grounds?

3. What lesson does Manka teach her husband?

4. In the poem "Things I Forgot Today," the speaker learns how important choices are each day of her life. How can small daily choices make our lives better?

5. In the essay "Young Hunger," why do you think the narrator changes her opinion of her godparents?

B. Choose two of the essay questions below. Answer them on a separate sheet of paper. Write one or two paragraphs for each one.

1. We make choices about the way we treat people. Explain how poor choices can hurt our relationships with other people. Use examples from the selections to support your answer.

2. Different events in our lives are important in making us who we are. Choose one of the selections in this unit. Explain how an important event changed the life of a main character.

3. We sometimes understand our relationships with others at a later time in our lives. Describe the way the narrator in "Young Hunger" feels about her godparents when she is eighteen years old and how her view changes when she is older.

Unit Seven

A DIFFERENT VIEW

Chapter 13 Imagine

▲ We can imagine a world of possibilities. Perhaps the symbols facing Itwesh in this Egyptian relief are some of the things he has imagined.

Chapter Learning Objectives

- Learn how repetition is used in poetry.
- Understand how dialogue gives clues about character.
- Learn to draw conclusions.
- Recognize simile.
- Learn about personification.
- Recognize analogy.

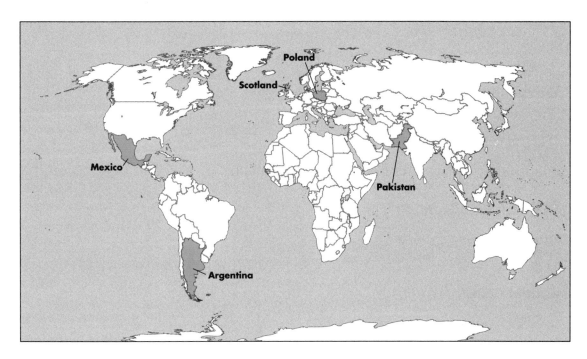

Mexico
from Homage to the Cookie Islands
a poem by Raúl Aceves

Pakistan
The Tiger and the Jackal
an adapted folktale retold by Ethel Johnston Phelps

Argentina
The Rebellion of the Magical Rabbits
an adapted story by Ariel Dorfman

Scotland
The Nose (after Gogol)
a poem by Iain Crichton Smith

Poland
The Bicycle
a poem by Jerzy Harasymowicz

Each of us sees the world in different ways. Sometimes what we see can lead us to imagine different things. In this chapter you are invited to share views different from what most people imagine. Among them, you will explore a strange land and bump into a walking nose.

from Homage to the Cookie Islands

a poem by Raúl Aceves

Words to Know

LITERARY TERM

repetition using a word or phrase more than once

SELECTION VOCABULARY

homage a show of respect

exist to be real

caramel smooth, soft candy

assured sure

lithograph a printed picture

The speaker in this poem thinks about his favorite food in a different way. The Cookie Islands may not be on any map. But the poet makes them seem very real.

————

The Cookie Islands are more real than geography because they are seen in the speaker's mind.

Marias are a popular type of Mexican cookie.

The Cookie Islands don't **exist** on any map.
How could they exist
    if they are more real than geography?

I would like to travel to the Cookie Islands
    to eat them with **caramel** sauce,
or better, to see if there
    really are three Marias and only one true sea.

▲ This early map of Western North America was drawn by
Cornelius de Jode in 1593.

I would go to sea if Maria were there
    and I would buy one box of islands
if I were **assured** it contained
    Marias on every island.
Of course, I would go to the Cookie Islands
even if I had to travel into a watercolor or
    lithograph

Poets use repetition to call attention to an idea. What words does the poet repeat in this poem?

Literature Practice

Answer these questions on a separate sheet of paper.

1. Why does the speaker want to travel to the Cookie Islands?

2. Why might the speaker have to travel into a piece of art to visit the Cookie Islands?

3. What does the speaker mean by saying the Cookie Islands are "more real than geography"?

4. Read the phrases and words the speaker of the poem repeats (*I would*, *if I*, *see*, and *sea*). What does the use of the repetitions tell you about the speaker?

The Tiger and the Jackal

an adapted folktale retold by Ethel Johnston Phelps

Words to Know

LITERARY TERM

dialogue the words spoken between two or more characters in a story

SELECTION VOCABULARY

thrashed waved wildly

turban a scarf wrapped around the head to form a kind of hat

slashed cut through

jackal a wild dog usually found in Africa or Asia

Imagine a world where animals talk not only to each other but to people. Such a place gives a different view of how people and animals would get along with one another. In this story a tiger and a jackal team up against a farmer and his wife. The tiger and the jackal soon discover that they are not as clever as they think.

There once was a farmer who went out with his oxen one morning to plow his field.

He had just finished plowing one row when a tiger walked up to him. The tiger said, "Good morning, friend. How are you today?"

"Good morning, sir. I am very well, sir," said the farmer. He was shaking with fear, but he thought it wise to be polite.

"I see you have two fine oxen," said the tiger. "I am very hungry. Take off their yokes at once, please. I plan to eat them."

Notice how polite the tiger and the farmer are to each other. The tiger goes along with the farmer's plan.

The farmer's courage returned to him. Now he knew the tiger did not plan to eat him. Still, he did not want to give up his oxen for the tiger's meal.

"My friend," said the farmer, "I need these oxen to plow my field. Surely a brave tiger like you can hunt for a good meal elsewhere."

"Never mind that!" said the tiger angrily. "Take the yokes off the oxen. I will be ready to eat them in a

This is a carved tiger head from China. ▼

moment." The tiger began to sharpen his teeth and claws on a stone.

"The oxen are very tough and will be hard to eat," pleaded the farmer. "My wife has a fat young milk cow at home. Spare my oxen, and I'll bring you the cow."

The tiger agreed to this. He thought a tender young cow would make a much easier meal for him than tough oxen. So he said, "Very well. I will wait here in the field while you go home and get the cow. But bring the cow back as quickly as you can. I'm very hungry."

The farmer took the oxen and went sadly to his home.

"Why do you come home so early in the day?" asked his wife. "It is not time for dinner!"

"A tiger came into the field and wanted to eat the oxen," said the farmer. "But I told him he could have the cow instead. Now I must bring him the cow."

"What!" she cried. "You would save your old oxen and give him my beautiful cow? Where will our children get milk? How can I cook our food without butter?"

"We'll have no food at all unless I plow the field for my crops," said the farmer angrily. "Now untie the cow for me."

"No, I will not give up my cow to the tiger!" said his wife. "Surely, you can think of a better way to get rid of the tiger!"

"No, I cannot. He is sitting in my field waiting for me, and he's very hungry."

His wife thought a moment. Then she said, "Go back to the tiger and tell him your wife is bringing the cow. Leave the rest to me."

The farmer did not like to go back to the tiger without the cow. But he had no better idea, so he walked slowly back to the field.

"Where is the cow?" roared the tiger angrily.

The dialogue gives you clues about the husband and wife as characters.

"My wife will bring the cow very soon," said the farmer.

At this, the tiger began to prowl about. He growled and **thrashed** his tail. The poor farmer's knees shook in terror.

Why do you think the wife dresses up as a man?

In the meantime, his wife dressed herself in her husband's best clothes. She tied a **turban** very high on her head to make her look very tall. She took a long knife from the kitchen and put it into her belt. Then she put a saddle on their pony and rode off to the field.

As she drew near, she called out to her husband in a loud voice. "My good man, are there any tigers about? I've been hunting tigers for two days, and I'm hungry for tiger meat!" She **slashed** the air above her head with the knife in a very threatening way.

The farmer was so surprised he could not answer.

"Aha!" cried his wife. "Is that a tiger I see hiding in the grass? I ate three tigers for breakfast the other day. Now I'm hungry for more!" She started to ride toward the tiger.

These words frightened the tiger. He turned and bolted into the forest. He ran so fast he knocked over a jackal. The **jackal** had been sitting and waiting to feast on the oxen's bones when the tiger had finished his meal.

"Why are you running away?" called the jackal.

"Run! Run for your life!" cried the tiger. "There is a terribly fierce horseman back in the field! He thinks nothing of eating three tigers for breakfast."

"That was no horseman," laughed the jackal. "That was only the farmer's wife dressed up as a hunter."

The tiger came back slowly. "Are you sure?"

Notice how the dialogue helps you learn more about the tiger and the jackal.

"Did the sun get in your eyes? Didn't you see her hair hanging down from the turban?" asked the jackal impatiently.

The tiger was still not sure. "He looked like a hunter, and he swung that big knife as if he were going to kill me!"

"Don't give up your meal so easily," cried the brave jackal. "Go back to the field. I will follow and wait in the grass."

The tiger did not like that idea at all. "I think you want me to be killed!"

"No, of course not," said the jackal. He was hungry and eager for a meal. "If you like, we will go together, side by side."

The tiger was still not sure of the jackal's purpose. "You may run away and leave me after we get there."

"We can tie our tails together," said the jackal. "Then I can't run away."

The tiger thought this a good idea. So they tied their tails together in a strong knot. Then they set off together for the field.

The tiger does not seem to trust the jackal. Find clues in the dialogue that show this is true.

In this scene by an unknown Indian artist, animals and people are living side by side. The tiger and the jackal appear to be talking to one another just as they do in the story. ▼

The farmer and his wife were still in the field. They were laughing over the trick she had played on the tiger. Suddenly they saw the tiger and the jackal trotting toward them with their tails tied together.

The farmer shouted to his wife, "Now the tiger has a jackal with him. Come away! Hurry!"

The wife said no, she would not. She waited until the tiger and the jackal were near. Then she called out, "Dear Mr. Jackal, how very kind of you to bring me such a nice fat tiger to eat. After I eat my fill, you can have the bones."

When the tiger heard this, he became wild with terror. He forgot the jackal, and he forgot the knot in their tails. He leaped for the tall grass. Then off he ran, dragging the jackal behind him over the stones and through thorn bushes.

The jackal howled and cried for the tiger to stop. But the howls behind him only scared the tiger more. He ran on until they both dropped in a heap. They were more dead than alive.

As for the farmer, he was very proud of his wife's clever trick. The tiger never came back to their field again.

The ending suggests that the tiger believed the wife. Why do you think he did not believe the jackal?

Literature Practice

Answer these questions on a separate sheet of paper.

1. What is the main problem the farmer has to solve?

2. What do you learn about the farmer's wife from the dialogue?

3. How did the jackal convince the tiger to go back into the field?

4. The tiger never returns to the farmer's field. Why do you think he stayed away?

The Rebellion of the Magical Rabbits

an adapted story by Ariel Dorfman

Words to Know

LITERARY TERM

drawing conclusions forming an opinion about what a story
means based on information from the story

SELECTION VOCABULARY

existed could be found anywhere

adviser someone who gives
information to or guides
someone else

traitor someone who works against
his or her own government

darkroom a place where film is
turned into pictures

---

*Imagine being told that what you see is not really there.
When King Wolf takes over the land of the rabbits, he
declares his way of seeing the world as the only way to
see things. His message is that rabbits do not exist.
The rabbits, however, have an important message of their
own to deliver.*

Now that the wolves have taken over the land of the rabbits, there is a new King. How does he feel about the rabbits?

When the wolves took over the land of the rabbits, the leader of the pack declared himself King. Then he said that the rabbits no longer **existed**. It would now be against the law to even say their name.

To be on the safe side, the new Wolf King went over every book. With a big black pencil, he crossed out every word about rabbits. He also tore out every picture of a cottontail. He did not stop until he felt sure that no trace of his enemies was left.

But an old gray fox, the Wolf's **adviser**, brought bad news.

"The birds, Your Wolfiness, keep saying that they have seen some . . . some of those creatures."

"So how come I don't see anything from way up here, on my throne?" asked the Wolf.

"In times like these," answered the fox, "people must see to believe."

"Seeing is believing? Bring me that monkey who takes photos, the one who lives nearby. I'll teach those birds a lesson."

The monkey looked at his wife and daughter. "What can the Wolf of all Wolves want with me?" he asked.

The monkey's daughter had an answer. "He must want you to take a picture of the rabbits, Dad."

"Quiet, quiet," said her mother. "Rabbits don't exist."

But the monkey's daughter knew that rabbits did exist. True, the rabbits no longer came to visit her as they had before. She had not seen them since the wolves had taken over. But in her dreams she still heard their voices singing nearby. When she awoke, there was always a small gift beside her bed.

What creatures have the birds seen?

How things are seen is important in this story. The Wolf King feels people will believe he is King if they see him as the King in pictures.

This is an ancient work from Algeria. The artist is unknown. ▼

Different names are used for the Wolf. Think about why he might have these names.

The monkey wants his daughter to know that she can only see what the King says everyone must see. No one can question the King.

"That's why I sleep well," said the little girl. "That's why that General Wolf must need the photo. Then he can sleep well. You'll bring me a picture of the rabbits, won't you, Dad?"

The monkey felt fear crawl up and down his fur. "Send this little girl to her room," he told his wife. "Keep her there until she understands that we just don't talk about certain things."

The King of the Wolves was not in the best of moods when the monkey came in. He said to the monkey, "You're late. I'm in a hurry. I need a picture of each important act in my life. All my acts, let me tell you, are of the greatest importance. Can you guess what we're going to do with those pictures? You can't? We're going to put one on every street, inside every bush, in every home."

The monkey was shaking so hard that no words came out.

The Wolf King said, "Now the birds will think twice before talking any nonsense about rabbits. Understand?"

The monkey understood very well. His shaking paw immediately clicked the button of the camera. He had taken the first picture.

"Go," roared the Wolf, "and develop it. I want it on every wall in the kingdom."

The monkey returned some minutes later. He did not dare enter the throne room. Instead, he asked one of the soldiers to call the Wolf's adviser, the fox. Without a word, the monkey passed the fox the picture he had just taken.

The fox blinked once. Then he blinked again. In a corner of the photo there was something. It was not the strong, fierce figure of the King. In the corner was the beginning of an ear.

The ear in the photo made the fox angry. What kind of an ear is it?

"You blind monkey!" said the fox. "How come you didn't notice that this . . . this thing was there? Can't you aim that camera of yours?"

"If it could get into the picture," the monkey

answered, "it was because you and your guards let it get close."

"It won't happen again," the adviser promised. "Rub out that . . . ear before His Wolfiness finds out."

From his bag, the monkey took out a special liquid. He used it to remove anything that might bother his customers. The annoying ear began to disappear.

The King of Wolves was pleased with the picture. He ordered it sent all over the kingdom. Two hours later he went on a tour of his kingdom. He wanted to make sure that not a single window was without his picture. "Not bad," he said, "but this photo is already getting old. People should see my latest deeds. Take another. Quick. Show me scaring these pigeons—right away. Bring it to me immediately. You took too long last time."

But the monkey wasn't able to obey this time either. Once again he had the adviser called secretly.

"Again?" asked the fox. "It happened again?"

Except that now it was worse than before. A whole corner of the new picture was filled with the face of a rabbit winking an eye.

"We've got to do a better job of guarding the King," muttered the fox. "Meanwhile, rub that out."

"Wonderful," shouted King Wolf when finally he was given the picture. "Look at the frightened faces of the pigeons trying to escape. I want a million copies. I want them on milk cartons and on the coupons inside cereals. Onward. Onward. Let's go and smash up a dam. Come on, monkey. Fame awaits us both."

The beavers had been working summer and winter for three years. They were building a beautiful dam to get water to a distant valley.

The Wolf of Wolves climbed a tree. "I want you to shoot the exact moment when my feet crash into the middle of the dam. If you miss the shot, next time I'll fall on top of you. Then I'll have to get myself another photographer. Are you ready?"

The King is proud and determined to prove he is the best King. Now the author shows you another side of him. What is it?

What do the rabbits'
positions in the pictures
tell you about how they
feel toward the Wolf
King?

Not only was the monkey ready, but so was the
adviser. The fox was breathing down the old monkey's
back. He was staring over his shoulder, watching,
listening. Nothing could escape those alert eyes.

So neither the monkey nor the fox could believe it
when they saw the picture. There at the bottom was a
rabbit resting on his side as if he were relaxing at a
picnic. Next to him, another rabbit had raised her paw
and was boldly thumbing her nose.

"They are everywhere," said the fox. "Let me tell
you, our lives are in danger."

"Let's start rubbing them off," the monkey said
wearily.

His Wolfhood the King yelped with pleasure when
he saw the picture. There was not a single shadow of a
rabbit.

"Send it out!" he shouted. Then the King said,
"What are we going to do now for some fun?"

"We could rest," the monkey suggested. His paws
were peeling from the strong fluid he used on the
pictures.

The Wolf looked at him as if he were a stone. The
Wolf said, "Who asked you for an opinion? I'm in
charge here. That's why I was born with these teeth.
We'll go on until there's no more light."

In each new photo, there were more and more
rabbits. The King Wolf did many terrible things. He
destroyed sugar mills. He shook squirrels out of their
trees and hid their nuts. He stripped ducks of their
feathers. As the King became more frightful, his
pictures changed. More rabbits of every color danced
around the edges of the photographs.

The King's pictures are
changing. As his acts
become worse, the
rabbits appear more
often.

The pictures the monkey took were beginning to
look strange. There were blank spaces everywhere.
The monkey knew that the only solution was to get his
Wolfiness to sit up high on a raised throne. Rabbits live
underground. They wouldn't be able to wiggle their
way into the frame of the photograph.

The next morning the monkey and the fox rushed to see the new throne. The King's seat was now set high on top of four huge wooden legs.

"I want two shots," His Wolfhood demanded. "One will be of me approaching my throne. The other will be of me sitting on it, enjoying the fresh air."

This time, when the photos were developed, there was not so much as a sign of a rabbit.

"Didn't I tell you? Didn't I tell you the rabbits don't exist?" the adviser asked the monkey. He was thrilled. "It was just a matter of your aiming the camera properly."

Artist Michelle Puleo calls this painting *Fox*. In the story, a fox is a special adviser to King Wolf.▼

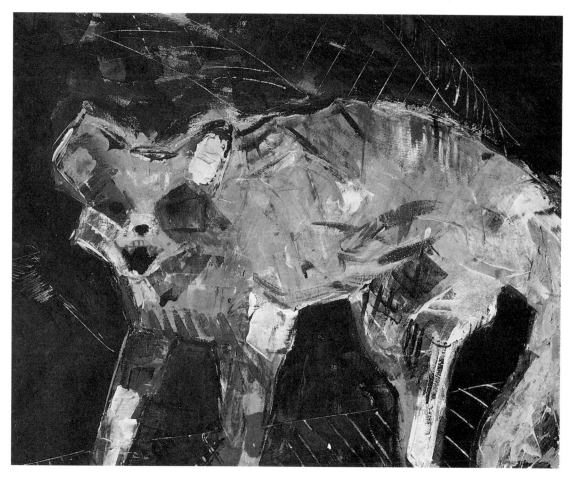

Cameras give pictures of what is really seen. The monkey did aim the camera properly. The rabbits do exist.

The white spots are places where liquid covers up pictures of rabbits.

The rabbits have reappeared on the King's photos. The monkey's daughter is happy.

For the next few days, there were no more unpleasant surprises. The Wolf of Wolves felt happy. He let his officers run things while he posed for pictures. He was pictured giving commands, making speeches, and signing laws. He looked over the shots carefully. "Congratulations," he said to the monkey. "You're being more careful. I don't see any more of the white spots that spoiled my first pictures."

But one morning, the monkey was awakened by his daughter's voice. "They're back, Dad," she whispered in his ears. "Those pictures you took sure are magical."

In one set of photos, there was a small army of rabbits at the foot of the towering throne.

The adviser was waiting. The monkey could see he was upset.

"How many this time?" the monkey asked.

"The photos are being taken care of," the fox said grimly. "But the birds have got wind of what happened. Now they're telling everyone that those . . . those awful animals exist. His Wolfiness said if those birds didn't keep quiet, he would make them disappear."

But the adviser had another idea. The Wolf of All Wolves should make a recording of one of his latest speeches. Then he should tie it around the necks of the birds. They would have to carry not only the photos, but also the King's words, all over the kingdom. Nobody would be able to hear any of their songs.

"Hearing is believing," blared His Wolfiness.

The old monkey's life had become more than he could stand. In every picture, there was a rabbit part. Sometimes it was a curious nose. Sometimes it was a pair of furry ears. There were even pictures with white whiskers.

The monkey felt dizzy.

Then one night, very late, the old monkey was awakened by an angry shake. It was the adviser with fierce soldiers at his side. The King Wolf had sent for him.

The Wolfiest of Wolves was waiting for the old monkey. The King Wolf was sitting on his throne. Around each leg of the throne, hundreds of guards kept watch.

"Monkey, you are a **traitor**," thundered the King. "Your pictures are being used by people who say that rabbits are plotting against me. I hear they are planning this very night to overthrow me. Tonight, you are going to take another picture. If a single rabbit shows its nose, I will make you eat the picture. Then I'll eat you and not only you, but your wife and your daughter. Now. Take that picture."

The monkey stood behind his camera. He aimed it at the throne. He let out a moan. Up until then, the rabbits appeared only when the picture was developed. Now the rabbits were directly in front of the camera. They chewed away at King Wolf's throne. They also chewed the swords of the guards.

The rabbits chew the legs of the throne. What do you think will happen to King Wolf?

"What's the matter?" bellowed the King Wolf. He did not look down. He wanted his picture to be perfect.

The monkey moved the camera nearer to the throne. He hoped that this way the rabbits would not show up in the picture. The rabbits moved faster than he did. They scrambled up the legs of the throne.

"Hurry up!" ordered the Wolf of Wolves.

The monkey closed his eyes very tightly. It was better not to see what was going to happen. The very moment he clicked the camera, he heard a very loud noise. He knew what he was going to see when he opened his eyes. Still he could not believe it. Like an old tree rotten to the core, the throne came crashing to the ground. With it came the King of Wolves. The monkey blinked. There at his feet lay the Biggest, Baddest, the Most Bragging Wolf in the World. His ribs were broken. His black fur was torn by the fall. His yellow eyes were red. He was wailing in pain.

The King's throne is compared to a rotten tree. The roots of his power are as rotten as the roots of the old tree.

"Monkey," squeaked the would-be Wolferor of the World. "This picture . . . you have my approval not to show it."

At that moment, all the lights in the palace went out. The monkey grabbed his camera and his bag. Clutching them to his chest like a treasure, he fled.

His daughter was waiting for him at the door of the house.

"Wait," he said to her. "Wait. I've brought you something. Without another word, he raced into his **darkroom** to develop the last picture.

When he came out a few minutes later, his daughter and wife were standing on chairs. They were taking down the pictures of the Wolf King.

"Here," the old monkey said to his daughter. "Here, this is the picture you've been asking for all this time. I've finally brought you your present."

"Thanks, Dad," the little girl said. "But I don't need it anymore."

She pointed around the room. She pointed toward the street and across the fields. There the sun was beginning to rise. The world was full of rabbits.

The monkey's wife and daughter take down the pictures of the King. Why have they decided to do this now?

Literature Practice

Answer these questions on a separate sheet of paper.

1. How does the Wolf King show he is very important?

2. The King wants to believe that rabbits do not exist. How do the monkey and the fox help him believe this?

3. What clues in the story show that the rabbits want to upset the King?

4. What conclusions can you draw about the kind of ruler the king is?

A Few Famous Rabbits

In "The Rebellion of the Magical Rabbits," we learn that the world of the story is full of rabbits. Actually, the real world is also full of rabbits. Rabbits live in North America, South America, Europe, Africa, and Australia.

As a symbol, the rabbit is usually said to bring good luck and long life. But in reality, rabbits are not appreciated. They destroy plant life.

In stories, rabbits are popular. Some are even famous. Here are some you may already know about.

Rabbit is a friend of the bear Winnie-the-Pooh. Rabbit is a quiet, friendly, hardworking bunny who grows wonderful carrot gardens.

Among some Native American nations, rabbits represent the beginning of life. Manabozho is honored in Algonquin legend for creating life and the earth.

Peter Rabbit is the famous rabbit from "The Tales of Peter Rabbit." He always manages to get into trouble. Flopsy, Mopsy, and Cottontail are his three sisters.

Zomo is the hero of many Nigerian folktales. This rabbit is usually a trickster figure, which means that he does things to outsmart larger and stronger animals.

The Nose (after Gogol)

a poem by Iain Crichton Smith

Words to Know

LITERARY TERMS

personification giving human characteristics to non-living things

simile a comparison of two things using *like* or *as*

SELECTION VOCABULARY

flower to become as good as possible; to reach full growth

scents nice smells

bowling rolling quickly

staggered moved unsteadily

Follow the travels of a nose that decides it needs a life of its own.

———⊗⊗⊗———

Gogol was Nikolai (NIH-koh-leye) Gogol, a Russian writer. In 1836 he wrote a story called "The Nose." In it, a nose leaves its owner and behaves like a person.

The nose went away by itself
in the early morning
while its owner was asleep.
It walked along the road
sniffing at everything.

It thought: I have a personality of my own.
Why should I be attached to a body?
I haven't been allowed to **flower.**
So much of me has been wasted.

▲ This is a limestone sculpture of the head of Hera. The nose has been destroyed. In the poem, the nose itself decides to leave the face of its owner.

And it felt wholly free.
It almost began to dance
The world was so full of **scents**
it had had no time to notice,

when it was attached to a face
weeping, being blown,
catching all sorts of germs
and changing color.

But now it was quite at ease
bowling merrily along
like a hoop or a wheel,
a factory packed with scent.

And all would have been well
but that, round about evening,
having no eyes for guides,
it **staggered** into the path
of a mouth, and it was gobbled
rapidly like a sausage
and chewed by great sour teeth–
and that was how it died.

The mouth gobbles the nose rapidly. How does the simile "like a sausage" add to the picture in your mind?

Literature Practice

Answer these questions on a separate sheet of paper.

1. How is the nose like a person?

2. What does the nose discover in its travels?

3. What is one simile that the writer used? Name the items being compared.

4. What happens when the nose meets the mouth?

The Bicycle

a poem by Jerzy Harasymowicz

Words to Know

LITERARY TERM

analogy a comparison between two things that are very different

SELECTION VOCABULARY

romps active play

glade an open area in the woods

buck male goat

poacher a person who hunts illegally

trophy something taken in hunting to show one's success

In this poem a bicycle is able to see and think like a person. Left alone by tourists, it decides to join a herd of mountain goats. In a short time, the bicycle begins to see the world from a goat's point of view.

once
forgotten by tourists
a bicycle joined
a herd
of mountain goats

with its splendidly turned
silver horns
it became
their leader

with its bell
it warned them
of danger

With silver horns, a bicycle looks like a goat. As you continue to read, notice the ways the bike acts like a goat.

▲ This is a detail from a batik sarong from Idonesia.
Bicycles, fans, old-fashioned record players, and umbrellas
cover the sarong.

with them
it partook
in **romps**
on the snow covered
glade

the bicycle
gazed from above
on people walking;
with the goats

it fought
over a goat,
with a bearded **buck**

it reared up at eagles
enraged
on its back wheel

it was happy
though it never
nibbled at grass

There are some things
that goats do that a bike
cannot do. What are
they?

or drank
from a stream
until once
a **poacher**
shot it

tempted
by the silver **trophy**
of its horns

and then
above the Tatras was seen
against the sparkling
January sky

The Tatras are mountains
in Eastern Europe.

the angel of death erect
slowly
riding to heaven
holding the bicycle's
dead horns.

▲ This sculpture by an unknown artist is called *Stone Ram in Kong Woods*.

Literature Practice

Answer these questions on a separate sheet of paper.

1. What does the bicycle do when it is forgotten by the tourists?

2. How does the bicycle use its bell?

3. How does the bicycle die?

4. In the poem, the poet draws an analogy between the bicycle and a goat. In what ways is the bike like a goat?

From Boneshakers to Bicycles

Before 1900, few people rode bicycles. The early bikes were uncomfortable and even dangerous. They had wooden wheels and gave very rough rides. Not surprisingly, early ones were called "boneshakers."

Then, bicycles were improved. In 1888 an Englishman named Dunlop introduced air-filled rubber tires. The rubber tires made the ride smoother. Bicycles became very popular. Millions of people all over the world bought them. In 1895, 20 million bicycles were sold. Bicycles had become a huge fad.

People began to worry. They thought bicycles would ruin the country. Store owners feared no one would shop. People might spend all their money on bicycles. Schoolteachers thought people would stop reading. Theater owners said no one would come to see their plays. Everyone would be riding a bicycle. Doctors reported that bicycles might cause strange diseases.

Of course, none of this happened. The world was not ruined because of bicycles. By 1910 the bicycle fad ended. Everyone was talking about a new machine. The car had arrived.

Chapter Review

Summaries

- **Homage to the Cookie Islands**—The Cookie Islands are not on any map. The speaker wants to eat and explore them. The speaker would travel great distances to visit these islands.

- **The Tiger and the Jackal**—A tiger wants to eat a farmer's oxen. The tiger agrees to eat a cow instead. The farmer's wife plans a way to scare off the tiger. A jackal explains the wife's trick to the tiger. The jackal and the tiger try to outsmart the farmer and his wife. The plan doesn't work.

- **The Rebellion of the Magical Rabbits**—When wolves conquer the land of the rabbits, the Wolf King decides that rabbits no longer exist. The King hires a monkey to take pictures of all that the King does. That way, everyone will see just what the King wants them to see. One day, the throne collapses. Rabbits have chewed its legs. The King falls and loses his power. The rabbits return.

- **The Nose (after Gogol)**—A nose leaves its owner. When it was attached to its owner's face, it caught colds. Now it can travel. It has no eyes, though, and it walks in front of a mouth. The mouth eats it up.

- **The Bicycle**—A bicycle joins a herd of wild goats. The bicycle becomes the leader. It acts like the goats. It is happy. One day a hunter shoots it. The angel of death rides the bicycle to heaven.

Chapter Quiz

Choose the letter of the correct answer. Rewrite the sentences on a separate sheet of paper.

1. To reach the Cookie Islands, the speaker in "Homage to the Cookie Islands" might have to
   a. study geography.
   b. eat caramel sauce.
   c. travel into a watercolor.
   d. buy three boxes of islands.

2. In "The Tiger and the Jackal," the farmer wants to give his wife's cow to the tiger because he
   a. does not need the cow.
   b. thinks he should be polite.
   c. will buy a new cow.
   d. wants to get rid of the tiger.

3. The Wolf King in "The Rebellion of the Magical Rabbits" wants everyone to believe
   a. his adviser is wise.
   b. he is a great leader.
   c. the birds are important.
   d. that rabbits are everywhere.

4. The nose in the poem "The Nose" leaves its owner and
   a. begins to weep.
   b. goes to sleep.
   c. chews a sausage.
   d. enjoys being free.

5. In "The Bicycle," the bicycle's horns
   a. scare off eagles.
   b. tempt a poacher.
   c. scare the goats.
   d. are lost in the Tatras.

Thinking and Writing

Answer the following questions on a separate sheet of paper.

1. Why would someone want to pay respect to an imaginary place like the Cookie Islands? Include examples from your own experience about the things you respect.

2. What do you learn about the tiger and the jackal from dialogue? Give examples from the story to support your answer.

▲ It is difficult to believe that something is not about to happen in Henri Rousseau's *The Sleeping Gypsy*. The dark night and bright moon add to the feeling of suspense.

Chapter Learning Objectives

- Understand foreshadowing.
- Identify the narrator of a story.
- Learn about making predictions.
- Recognize the mood of a poem.
- Learn about first-person point of view.

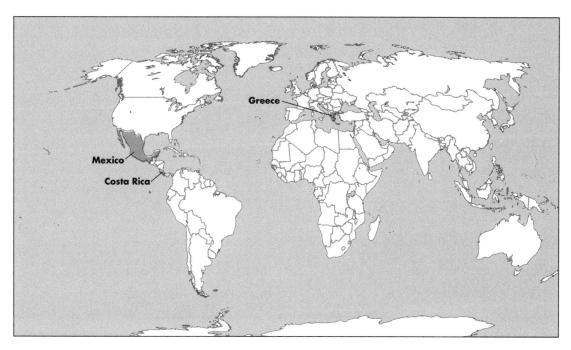

Costa Rica
The Cegua
an adapted folktale retold by Robert D. San Souci

Greece
The Cyclops
adapted from The Odyssey *by Homer*

Mexico
The Street
a poem by Octavio Paz

The thrill of watching a horror movie is the single, scary moment before something happens. As frightened as you may be, you are anxious to know what will happen next. Suspense in stories and poems leaves you feeling the same way. Writers create suspense in different ways. In the next chapter, experience different views of ghosts, the unknown, and a monster.

The Cegua

an adapted folktale retold by Robert D. San Souci

Words to Know

LITERARY TERMS

foreshadowing clues that suggest what will happen later in the story

mood the feeling a story or poem gives the reader

SELECTION VOCABULARY

sulfur an element that has a bad smell when it burns

mantilla a scarf worn over a woman's head and shoulders

faint so soft it is hard to hear

hacienda a big ranch

Sometimes, readers feel suspense more than the characters do. In this folktale, a young man laughs at a warning. He thinks the stories about a terrible creature are nonsense. Then he rides out alone one dark night.

One evening, a young man rode his horse out of San José, the capital of Costa Rica. He was on his way to visit his friend's ranch. His friend lived in a lonely area. The young man wasn't sure which road to take to get there.

The young man stopped at a *cantina*. He wanted to get something cool to drink and ask directions.

The owner of the cantina brought him a glass of lemonade. He told the young man he still had a long way to ride. The owner said, "You should stay here

A *cantina* is a place to eat and drink.

tonight. I can give you a room for a few pesos. No one rides on these roads after dark."

The young man shook his head. He said, "I have to reach my friend's ranch tonight."

The owner shook his head. He said, "Only a fool would risk meeting the *Cegua*."

The young man said, "The Cegua! What kind of creature is that?"

The owner smiled. He said, "*Señor*, don't people in San José know what the Cegua is? It is very scary!"

The young man said, "I've never heard of such a thing. Bring me another lemonade, and please tell me what you know about this Cegua."

The owner brought him another lemonade and sat down. He said, "The Cegua will make you lose your mind. Even strong, healthy men have gone mad from the sight of it. Some have even died of fear."

The young man said, "If the Cegua is such a terrible thing, why haven't I heard of it before?"

The owner said, "It likes certain parts of the country. We have the bad luck to be one of those places. For that reason, no one here rides alone after dark. If someone must travel at night, he always goes with a friend."

The young man laughed. He said, "Why? Doesn't the Cegua like crowds?"

The owner said, "The Cegua only appears to someone traveling alone. It appears as a beautiful young woman. It smiles sadly and begs for a ride. But oh, if you stop to help it! That will be the end of you."

The young man said, "Why? What does it do?"

The owner said, "When the rider looks at it, the beautiful young woman is gone. The creature riding with him has a huge horse's head with long fangs. Its eyes burn red, like hot coals. Its breath stinks of **sulfur.** It will hiss, then bury its claws in the rider's shoulder. The horse knows something terrible is on his back.

The *peso* is the basic unit of money in Mexico and in several Central and South American countries.

Cegua (SEG-wuh)

Señor means "Mister" in Spanish.

The cantina owner's story hints at something that will happen later. This clue also helps to build suspense.

Two important things happen at this point. The reader is given more clues about the Cegua, and the suspense is increased.

He will dash off like a wild thing. No one will be able to stop him."

The young man said, "Then what happens?"

The owner said, "Sometimes we never see them again. Sometimes we find them dead the next day. If they are alive, they have gone mad from the sight of the Cegua."

The young man said, "Nonsense," and stood up. He tossed a few coins on the table to pay for the lemonade. He said, "I must leave now. I want to reach my friend's ranch tonight."

The owner shrugged his shoulders. He took the coins and turned away. He thought to himself, "You can't argue with a fool."

The young man untied his horse from the hitching post. The owner of the cantina had showed him which road to take.

The night was warm. The only sound was the *clop-clop* of the horse's hoofs on the stones in the road.

The young man rode around a bend. Suddenly, he saw someone standing in the shadows.

The suspense increases as you wait to see if the young woman is really the Cegua.

The young man slowed his horse. He saw a beautiful young woman with a pale face. She wore a black lace **mantilla.** In the moonlight, he could see that she had curly black hair, dark eyes, and deep red lips.

The young woman said, "Señor, I am very tired. But I must go to see my mother. She is sick. Would you take me to *Bagaces*?" Her voice was sweet, but she sounded tired and weak. The young man was afraid that she might faint.

Bagaces (bah-GAH-sehs)

The young man climbed down from his horse. He took off his hat and bowed. He said, "Of course, I will take you. My friend's ranch is close to Bagaces. You can spend the night there. In the morning I will take you the rest of the way."

The young woman said, "You are very kind, señor." Her voice was a **faint** whisper. The young man had to lean close to hear her.

▲ A figure on horseback covers the inside of a Navajo bowl.

The young man helped her onto the horse. Then he got on in front of her. They took off at a good speed.

The moon and stars made the land look silver. The young man tried to talk to the beautiful young woman, but she didn't answer. She leaned her head against his back. She held on to his shoulders. The young man thought she must be afraid that she might faint and fall from the horse.

Suddenly, the horse started going faster. The young woman dug her fingers into the young man's back. The young man thought she must be afraid of falling. He was too polite to tell the young woman that her nails were digging into his skin.

Then the young man felt sharp teeth on his neck. Only the collar of his coat saved his skin. He heard an awful cry. No human voice could make such a sound.

The young man wrapped the reins around one of his hands. With the other hand, he tried to get her fingers off his shoulder. In the moonlight, he saw that her fingers were too white to be skin. They were bone.

He heard another awful cry. He smelled the creature's terrible breath. It smelled like sulfur. The fingers on his shoulders seemed to grow stronger. Her jaws snapped again at his neck. This time, there was blood.

Then he could see his friend's ranch up ahead. He thought he heard dogs barking. Lights were on in the **hacienda.** People were running up the road toward him. They carried torches.

There was a great scream from the creature. It pulled him backward. The horse reared up on its back legs. Then it fell. The young man and the creature fell, too.

The young man was knocked out. When he opened his eyes, his friend was staring at him. The friend asked if he was all right. The young man nodded. He was still shaking. He touched the back of his neck. It was bloody.

Here is an example of foreshadowing. Why do you think the horse moved faster?

The young man sees his friend's ranch ahead. Will he ever arrive there? There would be less suspense if you knew.

▲ This painting of a young woman is *Spanish Dancer Wearing a Lace Mantilla* by Mary Cassatt.

He looked around. All he saw were friendly faces, looking at him. One man was holding his horse.

The young man asked his friend, "Where is it? Where is the creature?"

His friend said, "What creature?"

The young man said, "The Cegua."

His friend laughed. He said, "I think you are very tired from your trip. The Cegua is a story to scare children. That's all. Still, you should not ride alone at night. These lonely roads can be dangerous in the dark."

The young man said nothing. The night breeze brought the smell of sulfur to his nose. It made him shiver just a little.

Literature Practice

Answer these questions on a separate sheet of paper.

1. What is the Cegua?

2. Why do you think the young man ignores the warning he gets from the cantina owner?

3. Why does the Cegua look like a young woman in need of help at first?

4. What early clues do you have about what will happen in the story?

5. What do the young man's friends think of his story?

The Cyclops

adapted from The Odyssey *by Homer*

Words to Know

LITERARY TERMS

narrator a person who tells the story

making predictions using what you know and what you
    have read to tell what might happen next in a story

SELECTION VOCABULARY

woes terrible problems or suffering

fierce violent

savage dangerous and wild

kids young goats

fuddled confused

---

*You can feel the suspense when a character describes a
scary event from the past. As this story begins, Odysseus
says that he had many troubles on his voyage home. With
this hint at what will happen later, the story's suspense
starts to build.*

I am Odysseus, son of Laertes. The whole world talks
of my skill in battle, and my fame has reached the
heavens. My home is under the clear skies of Ithaca.
Let me tell you now of our voyage as we came home
from Troy. It was a terrible voyage, for the gods sent
me many **woes.**

First, the wind brought me to the land of the
Cicones. My men and I fought the Cicones in the city

Odysseus (oh-DIH-SOOS),
son of Laertes (lay-ER-
teez), is the narrator .

Cicones (si-KOH-nes)

of Ismarus. We killed the men in battle. Then we divided up the wealth. Each of my men got his share. I said we must escape right away. But my men wanted to stay. Meanwhile, the people of the city sent for help from their neighbors. More Cicones came to fight. Many of my men were killed. We sailed away from Ismarus with heavy hearts. We were sad for the loss of our dear friends, but glad of our own escape.

We set sail for home, but the winds blew us off course. For nine days I was chased across the seas by those winds. But on the tenth day, we reached the country of the Lotus-eaters. This is the race of people who eat the flowery Lotus fruit. I sent two men to find out what kind of people the Lotus-eaters were. The Lotus-eaters gave them lotus to taste. Once the men had eaten the lotus, they had no wish to come back to the ship. All they wanted was to stay with the Lotus-eaters, eat the lotus fruit, and forget all thoughts of coming home. I had to use force to bring them back to the ships. I ordered my men to leave the land of the Lotus-eaters as fast as they could.

We sailed on with heavy hearts. We came to an island where there were a great number of wild goats. We took our bows and long spears from the ships and began shooting at the goats. Then we sat down to a fine meal. As we sat, we looked across the water to the nearby island of the Cyclops. The people on the island of the Cyclops are **fierce**. They have no laws. They never lift a hand to plant or plow food. They just leave everything to the gods.

The next morning, I set out for the island of the Cyclops. When we arrived, I took twelve of my best men with me. The rest stayed to guard the ship.

As I set out, I took some food and filled a goatskin with sparkling water. The water had a special potion that would make a man or beast drowsy. I had to be prepared. I had a feeling we would find ourselves face to face with some **savage** being of great strength.

Once again, Odysseus and his men sail away "with heavy hearts." How do you predict they will leave the next place on their journey?

We came to the cave of a Cyclops, but he was away with his goats and sheep. We went inside and looked in amazement at everything. There were baskets of cheeses, pails and bowls for milking, and many lambs and **kids.**

My men begged me to take some of the cheeses and the lambs and kids back to the ship and sail away. It would have been better if I had agreed. But I wished to see the owner of the cave. I hoped to receive some friendly gifts from him.

At last the Cyclops came with his flocks of sheep and goats. He carried a huge bundle of wood and threw it down with a great crash. We were so

The Cyclops (sy-klahps) is a monster in Greek myths. It has a single eye in the middle of its forehead.

This is a detail of the *Blinding of the Cyclops* as it appears on a Greek jar from the 6th century. ▼

frightened we ran to the back of the cave. The Cyclops picked up a huge stone and closed the entrance to the cave. Then he began to milk his sheep and goats. When he had finished, he lit the fire and saw us.

In a booming voice, he said, "Strangers! Are you traders or pirates?"

The voice and the sight of the monster filled us with panic. But I managed to answer him. I said, "We are on our way back from Troy. We hope to be your guests, good sir. Remember, it is your duty to the gods, especially Zeus. He is the friend of guests."

The Cyclops said, "Stranger, you must be a fool. We Cyclops care nothing for Zeus or the rest of the blessed gods. We are much stronger than they are."

The cruel monster jumped up. He reached out to my men and snatched a couple. He dashed their heads against the floor as though they had been puppies. Then he tore them to pieces and ate them. We watched, weeping. We lifted our hands to Zeus in horror at the terrible sight.

When he finished his meal, he lay down to sleep. At first, I thought I would gather my courage and stab him with my sword. But then we would be trapped inside the cave. The door was impossible to move. So with sighs and groans we waited for the blessed light of day.

As soon as Dawn appeared, the Cyclops milked his ewes and goats. Then he snatched up a couple of my men for his meal. When he had eaten, he drove his sheep and goats out of the cave. I watched him go, with murder in my heart. I tried to think of how to pay him back. The best plan I could think of was this.

In the pen, the Cyclops had a huge staff of green olive-wood. I told my men to smooth it down. I sharpened it to a point. Then I hardened it in the fire and hid it under some loose rocks.

Evening came, and with it came the Cyclops. He drove in his flocks and closed the great stone door.

In Greek mythology, Zeus (ZOOS) rules all of the gods.

The monster's horrible actions add to the suspense. You wonder what will happen to Odysseus and the other men.

Can you predict what Odysseus plans to do?

After he milked his sheep and goats, he snatched up two more of my men and ate them.

I went up to him with the sparkling water I had brought in the goatskin. I said, "Here, Cyclops, I brought you a cool drink. I hope you will take pity on me and help me on my way home."

The Cyclops took the sparkling water and drank it up. The delicious drink gave him such pleasure that he said, "Give me more, please, and tell me your name."

I handed the Cyclops another bowl of the sparkling water. Three times I filled the bowl for him. Three times the fool drank every bit. When the special potion had **fuddled** his wits, I said, "I'll tell you my name. In return, give me the gift you promised me. My name is Nobody."

The Cyclops said, "I will eat Nobody last. This shall be your gift."

As soon as he had spoken, the Cyclops fell over. I went at once and put the olive-wood pole in the fire to make it hot. My men gathered around me. A god now gave them great courage. Taking the pole, we drove the sharp end into the Cyclops' eye.

The Cyclops gave a terrible shriek. He pulled the pole from his eye and threw it away from him. He shouted for other Cyclopes to come. The Cyclops' neighbors gathered outside the cave. They said, "What on earth is wrong with you, Polyphemus? Is somebody trying to kill you?"

Polyphemus said, "O my friends, it is Nobody."

The neighbors said, "If Nobody is hurting you, you must be sick. All you can do is pray to your father Poseidon."

The neighbors went away. Polyphemus moaned in pain. He pushed away the stone from the doorway and stretched out his arms. He was hoping to catch us as we slipped out of the cave. He must have thought I was a fool!

Remember what Odysseus said about the special potion. What will happen when the Cyclops drinks the water?

Odysseus tells the Cyclops that his name is Nobody. This creates suspense as you wonder how Nobody will fit into the escape plan.

Polyphemus (PAH-lee-fee-MUHS) is the name of the Cyclops.

Poseidon (puh-SEYE-duhn) is the Greek god of the sea.

▲ The Island of the Cyclops is near large mountains. These are *Point of Rocks at Port-Goulphar* by Claude Monet.

Meanwhile, I was trying to hit on some way to save us. I thought up plan after plan. This was the plan that finally seemed best. I wove together willow twigs from the Cyclops' bed. With these, I tied groups of three rams together. Under the chest of each middle ram, we tied one man. For myself, I chose one big ram who was the pick of the whole flock.

When Dawn came, the goats and rams ran out of the cave. The Cyclops ran his hands along the backs of each animal as it passed him. But the idiot never noticed my men were tied under the chests of his own rams.

When we were all a little distance from the cave, I untied my men. We drove Polyphemus' flock of goats and sheep onto our ship. The men took their places at the oars and began to row.

Before we had gone very far, I shouted out to Polyphemus, "Your crimes have caught up with you! Now Zeus and the other gods have paid you!"

The Cyclops was in a rage. He tore the top from a great rock and threw it at us. The rock fell just ahead of our ship. The water rose up in a great swell and drove us back toward the beach. My crew rowed as fast as they could. We escaped once more.

My men tried to hold me back, but my temper was up. I shouted once more to the Cyclops: "It was I who put your eye out, Cyclops! I am Odysseus, the son of Laertes!"

The Cyclops gave a groan. He cried, "Alas! A great prophet warned me that a man called Odysseus would rob me of my sight." The Cyclops lifted his hands to the starry heavens. He said, "Hear me, Poseidon. If I am your son, let Odysseus never reach his home. Or if he does, let him come late, in terrible woe. Let him find trouble in his home."

Once again the Cyclops picked up a huge boulder and threw it. But this one made a wave that carried us farther away. We reached the island, where the rest of

Even though the Cyclops is wounded, the suspense is still building because the men still have to escape.

The suspense reaches its greatest point when the fleeing men are pushed back toward the shore.

How might the Cyclops' parting words foreshadow the rest of Odysseus' voyage home?

my men and ships were waiting. We unloaded the Cyclops' flock and divided it among us.

As soon as Dawn appeared the next day, we set sail once more. We were sad for the dear friends we had lost, but glad at our own escape from death.

Literature Practice

Answer these questions on a separate sheet of paper.

1. What is the Cyclops?

2. What danger do Odysseus and his men find in the cave of the Cyclops?

3. What plan does Odysseus create to hurt the Cyclops?

4. How do Odysseus and his men escape from the cave?

5. What early clues do you have about what will happen in the story?

An Unhappy Odyssey

Battling a man-eating, one-eyed monster was just the beginning for Odysseus and his crew. "The Cyclops" comes from a long, ancient Greek poem called *The Odyssey*. The poet Homer tells of the incredible challenges that Odysseus must face. Here are just some of them:

Bad Winds. Odysseus receives a bag that holds winds that would keep his ships from reaching home. With the bad winds in the bag, Odysseus sails directly home. But when his curious crew opens the bag, the winds escape and blow the ships far from home again.

Giants. A race of giants throw huge stones at the ships. Only one ship survives the attack.

A Crew of Pigs. A woman turns the crew into pigs. Luckily, Odysseus is spared. He convinces the woman to turn the crew back into men.

Sea Monsters. The ships must sail through a narrow stretch of water where two monsters live. One monster has twelve feet, six heads, and sharp teeth. It sits on a rock and threatens travelers. The other monster swallows the sea and spits it back out.

Angry Gods. Just when it seems that the men will make it home, the crew steals cattle from the sun god. As punishment, a thunderbolt hits the ships. Only Odysseus survives.

The Street

a poem by Octavio Paz

Words to Know

LITERARY TERM

first-person point of view the use of the words *I, me,* and *my,* to tell
a story

SELECTION VOCABULARY

stumble trip   **pursue** chase after

Long and *silent* are
some words that set
the mood of the poem.
Can you find any others?

A long and silent street.
I walk in blackness and I **stumble** and fall
and rise, and I walk blind, my feet
stepping on silent stones and dry leaves.
Someone behind me also stepping on stones, leaves;
if I slow down, he slows;
if I run, he runs. I turn: nobody.
Everything dark and doorless.
Turning and turning among these corners
which lead forever to the street

The speaker says the
same street appears at
every corner. What do you
think is really happening?

where nobody waits for, nobody follows me,
where I **pursue** a man who stumbles
and rising and says when he sees me: nobody

◀ This painting of an empty street in *Village in Bolivia* is by Lino Eneas Spilimbergo.

Literature Practice

Answer these questions on a separate sheet of paper.

1. The speaker is a character in the poem. How can you tell?

2. What are some of the speaker's actions?

3. What is the street like? Give details from the poem.

4. How does the poet describe what the speaker feels? Explain your answer.

Chapter Review

Summaries

- **The Cegua**—Although warned about traveling after dark, a young man ignores the advice. He does not believe the tale about the Cegua, a terrible creature who attacks travelers. While going to his friend's ranch, the young man meets a woman. He allows her to travel with him. The woman turns into the Cegua. The young man manages to rid himself of the horrible creature. When he arrives at the ranch, his friend does not believe his story.

- **The Cyclops**—On their voyage home from Troy, Odysseus and his men reach the island of the Cyclops. They get trapped inside the cave of the Cyclops, a fierce monster. Odysseus thinks of an escape plan. He gives the Cyclops a special potion. Then Odysseus and his men blind him with a sharp pole. They escape by hiding beneath rams that are tied together. The blinded Cyclops chases them, but they reach their ship and sail away.

- **The Street**—The speaker is on a long, dark street. Frightened, he thinks he hears someone behind him. He feels the person stopping and moving at the same time he does. But he sees no one.

Chapter Quiz

Choose the letter of the correct answer. Rewrite the sentences on a separate sheet of paper.

1. In "The Cegua," the young man
   a. travels with a friend.
   b. travels to another country.
   c. laughs at the story.
   d. owns a ranch.

2. The young man's friend, the rancher, said the Cegua was
   a. a danger to travelers.
   b. a helpless woman.
   c. someone he met in town.
   d. only a scary story.

3. The Cyclops falls down because
   a. he trips over Odysseus.
   c. the rams trip him.
   b. a special potion makes him drowsy.
   d. he cannot see.

4. Odysseus and his men escape the cave by
   a. asking Polyphemus' neighbors for help.
   c. tying themselves underneath the rams.
   b. drinking a special potion that makes them invisible.
   d. sailing away.

5. The mood of "The Street" shows that the speaker is
   a. talking to a stranger.
   c. worried and nervous.
   b. waiting for someone.
   d. happy and relaxed.

Thinking and Writing

Answer the following questions on a separate sheet of paper.

1. In "The Cegua," the young man's friend says the story is used to scare children. Why do you think the cantina owner tells the young man about the Cegua?

2. In "The Cyclops," Odysseus creates two plans to escape the monster. How does the way he tells about each plan help to create suspense?

3. The speaker in "The Street" is very frightened. Do you think his experience is real or imagined? Explain your answer.

Unit Seven Review

A. The following questions are about some of the selections you read in this unit. Answer each question by writing one or two sentences on a separate sheet of paper.

1. In "The Tiger and the Jackal," how does the wife show she is smarter than the tiger?

2. Why does the monkey in "The Rebellion of the Magical Rabbits" try to obey the King's wishes?

3. In "The Bicycle," the poet shows the ways in which a bicycle and a goat are the same. In what ways are the bike and the goat not the same? Give examples from the poem to support your answer.

4. What details at the end of the story suggest that the Cegua was real to the young man?

5. "The Cyclops" begins with Odysseus' stories about the Cicones and the Lotus-eaters. How do these details foreshadow what happens with the Cyclops?

B. Choose two of the essay questions below. Answer them on a separate sheet of paper. Write one or two paragraphs for each one.

1. Sometimes we decide it is time to change how we see things. We would like to experience the world in a new way. What new experiences change the view of the world for some of the characters in the poems and stories in this unit?

2. In "The Rebellion of the Magical Rabbits," the King Wolf wants everyone to see the world as he believes it should be seen. How do the pictures the monkey takes of King Wolf show a real view of the world?

3. In "The Cegua" and "The Cyclops," suspense builds as the characters struggle against frightening creatures. Which tale did you find more suspenseful? Use details from the story to support your answer.

Appendix

* In this index, you will find selections grouped according to the author's place of birth or the country from which a story comes. Each map shows one of the continents of the world. Each country appears in the continent where it is located.

GLOSSARY

adviser someone who gives information to or guides someone else

alms money given to help the poor

ancestor a person who lived long ago and is related to someone living many, many years later

ancestors the family or group a person comes from

Anglo-Indian English and Indian

anvil an iron block where hot pieces of metal are hammered into shape

appetite desire for food

apprentice a person who works for an experienced worker to learn a skill

armor a covering that protects a fighter in a battle

ashamed feeling guilty or sorry for something done wrong

assured sure

baboon a large monkey

bait something, usually food, that attracts animals to a trap

bamboo a kind of tropical grass that has hollow woody stems

bar mitzvah a ceremony celebrating the beginning of adulthood for a thirteen-year-old Jewish boy

befriended made friends with

bellows a hand-operated machine that creates a current of air so a fire will burn

blade a single stem of grass

bleats the cries of a goat, sheep, or calf

bounds moves forward quickly with leaps and jumps

bowling rolling quickly

brambles prickly bushes

brigade a group of people organized for a specific purpose

brim the top edge of a jar or container

brow forehead

buck male goat

bulwarks strong supports

captured caught

caramel smooth, soft candy

career the work a person chooses to do in life

cast off sent or driven away

cemetery a place for burying the dead

challenged called to a fight or contest

chuckling quietly laughing

civil service having to do with the part of the government that deals with employment

civilized educated or refined

clatter a sharp noise

clever smart and quick

clumsiness awkwardness

cocked turned to one side

collapsing caving in or falling down

collide crash or bump into

composed calm, peaceful

cottage a small house in the country

cowardly lacking courage

crackles makes a crisp snapping sound

crossbow a weapon like a bow and arrow that was used by people long ago

crumple fold or wrinkle

cubbyhole a small shelf or cupboard, often used to store things

culture the customs and beliefs of a group of people

custom a usual way of acting

cypress a kind of evergreen tree or shrub

darkroom a place where film is turned into pictures

dazzling bright

dedicated devoted

dense thick or crowded

despair sadness

discolored stained, spoiled in color

dishonest untruthful

dowry money or belongings that a woman brings to a marriage

drought a long time without rain

embroidery detailed needlework on cloth

Eskimos people native to the Arctic coastal areas of North America

exhausted very tired

exhibit show of art work

exist to be real

existed could be found anywhere

explanations answers

failings faults or weaknesses

faint so soft it is hard to hear

felled cut down

feud a long quarrel between families

fierce violent

firmness solid manner

flesh the soft parts of an animal's body that are covered with skin

flexible easy to bend

flit to move about with quick motions

flouncing moving in big, jerking motions

flower to become as good as possible; to reach full growth

forbid to order not to do something

fragrance a sweet or pleasing smell

fuddled confused

furiously fiercely, angrily

furrier someone who makes and sells clothing made out of furs

Gaelic a language once widely spoken in Ireland and Scotland

game wild animals hunted for sport or for food

gauze a thin, see-through cloth used for bandages

gazelle a small, fast antelope

generations the time between the birth of parents and the birth of their children

glade an open area in the woods

glittered sparkled or shined

glorious wonderful

gnawed chewed

goblet a drinking glass

godparents people who sponsor, or agree to be partly responsible for, a child at its baptism

gourds fruits that have thick skins or rinds

gradually slowly

grieve to feel or show great sadness

groaned made a deep, sad sound

grudge a strong, continuing feeling of hatred or ill will against someone

guarded cautious or watchful

gulp a large swallow

gushed flowed or poured out quickly

hacienda a big ranch

harness the leather straps and metal pieces used to attach a horse to a plow

harvest time of year when ripe crops are gathered

Hasidim a group of Jewish people who follow strict teachings of Judaism

headmaster school principal

headmistress school principal

helmet a strong hat that protects the head

hesitate to pause

hesitated stopped for a moment

hobble to walk with a limp

Holocaust the killing of European Jews and others by the Nazis during World War II

homage a show of respect

homespun loosely woven home-made cloth

hospitable friendly and generous

houseboy a boy or man hired to do housework

huddled crowded close together

humbly with meek or modest feeling

immortal living forever

inactive not active

innocent free of guilt

innocence being free of guilt

insult something said that hurts someone's feelings

intense extreme in strength or size

interwoven woven together

intruder a person who doesn't belong in a certain place

invaders people who take over other people or places

jackal a wild dog usually found in Africa or Asia

judgment decision

kids young goats

languid weak or without energy

lantern a covering for a light

lashed moved or waved suddenly and violently

lawsuit a disagreement brought to court

lever a rod or bar used to lift things

lithograph a printed picture

loaf to pass the time doing little or nothing

lodger a person who rents a room

loom a machine on which cloth is woven

looter someone who steals openly

lucid clear

mangled cut and bruised

mansion large house

mantilla a scarf worn over a woman's head and shoulders

manure animal waste

mare a female horse

marketplace a public square where goods are bought and sold

meddle to step into another person's business

messenger person who carries news or other information

milky like milk in color or form

ministers people who help the king run the country

mischief action that bothers or annoys others

misery great pain, suffering

misplaced wrongly placed

nobility high social class

nugget a small lump of gold

numb without feeling, as from cold

oaths promises that one will speak the truth

ooze soft mud at the edge of a body of water

ordinariness the state of being common

outcast a person whom other people do not accept

overjoyed very happy and satisfied

overtook caught up with and passed, as in a race

pagan not religious

panting breathing rapidly in short gasps

parched very dry

peat a dirt-like substance that is dug up, dried, and burned as fuel

peddler a person who sells things

perched sat or rested on something

perished died

pillars tall columns

poacher a person who hunts illegally

porter a person who carries things for other people

possibility chance

priceless of great worth

proper correct

proposed offered marriage to someone

pumice a type of rock, sometimes used to scrub away dead skin

pursue chase after

quarrel an argument

rabbi the leader of a Jewish house of worship

rabble a noisy crowd of people that is hard to control

rays arms

reassure to make a person feel confident

rebel a person who is against the ruling government

reef a ridge of coral in the sea

reel a spool attached to a fishing rod on which the fishing line is wound

relics objects that have been left behind, usually by a culture or group of people

remains stays behind

resembles looks like

reserves extra supplies

respects has a high opinion of

romps active play

routines regular ways or patterns of doing things

sacrificed given unselfishly

sacrifices offerings of valued objects

satin a smooth, shiny material

savage dangerous and wild

scaly covered with scales

scarcely just barely, hardly

scents nice smells

scolded told someone angrily what he or she did wrong

scuffed scratched or scraped

scuttling running in a hurry

serene calm and peaceful

severed separated, broken apart

Shabbat the period from Friday evening to Saturday evening, a time of rest and worship for Jews

shabby worn out

shattered broke into many pieces

shelter a place to live

shimmering shining

shrine a place where people pay respect to a god

shriveled wrinkled, often from being in water

shuttle a card or spool that moves thread back and forth to weave cloth

slashed cut through

slay to kill

slender thin

slimy slippery, wet, and smooth

slithering sliding smoothly, like a snake

snarling growling angrily with the teeth showing

sneer an expression that shows dislike

sneering raising one corner of the upper lip in an unpleasant way

solemnly seriously

solid strong, not thin or skinny

sorrow great sadness

soy a salty brown sauce made from soybeans

splendor grandness

spring a source of water

sprouted took root, began to grow

spumed foamed or frothed

squabbled quarreled noisily over a small matter

squadron a group of military people

staggered moved unsteadily

stale not fresh; tasteless

steppe a large area of dry, flat, grass-covered land

stingy unwilling to spend money

stranded forced onto the shore

stubborn firm

stumble trip

sulfur an element that has a bad smell when it burns

superior as if of greater importance or value

swiftest fastest

Talmud a collection of ancient writings that form the basis of Judaism

tantrum a display of bad temper or anger

thatched covered with straw or grass

thrashed waved wildly

threepennybits coins used in Great Britain

thrifty not wasteful, economical

thrive grow

Torah a book that contains Jewish law and literature

torso trunk

traitor someone who works against his or her own government

treadle a pedal pushed by the foot to operate a machine

tripod a stand with three legs

trophy something taken in hunting to show one's success

turban a scarf wrapped around the head to form a kind of hat

tusk a long, curving tooth that usually grows in pairs and sticks out of the sides of the mouth of an elephant

twilight faint light after sunset

udders baglike parts of a cow or goat that hold milk

veranda a large, open porch

vibrant full of energy

wallaby a small kangaroo

warehouse a place where food or other products are stored before they are taken to stores or markets

waterchestnuts water-loving plants found in Asia and Africa

wearily in a tired way

weariness tiredness

whirlpool fast-moving water from the sea that turns in a circle

whitewash a mixture that is used like paint to make something white

whitewashed painted white

wince to draw back in pain or distress

withered dried up, shriveled

witness a person who sees or hears something

woes terrible problems or suffering

worthy having value or honor

wretch a very unhappy person

HANDBOOK OF LITERARY TERMS

alliteration the repeating of consonant sounds that begin words

analogy a comparison between two things that are very different

autobiography a story of a person's life written by the person

character clues thoughts, actions, and words in a story that help the reader find out what a character is like

chronological order the order in which events happen

climax the most exciting part of a story that comes near the end

clues about character thoughts, actions, and words in a story that help the reader find out what a character is like

concrete words words that describe things that the reader can see, hear, feel, smell, or taste

conflict a fight or battle between two or more characters; the problem that needs to be solved in a story

description words that create a clear picture of a person, place, or thing

descriptive details details of how something looks, feels, smells, or tastes

dialogue the words spoken between two or more characters in a story

drawing conclusions forming an opinion about what a story means based on information from the story

essay a brief piece of writing that develops a single idea

fable a very short story, usually with animal characters, that teaches a lesson

first-person point of view the use of the words *I*, *me*, and *my*, to tell a story

flashback a scene or story that takes place before the main events of the larger story

folktale a story handed down for many years among the people of a community or region

foreshadowing clues that suggest what will happen later in the story

free verse poetry that is without regular rhyme or meter

hero the main character in a story

image word or phrase that helps the reader to experience how something looks, sounds, tastes, or feels

imagery words that help the reader to "see" how something looks, sounds, feels, or tastes

internal conflict the struggle a character has in making a difficult decision

irony of situation an event that is not expected

main character the central figure in a story

making predictions using what you know and what you have read to tell what might happen next in a story

memoir a true story about events that an author has lived through

metaphor a way of comparing two unlike things

mood the feeling a story or poem gives the reader

myth a story from the past that explains how things began

narrator a person who tells the story

nonfiction a story that is about real places, people, and events

personification giving human characteristics to nonliving things

plot the action or series of events in a story

repetition using a word or phrase more than once

resolution the point at which the conflict in a story ends

rhyme the repetition of sounds in the words of a poem; words that sound alike

setting the time and place in which a story occurs

simile a comparison of two things using *like* or *as*

speaker the character who speaks in a poem

stanza a group of lines in poetry

story-within-a-story one story within another story; a character from the outer story tells the inner story to another character

surprise ending an ending of a story that is not expected

symbol a thing that stands for itself and something else

theme the main idea of a story or poem

third-person point of view someone other than a character is telling the story or poem

tone the feeling the author shows toward the subject of the story

Index of Authors and Titles

Acknowledgments

Grateful acknowlegment is given to authors, publishers, and agents for permission to reprint the following copyrighted material. Every effort has been made to determine copyright owners. In the case of any omissions, the Publisher will be pleased to make suitable acknowlegments in future editions.

Unit 1

"Arachne," from *Greek Myths.* Copyright © 1949, renewed 1977 by Olivia E. Coolidge. Reprinted by permission of Houghton Mifflin Co. All rights reserved.

"Lather and Nothing Else" by Hernando Téllez. Reprinted by permission from *Americas*, a bimonthly magazine published by the General Secretariat of the Organization of American States in English and Spanish.

Fred Bigjim. "The Bering Coast," from *Raven Tells Stories: An Anthology of Alaskan Native Writing.* Edited by Joseph Bruchac. Copyright © 1991 by Fred Bigjim. Reprinted by permission of The Greenfield Review Press.

"The Golden Touch," from *Favorite Greek Myths* retold by Mary Pope Osborne. Copyright © 1989 by Mary Pope Osborne. Reprinted by permission of Schoastic, Inc.

"The Fly," from *The Toad is the Emperor's Uncle* by Mai Vo-Dinh. Doubleday, 1970. Reprinted by permsion of the author.

"By Any Other Name," from *Gifts of Passage* by Santha Rama Rau. Copyright © 1951 by Vasanthi Rama Rau Bowers. Copyright renewed. Reprinted by permission of Harper-Collins Publishers, Inc. "By Any Other Name" originally appeared in *The New Yorker*.

"The Small Cabin," *from Procedures for Underground, Selected Poems* 1965-1975. Copyright © 1976 by Margaret Atwood. Reprinted by permission of Houghton Mifflin & Company. All rights reserved.

"The Small Cabin," from *Selected Poems* 1966-1984 by Margaret Atwood. Copyright © Margaret Atwood 1990. Reprinted by permission of Oxford University Press, Canada.

Unit 2

"The Mountain of the Men and the Mountain of the Women," a Cambodian folktale told by Touch Neak, translated by Samol Tan and retold by Alice Lucas. © San Francisco Study Center. Reprinted by permission.

"The Endless Steppe," Copyright © 1968 by Esther Hautzig. Used by permission of HarperCollins Publishers. The excerpt is a condensed and revised version of the author's text.

"My Brilliant Career," by Miles Franklin from *I'm On My Way Running: Women Speaking on Coming of Age.* Copyright © 1983 Avon Books.

"Unanana and the Elephant," from *African Myths and Legends* by Kathleen Arnott. Copyright © 1962. Reprinted by permission of Oxford University Press.

Unit 3

Four Japanese Haiku. Translated from the Japanese by Harold G. Henderson and David Ray

"Zlateh the Goat," from *Zlateh the Goat and*

Other Stories by Isaac Bashevis Singer. Text copyright © 1966 by Isaac Bashevis Singer. Reprinted by permission of HarperCollins Publishers, Inc.

E. E. Cummings. 'maggie and milly and molly and may," copyright © 1956, 1984, 1991 by the Trustees for the E. E. Cummings Trust, from *Complete Poems: 1904-1962* by E. E. Cummings, edited by George J. Firmage. Reprinted by permission of Liveright Publishing Corporation.

"The Earthworm," by Harry Martinson reprinted from *Friends You Drank Some Darkness: Three Swedish Poets*, chosen and translated by Robert Bly. Beacon Press, 1975. Copyright 1975 by Robert Bly. Reprinted with his permission.

"Green Creek," excerpt from *Laughing Lost in the Mountains: Poems by Wang Wei* translated by Tony Barnstone, Willis Barnstone, and Xu Haxin © 1991 by permission of University Press of New England.

"The Cedar Chest," from *The Tree is Older Than You Are* by Naomi Shihab Nye. Translation by Judith Infante. Reprinted by permission of Judith Infante.

Unit 4

"How Odin Lost His Eye," from *Adventures with the Giants* by Catharine F. Sellew. Copyright © 1950 by Catharine F. Sellew; copyright © renewed 1978 by Catharine F. Sellew. By permission of Little Brown and Company.

"The Good Brother's Reward," from *Tales of a Korean Grandmother* by Frances Carpenter.

Copyright © 1973 by permission of Charles E. Tuttle., Co., Inc.

"The Rat Trap," by Selma Lagerlöf, translated from the Swedish by Florence and NaBoth Medin.

"The Friends of Kwan Ming," reprinted with the permission of Simon & Schuster Books for Young Readers, an imprint of Simon & Schuster Children's Publishing Division from *Tales From Gold Mountain* by Paul Yee. Text copyright © 1989 by Paul Yee and Simon Ng. A Groundwood Book/Douglas & McIntyre.

Unit 5

"Manners" from *The Complete Poems 1927-1979* by Elizabeth Bishop. Copyright © 1979, 1983 by Alice Helen Methfessel. Reprinted by Farrar, Strauss & Giroux, Inc.

Excerpts from *Anne Frank Remembered: The Story of the Woman Who Helped to Hide the Frank Family.* Reprinted with permission of Simon & Schuster from *Anne Frank Remembered* by Miep Gies with Alison Leslie Gold. Copyright © 1987 by Miep Gies and Leslie Gold.

"The Trout." Copyright by Devin-Adair, Publishers, Inc., Old Greenwich, Connecticut, 06870. Permission granted to reprint "The Trout" by Sean O'Faolain. All rights reserved.

Le Ly Hayslip. Excerpt from the book *When Heaven and Earth Changed Places*. Copyright © 1989 by Le Ly Hayslip and Charles Jay Wurts. Used by permission of Doubleday, a division of Bantam Doubleday Dell Publishing Group, Inc.

"Aunt Julia," from *Collected Poems* by Norman MacCaig. Reprinted by permission of The Estate of Norman MacCaig and Chatto & Windus.

Unit 6

"Clever Manka," from *The Shoemaker's Apron: A Second Book of Czechoslovakian Fairy Tales*, copyright © 1920 by Parker Filmore and renewed 1948 by Louise Filmore. Reprinted by permission of Harcourt Brace & Company.

"A Piece of String," from *The Best Short Stories of Guy de Maupassant*. Copyright © 1968. Reprinted by permission of Airmont Publishing Company, Inc.

"Dead Men's Path," from *Girls at War and Other Stories* by Chinua Achebe. Copyright © 1972, 1973 by Chinua Achebe. Used by permission of Doubleday, a division of Bantam Doubleday Dell Publishing Group, Inc., and Harold Ober Associates, Inc.

"Young Hunger," from the book *As They Were* by M.F.K. Fisher. Copyright © 1982 by M.F.K. Fisher. Reprinted by permission of Alfred A. Knopf, Inc.

"The Story of Washing Horse Pond," from *The Spring of Butterflies and Other Folktales of China's Minority Peoples*, translated into English by He Liyi. Copyright © 1985 by William Collins Sons & Co., Ltd. Used by permission of Lothrop, Lee & Shepard Books, a division of William Morrow & Company, Inc., and HarperCollins Publishers, Ltd.

"The Watch," from *One Generation After* by Elie Wiesel. Copyright © 1965, 1967, 1970 by Elie Wiesel. Reprinted by permission of Random House, Inc.

"Things I Forgot Today," from *Raven Tells Stories: An Anthology of Alaskan Native Writing*, edited by Joseph Bruchac. Copyright 1991. The Greenfield Press. Reprinted by permission of the publisher.

Unit 7

"Homage to the Cookie Island," by Raúl Aceves. Translated by Christopher Johnson.

"The Tiger and the Jackal," from *The Maid of the North: Feminist Folk Tales from Around the World*, edited by Ethel Johnston Phelps, © 1981 by Ethel Johnston Phelps. Reprinted by permission of Henry Holt & Co., Inc.

"The Rebellion of the Magical Rabbits," copyright © 1986 by Ariel Dorfman, reprinted by permission of The Wylie Agency, Inc.

" The Nose," by Iain Crichton Smith from *Love Poems and Elegies*. Reprinted by permission of Victor Gollancz, btd.

"The Bicycle," by Jerzy Harasymowicz, translated by Edmund Ordon from *San Francisco Review Annual #1*. Reprinted by permission of *San Francisco Review*.

"The Cegua," from *Short and Shivery: Thirty Chilling Tales* by Robert D. San Souci. Illustrated by Katherine Coville. Copyright © 1978 by Robert D. San Souci. Illustrations © 1987 by Doubleday, a division of Bantam Doubleday Dell Publishing Group, Inc. Used by permission of Bantam Doubleday Dell Books for Young Readers.

"The Street," by Octavio Paz from *Selected Poems of Octavio Paz*, copyright 1966. Reprinted by permission of the Indiana University Press.

Index of Fine Art

Fine Art and Photo Credits

p. 129:	Foto Marburg, Art Resource
p. 132:	Christie's Images
p. 136:	Alfred W. Jenkins, The Brooklyn Museum
p. 138:	Christie's Images
p. 142:	Art Resource
p. 144:	Superstock
p. 148:	Courtesy of the American Museum of Natural History
p. 154:	Art Resource
p. 158:	The Granger Collection
p. 160:	The Granger Collection
p. 164:	Purchase, The Brooklyn Museum
p. 168:	Gift of Dr. and Mrs. Stanley Wallace, The Brooklyn Museum
p. 171:	Christie's Images
p. 175:	Giraudon, Art Resource
p. 178:	Superstock
p. 181:	Corbis-Bettman
p. 185:	Art Resource
p. 190:	Christie's Images/Superstock
p. 192:	Giraudon, Art Resource
p. 194:	Corbis-Bettmann
p. 195:	Corbis-Bettmann
p. 196:	Corbis-Bettmann
p. 197:	Corbis-Bettmann
p. 201:	Scala, Art Resource
p. 204:	Culver Pictures
p. 207:	Art Resource
p. 210:	Art Resource
p. 216:	Corbis-Bettmann
p. 219:	Christie's Images
p. 233:	Anne Frank Foundation
p. 235:	Christie's Images
p. 241:	Christie's Images
p. 243:	Christie's Images
p. 248:	James Joern
p. 251:	Christie's Images
p. 252:	Christie's Images
p. 256:	Christie's/Superstock

Index of Maps

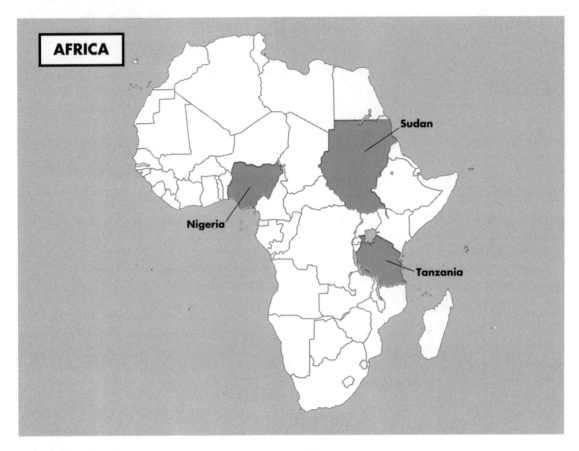

AFRICA

Sudan

Nigeria

Tanzania

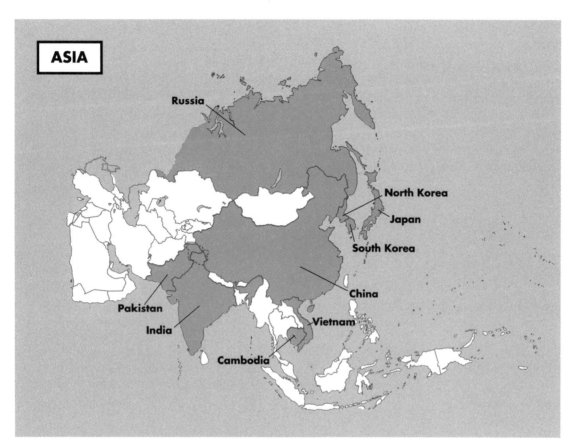

ASIA *(continued)*

Japan
Four Haiku
haiku by Bashō, Jōsō, Chiyo, and Skiki

Korea
The Good Brother's Reward
an adapted folktale retold by Frances Carpenter

Pakistan
The Tiger and the Jackal
an adapted folktale retold by Ethel Johnston Phelps

Russia*
The Old Grandfather and His Little Grandson
an adapted story by Leo Tolstoy

Vietnam
The Fly
an adapted story by Mai Vo-Dinh

When Heaven and Earth Changed Places
adapted from the autobiography of Le Ly Hayslip

*Russia is the biggest country in the world. Part of it is in Europe and part of it is in Asia.

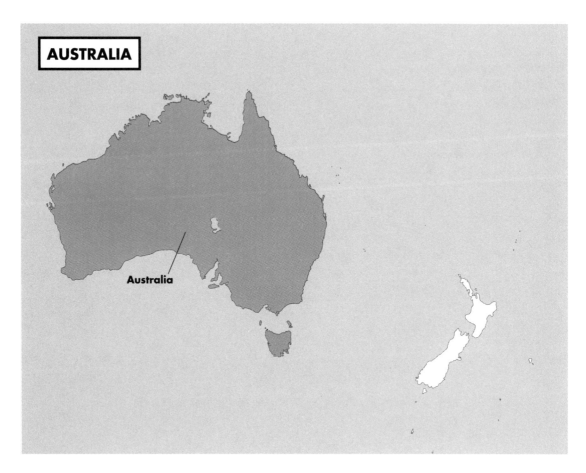

Australia
The Heroic Fisherman
an adapted myth retold by Louis A. Allen

My Brilliant Career
an adapted story by Miles Franklin

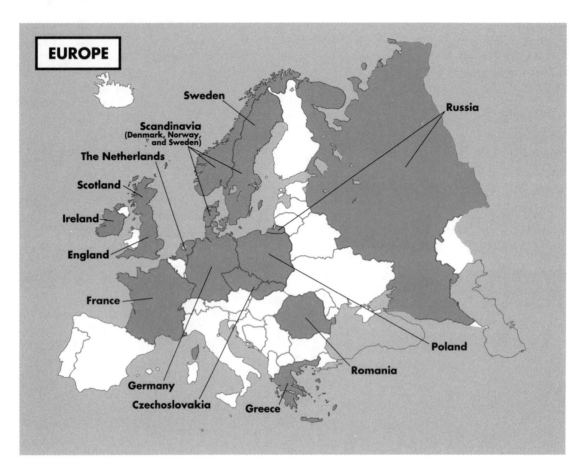

EUROPE

Sweden
Scandinavia
(Denmark, Norway, and Sweden)
The Netherlands
Scotland
Ireland
England
France
Germany
Czechoslovakia
Greece
Romania
Poland
Russia

* These are the borders of Czechoslovakia before it split peacefully in 1993. Today the western part is called the Czech Republic. The eastern part is called Slovakia.

** Russia is the biggest country in the world. Part of it is in Europe and part of it is in Asia.

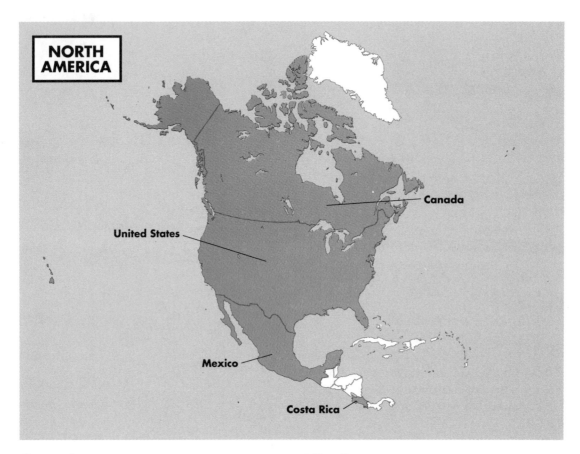

SOUTH AMERICA

Colombia

Chile

Argentina

Argentina
The Rebellion of the Magical Rabbits
an adapted story by Ariel Dorfman

Chile
The Horses
a poem by Pablo Neruda

Colombia
Lather and Nothing Else
an adapted story by Hernando Téllez